In Search of Central Europe

In Search of Central Europe

Edited by

GEORGE SCHÖPFLIN AND
NANCY WOOD

Polity Press

Copyright © this collection Polity Press 1989

First published 1989 by Polity Press
in association with Basil Blackwell.

Editorial Office:
Polity Press, Dales Brewery, Gwydir Street,
Cambridge CB1 2LJ, UK

Basil Blackwell Ltd
108 Cowley Road, Oxford OX4 1JF, UK

All rights reserved. Except for the quotation of short passages for the purposes of criticism and review, no part of this publication may be reproduced, stored in a retrieval system, or transmitted, in any form or by any means, electronic, mechanical, photocopying, recording or otherwise, without the prior permission of the publisher.

Except in the United States of America, this book is sold subject to the condition that it shall not, by way of trade or otherwise, be lent, resold, hired out, or otherwise circulated without the publisher's prior consent in any form of binding or cover other than that in which it is published and without a similar condition including this condition being imposed on the subsequent purchaser.

British Library Cataloguing in Publication Data

In search of Central Europe.
1. East Central Europe, history
I. Schöpflin, George   II. Wood, Nancy
943

ISBN 0-7456-0547-8

Typeset in Sabon on 10½/12pt
by Witwell Ltd, Southport
Printed in Great Britain by T. J. Press Ltd, Padstow

Contents

List of Contributors	vii
Acknowledgements	x
Introduction	1

PART 1 — 5

1. Central Europe: Definitions Old and New
   George Schöpflin — 7
2. What Is Europe, Where Is Europe? From Mystique to Politique
   Hugh Seton-Watson — 30
3. The Meaning of the Social Evolution of Europe
   István Bibó — 47
4. Central Europe: A Historical Region in Modern Times
   A Contribution to the Debate about the Regions of Europe
   Péter Hanák — 57
5. Intellectuals in East-Central Europe: Continuity and Change
   Zygmunt Bauman — 70
6. We, Central-European East Europeans
   Miroslav Kusý — 91
7. The European Ideal: Reality or Wishful Thinking in Eastern Central Europe?
   Miklós Duray — 97
8. Central European Attitudes
   Czesław Miłosz — 116
9. Central European Writers about Central Europe: Introduction to a Non-Existent Book of Readings
   Csaba G. Kiss — 125

PART 2 137

10 Milan Kundera's Lament
    George Schöpflin and Nancy Wood 139
11 Central Europe – What It Is and What It Is Not
    Egon Schwarz 143
12 Another Civilization? An Other Civilization?
    Milan Šimečka 157
13 Is the Russian Intelligentsia European? (A Reply to Šimečka)
    Jane Mellor 163
14 Who Excluded Russia from Europe? (A Reply to Šimečka)
    Mihály Vajda 168
15 Which Way Back to Europe? (A Reply to Mihály Vajda)
    Milan Šimečka 176
16 Central Europe Seen from the East of Europe
    Predrag Matvejević 183
17 Does Central Europe Exist?
    Timothy Garton Ash 191

Index 216

Contributors

Hugh Seton-Watson was Emeritus Professor of Russian History, School of Slavonic and East European Studies, University of London, until his death in December 1984. Among his books were: *Nations and States, Imperialist Revolutionaries* and *Decline of Imperial Russia*. The chapter included in this volume was his last published work.

István Bibó (1911–79) was an outstanding Hungarian political theorist and politician. He played an active role in the Hungarian revolution of 1956 and spent several years in prison in consequence. Towards the end of his life and after, his ideas became highly influential in the resurgence of Hungarian democratic thought. A collection of some of his writings in translation was being prepared at the time of publication.

Péter Hanák is a prominent Hungarian historian of the late nineteenth century. He is a Senior Research Fellow at the Institute of Historical Sciences, Hungarian Academy of Sciences, Budapest.

Zygmunt Bauman studied at Warsaw University and the London School of Economics. He graduated from Warsaw University, where he taught until 1968. Since 1971 he has been a Professor of Sociology at the University of Leeds. His most recent book is *Legislators and Interpreters: On Modernity, Post-Modernity and Intellectuals* (Polity Press, 1987).

Miroslav Kusý graduated from the Faculty of Philosophy at Charles University, Prague in 1954. Between 1957 and 1971, he was an Assistant Professor, and later a Professor in the Faculty of Philosophy at the Comenius University in Bratislava. Owing to his unorthodox political stance, he was forced to leave the University. Thereafter, and until 1976, he was employed at the Institute of Journalism in that city. He was dismissed from that post for 'organizational' reasons. After signing Charter 77, he was dismissed from his new employment in the Bratislava University Library. In recent years he has had various manual jobs, and he presently works as an urban sociologist for the Architectural Office of Bratislava. He is the author of several books on philosophy and his essays appear frequently in *samizdat* in Czechoslovakia.

Miklós Duray is a geologist, signatory of Charter 77 and well-known campaigner for the rights of the Hungarian minority in Czechoslovakia. He was arrested in November 1982 and charged with 'subversion'. His trial, which began in January 1983, was suspended the following month and he was released. In May 1984, he was again arrested for 'harming the interests of the Republic abroad', and released in 1985. He is the leading spokesperson and activist for the Committee to Defend the Rights of the Hungarian Ethnic Minority in Czechoslovakia, and the author of numerous studies of the minority question.

Czesław Miłosz was born in Lithuania in 1911 and grew up in Wilno. During the Second World War he was active in underground circles in Warsaw. In 1951, he broke with his government, left Poland and after ten years in Paris moved to the United States. He is Professor Emeritus at the University of California (Berkeley). He has published numerous books, the best-known of which is *The Captive Mind*, and a number of poetry collections. Czesław Miłosz was awarded the Nobel Prize for Literature in 1980.

Csaba G. Kiss is a literary historian and a Research Fellow at the Institute of Hungarian Studies in Budapest. He has written widely on Central European literary and political themes.

Egon Schwarz was born in Austria, and studied in Ecuador and the United States, graduating from the University of Washington in 1954. He has held a number of prestigious academic posts in Germany, New Zealand and the United States, and has been the recipient of numerous fellowships and awards, including the St George Medal, awarded by the City of Gorizia, Italy in 1986. In 1987 he was Distinguished Scholar at the Ohio State University, Columbus. He is the author of several books on German literature, including *Poetry and Politics in the Works of Rainer Maria Rilke* (1981) and *Literatur aus vier Kulturen: Essays und Besprechungen* (1987).

Milan Šimečka was born in Moravia in 1930. Since 1954 he has lived and worked entirely in Slovakia, writing in both Czech and Slovak. From 1954 he worked as a lecturer at Comenius University in Bratislava. After his expulsion from the Communist Party and dismissal from his university post in the course of the 'normalization' purges which commenced in March 1970, he has worked successively as a driver/chauffeur, building labourer, bulldozer driver and clerk. He was held in custody from May 1981 to May 1982 on a charge of 'subversion', which was subsequently dropped. He has been publishing *samizdat* essays and articles since 1975 and is acknowledged as one of Czechoslovakia's most talented independent publicists and thinkers. His book *The Restoration of Order* was published by Verso (London, 1984).

Contributors

Jane Mellor is a student of Russian and East European politics, living in London.

Mihály Vajda was born in 1935 in Budapest, where he studied philosophy and German literature. He was a pupil and close associate of György Lukács. From 1961–73 he was a Research Fellow in the Institute of Philosophy at the Hungarian Academy of Sciences. He was dismissed from this post for political reasons and has since engaged in various forms of freelance employment in Budapest. He has been a Visiting Professor at the University of Bremen, Columbia University and the New School for Social Research. His books in English include *Fascism as a Mass Movement* (1976) and *The State and Socialism* (1981).

Predrag Matvejević, essayist and literary critic, is Professor of French Literature at the University of Zagreb. In 1980, he was awarded the Legion of Honour by the French government. He is President of the Croatian PEN Club and since 1986 he has been Vice-President of International PEN. He is the author of numerous literary and political works, among them *Pour une poétique de l'événement* (10/18, 1979), *Pour une nouvelle créativité culturelle* (awarded the 'Prix de INA' in 1975), *La Yougoslavité d'aujourd'hui, question de culture* and *Lettres ouvertes, exercices de moralité*, a collection of seminal documents by Soviet, East European and Yugoslav thinkers and activists defending civil liberties and human rights in the Soviet Union and Eastern and Central Europe.

Timothy Garton Ash is an historian, author and journalist specializing in the contemporary history of Central Europe. He has written about the region for the *Spectator*, the London *Times*, the *New York Review of Books* and many other publications. He is the author of *The Polish Revolution: Solidarity* (1984) which won the British Society of Authors' Somerset Maugham Award, and '*Und willst du nicht mein Bruder sein . . .* ' *Die DDR heute* (1981), a book about East Germany. In 1986–7 he was Fellow at the Woodrow Wilson International Center for Scholars in Washington DC, where he worked on a book about the 'Yalta' division of Europe, a project he is now pursuing as a senior associate member of St Antony's College, Oxford. Timothy Garton Ash is Foreign Editor of the *Spectator*.

Acknowledgements

The editors and publishers are grateful to those who have given permission to reproduce material already printed elsewhere.

George Schöpflin, 'Central Europe: Definitions Old and New', commissioned for this volume. Copyright © George Schöpflin.

Hugh Seton-Watson, 'What Is Europe, Where Is Europe? From Mystique to Politique', reprinted from *Encounter*, July/August 1985, Vol. 65, No. 2. Copyright © Mary Seton-Watson.

István Bibó, 'The Meaning of the Social Evolution of Europe', extracted from Bibó István, *Összegyűjtött munkái*, Vol. 2 (Bern, European Protestant Hungarian Free University, 1984). Translation copyright © Peter Elkan.

Péter Hanák, 'Central Europe: A Historical Region in Modern Times', commissioned for this volume. Translated by Julian Schöpflin with the financial support of the Central and East European Publishing Project (Oxford).

Zygmunt Bauman, 'Intellectuals in East-Central Europe: Continuity and Change', reprinted with permission from *Eastern European Politics and Societies*, Vol. 1, No. 2, Spring 1987, pp. 162–8. Copyright © 1987 by the American Council of Learned Societies.

Miroslav Kusý, 'We, Central-European East Europeans', translation copyright © and permission to reprint from the Documentation Centre for the Promotion of Independent Czechoslovak Literature (CSDC). Translated by A. G. Brain.

Miklós Duray, 'The European Ideal: Reality or Wishful Thinking in Eastern Central Europe?', (1986) translated by A. G. Brain with the financial support of the Central and East European Publishing Project (Oxford).

Czesław Miłosz, 'Central European Attitudes', reprinted from *Cross*

Currents, a Yearbook of Central European Culture, No. 5 (1986). Copyright © Czesław Miłosz.

Csaba G. Kiss, 'Central European Writers about Central Europe: Introduction to a Non-Existent Book of Readings', reprinted with author's permission from *Valóság*, Vol. 30, No. 5, May 1987. Translation copyright © George Schöpflin.

Egon Schwarz, 'Central Europe – What It Is and What It Is Not', translation copyright © Egon Schwarz.

Milan Šimečka, 'Another Civilisation? An "Other Civilisation?"', reprinted from *East European Reporter*, Vol. 1, No. 2, Summer 1985. Translated by A. G. Brain.

Jane Mellor, 'Is the Russian Intelligentsia European? (A Reply to Šimečka)', reprinted from *East European Reporter*, Vol. 1, No. 4, 1986.

Mihály Vajda, 'Who Excluded Russia from Europe? (A Reply to Šimečka)', reprinted from *East European Reporter*, Vol. 1, No. 4, 1986.

Milan Šimečka, 'Which Way Back to Europe? (A Reply to Mihály Vajda)', reprinted from *East European Reporter*, Vol. 2, No. 3, 1987. Translation copyright © A. G. Brain 1987.

Predrag Matvejević, 'Central Europe Seen from the East of Europe'; a slightly shorter version of this essay, entitled 'Regard de Zagreb' originally appeared in *La Nouvelle Alternative*, No. 8, December 1987.

Timothy Garton Ash, 'Does Central Europe Exist?' reprinted with permission from the *New York Review of Books*, 9 October 1986. Copyright © 1986 Nyrev Inc.

The editors would also like to acknowledge the assistance of Jan Kavan of Palach Press (London), Daglind Sonolet, John Keane and A. G. Brain.

Introduction

Not all that long ago, the term 'Central Europe' was used almost exclusively by elderly survivors of Austria-Hungary and was dismissed by most people as a remnant, a sentimental leftover from the nostalgic days of Francis Joseph with no relevance to anything contemporary. The change has been quite extraordinary. After only a few short years, hardly a week passes without yet another essay or article on the topic. And not only has the quantity increased, the reassessment of what Central Europe is, what it meant historically and what its significance is today has offered subtle insights on the nature not just of the region itself, but on Europeanness as a whole.

The growth of material on Central Europe has come very largely from the area itself.[1] In the latter half of the 1980s, with the mounting political, economic and social crisis affecting the Soviet-type systems in force in the area, there was a growing search for alternative ideas and values through which the crisis might be understood. The revival of 'Central Europe' as such an ordering principle emerged as one of the important foci of this search. Central European intellectuals began to accept that Central Europe did, after all, matter to them and to the milieu they lived in. All but inevitably, this prompted them to explore two broad questions, what 'Central Europe' was and what it meant for the contemporary period. The answers were numerous and varied, but on one issue there was broad agreement: Central Europe existed, as did the problems raised by the need to define it.

This book is essentially devoted to discussing this, to reflecting the Central Europe debate in English (ironically, English is increasingly coming to replace German, once the natural *lingua franca* of Central Europe) and, at the same time, to contributing new perspectives on the meaning of Europe as a whole. It is noteworthy, that whereas in the 1970s, the word 'Europe' was widely used to mean only Western Europe, by the 1980s this usage had begun to change. The countries of Central and South-Eastern Europe, though unquestionably part of the Soviet sphere of power, were again felt to be within rather than excluded from the vaguely defined European fold. The psychological legacy of the division of Europe at Yalta was now subject to re-examination.

The debate is far from over. In a variety of languages and with great differences in approach – as is appropriate to the variety that Europeanness postulates – articles and essays appear all the time, so much so that it has now become all but impossible to digest them completely. The Central Europe debate has, in fact, spawned a variety of sub-debates. These include the *Mitteleuropa* question, which is essentially a discussion about the future of Germany, whether Germany's primary orientation should be Western or not, whether reunification is worth the price, what relations with East Germany should be and only after that does the question of how Germany should approach the (other) countries of Central Europe begin to arise.[2] Another sub-debate is the one in Yugoslavia, understandably, given that two of the country's republics – Croatia and Slovenia – see themselves rightly as Central European, whilst the remainder of the country is not. These issues are discussed in this volume, though its central focus lies elsewhere.

Taking Milan Kundera's essay 'The Tragedy of Central Europe' which effectively revitalized the debate, as a starting point, the Central European question has turned centrally on issues of Europeanness, the place of Soviet Russia and the future of Soviet-type systems in the area. But this immediately raised other questions, especially historical ones about the roots of Central European otherness and sameness,[3] about methodologies of identifying Central Europeanness and of distilling its essence.

The main contributions to the debate that had seen the light of day by early 1988 have found a place in this collection. Some of them are by Western writers, others by intellectuals living in Central Europe. We are confident that the debate will continue.

NOTES

1 The Czech *samizdat* journal *Střední Evropa* is expressly dedicated to this question; the Polish *samizdat* journal, *Nowa Koalicja* likewise deals with shared issues in the broad Central European area. *Nouvelle Alternative* (Paris) dedicated its eighth issue to this question. *East European Reporter* (London) has regarded the Central Europe debate as one of the most important issues to have arisen in *samizdat* and elsewhere for years and has given it extensive space.

2 Karl Schlögel, *Die Mitte liegt Ostwärts: die Deutschen, der verlorene Osten and Mitteleuropa* (Siedler Verlag, 1986). See also Werner Weidenfeld (ed.), *Die Indentität Europas: Fragen, Position, Perspektiven* (Hanser Verlag, 1985).

3 Jenő Szűcs's masterly essay, 'The Three Historic Regions of Europe', first appeared in *samizdat* in 1980, as part of the *Festschrift* volume dedicated to the great Hungarian political thinker István Bibó. Subsequently, it was published officially

in Hungary and then appeared in a variety of other languages. Jan Józef Lipski takes up some of these themes from a Polish perspective in 'Two Fatherlands – Two Patriotisms', *Survey*, Vol. 26, No. 4 (1982).

PART 1

1
Central Europe: Definitions Old and New
George Schöpflin

The idea of Central Europe became, unquestionably, one of the spectres that came to haunt the politics of Europe as a whole in the 1980s. Its re-emergence from near oblivion was welcomed by some, treated with incomprehension by others and rejected by yet others. All the same, it quickly established itself as one of the items on the political agenda of Europe. Thereby it immediately raised complex problems of definition and formation of political and cultural identities through a wide-ranging debate in Central Europe and in the West. The book as a whole is devoted to providing many of the arguments that have been put forward in this debate and this introductory article is concerned with definitions of Europe, of how and why Europe differs from Russia and America, in what ways Central Europe is a part of the broad European arena and what the longer-term implications of Central Europeanness might be.

Those who argue that Russia/Soviet Union are European tend to place their emphasis on a denial of contemporary political factors in their location of Russia. They stress these as being decisive in the decision to exclude Russia from Europe, implying thereby that we are dealing with a contingent, politically determined (and thus presumably politically reversible) phenomenon. I would like to submit that Russia may have had European elements in its culture, that it certainly contributed ideas and values to Europe and that individual Russians may indeed be Europeans, but it was not a part of the current of European cultural development and, most significantly, excluded itself from that current by the Russian Revolution and its aftermath. In this section, I would also like to take up another implicit point made by the protagonists of Russia as a European country – namely that the use of political criteria in this connection is arbitrary – and to counter this with the argument that it is no more and no less arbitrary than any other single criterion, economic, legal, aesthetic, religious or for that matter geographic.[1]

Hence the first substantive point may be put in the form of a question: 'did not the Russian intelligentsia and middle classes consider themselves fully European before 1914?' The answer is, 'some of them did, but many more did not'. The merest glance at the concerns and travails of the pre-Revolutionary Russian intelligentsia will show that both radicals and conservatives, left and right – if these terms can be applied to nineteenth century Russia – were in effect agreed on attempting to differentiate themselves from Europe, which they tended to identify with capitalist industrialization, materialism and the destruction of 'spiritual' values. There is, indeed, much to be said for the proposition that an autonomous Russian intellectual stratum developed much more recently than its counterpart in the West; that it was less deeply rooted in Russian society; and that it spent a great deal of time, effort and energy in looking for a role. This tended to draw it towards messianism, towards easy solutions for the Russian problem of what was to be the direction and goal of development. There was, of course, a stratum of individuals with Western values, which included a belief in moderate meliorism, but they were politically impotent and intellectually squeezed between the upper and nether millstones of neo-Slavophilism and the varieties of *narodnichestvo* (populism). In this context, Lenin and the neo-Leninist system were organically derived from one of the salient Russian traditions and were in no sense a radical breach with all aspects of that tradition.[2]

THE ROLE OF THE ENVIRONMENT

A second substantive point in this connection has been put in this form: 'the division of Europe has no rationale in geography and culture; no basis in nature or history'.[3] Here my disagreement is substantial, if not complete. As far as geography is concerned, while Russia may be contiguous with Europe, this says very little on its own. The crucial point, to my mind, is that European and Russian spatial relationships are utterly different and these, in turn, give rise to major cultural variations. To put it simply, whereas in Europe space – land – has been scarce and people relatively plentiful, in Russia the contrary prevailed. A look at the density of settlement in the two areas will reveal how enormous are Russian distances. Villages are few and far between and the Russian town was very unlike its European equivalent, in that it lacked the economic and political autonomy that characterized the latter. This difference in space is a determinant. It influences the pattern of organization, the intensity of communication, the needs of administration, the attitude towards decentralized power and, crucially, whether control should be primarily over land or over people, and thus the codes of conduct determining social and personal transactions. As far as this last is concerned,

Europe developed very early on a complex system for regulating land – the feudal system was partly about this – but there was much less of a need to control people.[4] The dominant European form of political organization – competitive loci of power and the insistence on the division of power and legitimation – are very alien to Russia and, indeed, were and still are viewed as antagonistic by Russians.

Nor are matters quite as straightforward as regards 'nature' as has been asserted. Climatic conditions are much harsher in Russia, untouched as it is by the Gulf Stream, with a markedly shorter growing season, and this is coupled with a much higher proportion of relatively marginal land than in Europe. The significance of this is that the agricultural surplus at the disposal of Russia's rulers was much more modest than in Europe and that it was far more difficult for Russia to escape the 'grain-trap' (just enough of a surplus to support organized social life, and not to generate investment into other areas) than it was for Europe.[5]

There is an argument that there is something of a link between the experience of agricultural prosperity and the corresponding regularity of food supplies and expectations of stability in other areas, notably in politics. Where societies have lived for generations with the fear that the coming winter will bring starvation, where accumulation is difficult because of the marginality of agriculture, the quest for external agencies of protection and support, coupled with an equivalent distrust of them, will be strong.[6] The contrast between Russia and Western Europe could hardly be greater. Central Europe, as might be expected, falls somewhere in between.

CULTURE AND HISTORY

The real differences, however, arise in culture and history, thereby making a discussion of European values essential. A cultural community is formed by shared experiences and by the perception of those experiences on the part of later generations. In this respect, history and culture merge. Self-evidently, there can be no such thing as 'total history', so that in all cases, 'history' consists of a set of choices. It follows from this, that the same community in different periods will give saliency to different experiences, according to some contingent need. My choices in this context have been governed by what I regard as significant in the context of the Europe – Central Europe – Russia debate and others will undoubtedly wish to select other experiences. Nevertheless, I would argue that my choices do qualify as an authentic representation of the European tradition. Inevitably, what follows here will be put together in a simplified and summary form; there will be numerous individual exceptions to my main propositions, but these do not, I believe, affect the broad thrust of my argument.

The events constituting Europe's cultural mainstream, then, can be defined by a short list of these shared experiences. These include the Judaeo-Christian and Hellenic heritage as transmitted by Christianity and evolving to medieval universalism, divine order grounded in faith, tempered by Renaissance values of scepticism and reason; the Reformation and the Counter-Reformation counterposing different special solutions to the problem of faith, eschatology, ontology; a synthesis of sorts offered by the Enlightenment, that all phenomena be subjected to reasoned criticism, to cognitive growth (expansion of knowledge in all spheres, no special status, privilege, the extension of the right to participate in politics notionally to all members of the political community, rather than any restriction by birth, but in reality to the growing entrepreneurial and professional classes). Romanticism and its political counterpart, Nationalism, can be regarded as reactions to the reductionist thrust of the Enlightenment, and Socialism to the incompleteness of the extension of political rights, inasmuch as it demanded the full enfranchisement of the new urban population. The 'long summer' of 1815-1915 elicited the response of impatience with the bourgeois values that were seen as having given rise to an age without higher aspirations.[7] The devastation of the Great European Civil War of 1914-45, the traducing of the European tradition by Hitler's New Order, the decline of Europe and its loss of autonomy to the superpowers in turn gave rise to the post-1945 a-nationalist currents, culminating in the European community, only to be followed by a revival of national identities as a political factor.[8]

The principal political methods and techniques generated by the *longue durée* of this cultural tradition – and in this context the contrast with Russia could hardly be greater – can be said to include the following. The central feature of the European approach to power is that it should be divided, that no ruler should be capable of uniting in his hands all political, legal, economic and religious power. The legitimation of power is likewise divided. The separation of secular from religious power and of legitimation, as embodied in the partly conflictual, partly co-operative relationship between kingship and papacy is unique. Canossa was the symbolic acting out of this institution. It encapsulates in itself the separation described here – it is inconceivable that the Tsar of Russia or any Asiatic ruler would ever have subjected himself to hair-shirt and rope as Henry IV did before Gregory VII. The institution proved to be a singularly effective instrument for maintaining this separation, both at the level of ideas and institutions.[9]

The church, furthermore, was inadvertently responsible for the emergence of an autonomous scientific and intellectual sphere, which was eventually to do great damage to the prestige and power of religion. By encouraging the founding of universities where learning might be pursued in an environment not controlled by the secular ruler, the church achieved two things. Learning was gradually emancipated from the repetition of previously amassed knowledge to be transformed into the investigation and assessment of phenomena and the development of ideas. This brought with it the idea of change and of innovation, ultimately leading to the questioning of the initial religious foundations of the project. The shift from rote learning to conceptualization was crucial because it led to the evolution of the autonomous scientific sphere, with its own autonomous rules and criteria not necessarily subject to those of religion and thus to church control. The result was the secularization of cognition (and the emancipation of other spheres), with its own functions, purposiveness and legitimacy. Learning could no longer be used for, say, display or the legitimation of religion without challenge. This helped to underwrite the emergence of a secular intelligentsia, enhanced individual power and offered the intellectual prestige on his/her own terms. No one would claim that this was an easy process – both Copernicus and Galileo had to struggle against those in the church who saw their ideas as dangerous to the power, status and prestige of the church. On the other hand, this process did not take place in Russia at all. The emancipation of the scientific sphere did not follow until the nineteenth century, independent investigation and an autonomous intelligentsia were always weaker than in the West and, correspondingly, dependence on the state was of a much higher order.

Analogous to this was the slow evolution of an autonomous, uncontrolled sphere of language. Literacy, helped by the printing revolution, gradually undermined the monopoly of the church and the ruler over the language of discourse in all spheres. In this connection, the intellectual revolution set in train by the Reformation was crucial. By the eighteenth century, the control of public discourse had slipped entirely from the control of both church and state, despite rearguard actions by both to retain their power in this sphere. Obviously, the existence of only partially supervised urban concentrations, with their own economic base, was enormously helpful in promoting this development.

The reciprocity of rights, the proposition that the ruler owed a duty to his subjects, coupled with the existence of a separate legal sphere through which that duty could be enforced, were vital. It was in this area too, that much-maligned feudalism helped to institutionalize reciprocity of rights, inasmuch as the feudal contract – both a legal and a political act – expressly envisioned two sides with rights attaching to both. The fact that enforcement may have been difficult (e.g. Magna Carta) does not invalidate the principle.[10] Equally, this was expressed in the emerging autonomy of urban communities and the rise of the city as a centre of autonomous activity and exchange under the supervision of neither the secular nor the religious authorities. The independent city also had its role in preserving and promoting the market, the autonomy of economic transactions, in the development of the technologies of administering money, the specialization of skills and the emergence of a concept of economic growth with its own patterns of causality, not subject to the benevolence of the ruler or divine providence.[11] The Russian city, especially with the deliberate destruction of Novgorod by Ivan the Terrible in 1570, was systematically suppressed as a centre of autonomy and integrated into the Russian concept of power.

The regulatory role of the state in Europe lies somewhere between complete social autonomy and full-blown state control. The European tradition is, in a word, etatistic. It recognizes that in some respects the state does know better than the individual or groups, but that in others it does not. The twentieth century has seen an ever-increasing role for the state and latterly a reaction against this trend.[12] How the limits of state and society are to be defined though is the subject of a continuous debate, sometimes explicit, sometimes less so. Here again, the contrast with Russia could hardly be greater. The Tsar and those seeking to replace him in the nineteenth century sought not to lessen the power of the state over the individual, as happened in Europe to a very large extent, but to replace the ruler because they believed they would make a better job of ruling by reason of their superior world-view. The nineteenth (and twentieth century) Russian intelligentsia was united in despising liberal values and viewed with alarm the diversity of Europe as anarchic. Solzhenitsyn's strictures on the West are the lineal descendants of the ones made by nineteenth century Russian travellers who were, for the most part, appalled by what they saw in Europe.

In essence, both in domestic politics and in the international sphere, the solutions to the problem of power devised in Europe gave the competitive aspect of different foci of power the greatest emphasis. Competing groups, moderated by an autonomous institutional framework, and the tacit recognition of ground-rules, were paralleled internationally by competing polities with an equivalent, albeit weaker, set of rules. The aspect of this that demands particular attention is the rejection of the patrimonial state, where the ruler commands all power and his subjects are not citizens but chattels, coupled with the concept of imperium, the divinely ordained ideology of a world centre with a world mission. The last has been characteristic of Russia both before and since 1917. It implies a far greater homogenization in all spheres than is acceptable in the European tradition. It is worth stressing here that there is nothing inherently right or wrong about either tradition; it is their irreconcilability that is at issue.

In all, therefore, Europe has developed values specific to itself and these appear to be immanent, as well as ineradicable. Some of these may, indeed, be found in other cultures, but their particular combination is unique to Europe. Here again what follows is little more than a rough and ready checklist of ideas.

THE LEGACY OF RELIGION

First there is the legacy of Western Christianity. The contrasting models of behaviour derived from the two forms of the Christian tradition differ in that Western Christianity has long insisted that internal belief and external behaviour should as far as possible be in conformity, if not indeed congruent, that it is the individual's transcendental duty to stand up and be counted. This pattern is specific to Western Christianity, which was, if anything, reinforced by the Reformation, and is much less important in Orthodoxy.[13] Eastern Christianity has not stressed this, but has contented itself with external conformity, with ritualistic observance.

This dichotomy is connected with Europe's division of power as contrasted with the homogenization of power, notably as expressed in Caesaropapism. The argument is essentially this: in the West, culture, society and power were fragmented and competitive, with conflicting and complementary duties and obligations to different secular rulers. The universal church thereby became the dominant integrative institution, which sought to create a particular order, regularity, similar observance of rules and the like. To achieve this, it placed great emphasis on the internalization of values, not least because it lacked the secular power to enforce this. Indeed it understood that its power lay precisely in the spiritual realm, in the mystery which it controlled. (This is clearly one of the meanings of Canossa). Thus it was essential from the Church's point of view to ensure that its power should subsist through the universal acceptance of its values. Hence the Church's insistence on controlling that which was God's and arguing that in some matters even the highest ruler was subordinate to the Church. The stress placed on sincerity, openness, honesty etc. in Western political life is a testimony to the enduring nature of this value.

In the East, this compulsion was weaker because of the persistence of the imperial tradition (Byzantium, Muscovy, Tartars) which precluded fragmentation. In this way, the ruler was able to integrate the Church into the framework of secular power and thereby exercise control over religious areas. Both in Byzantium and in Muscovy, where the Byzantine tradition was reinforced by the influence of Islam, the ruler used religion to strengthen the myth of legitimation that 'empire' was divinely ordained, so that religion could never emerge as an autonomous, competitive value in the way that it did in Europe.

By contrast, the idea of internalization is much less salient in Russia, where the ability of individuals to live with two contradictory sets of values (with the result that the meaning to be attached to words becomes situational and relativized rather than absolute) has received regular attention.[14] This particular aspect of Russian culture has been adopted under the Soviet system, often as a ready-made strategy of survival, and can be said to constitute a crucial part of it. It makes it extremely difficult for Western interpreters to make sense of Russian discourse if they fail to take into account the very different cultural context of Soviet statements.

PLURALITY OF VALUES

At the heart of the European value system is the proposition that society is creative and the state is reactive. Individuals and groups organized in regulated institutions, with autonomy protected by regulated procedures, generate change. The state is there to act as the protective framework, to prevent particular groups in society from establishing dominant or despotic positions. The acceptance of competing and overlapping criteria by which decisions are made, the rejection of the reductionism to a single overarching rationality (with the result that different problems can have contradictory but legitimate solutions depending on the circumstances) are central to this interpretation of the European tradition. Hence Europe has evolved a plurality of value systems, a multiplicity of codes of conduct, with equal value placed on very different and conflicting criteria. These may be the interests of the state *v.* those of society; utilitarian value *v.* aesthetic; innovative *v.* traditional; urban *v.* rural; hierarchy *v.* equality; legal *v.* political; universal *v.* local; economic (i.e. market) *v.* welfare, and so on. The European cultural tradition, therefore, should be seen as a continuous debate, in which no solution is permanent, in which the transcending of existing solutions is given the highest value,[15] in which the margin of argument changes continuously (making it essential for the views of utopians and dogmatists of every kind to be given an airing, otherwise the debate will slide into stultification), in which no one individual or group can have an intellectual monopoly and in which at every level there is tension. The accompanying institutional framework has been constituted to safeguard and mediate in this debate.

Russia is critically different in this context. The whole pattern of Russian development suggests that the overarching Russian criterion is that of power and the legitimation of power. The maximization and centralization of power, whether political, economic, social, legal, aesthetic, etc. are the imperatives of Russian tradition. All that has changed since the days of the Tsars is that the eschatology of power is different and the techniques of power have improved. But qualitatively there is not that much to differentiate the two in this particular respect. The ruler knows best; the individual does not. Obviously, this proposition is not intended to suggest that all decisions in all circumstances are taken by the criterion of power, as defined here, but as a general trend, and as the broadly accepted framework the proposition appears to be valid.

What also follows from this is that the distinction between private and public, between the sphere of individual morality and regulation by the state, is weak to non-existent in the Russian tradition. The main currents of nineteenth century Russian thought were united in their belief that the role of the state included the moral supervision of society, albeit from different starting points. The Revolution adopted this and adapted it to the new conditions, but the essence has remained unchanged. In this context, myths of social harmony had far greater appeal in Russia both in the last century and in this one. The near obsession with the peasant commune on one side and community (*sobornost*) on the other, which were seen as the possible basis for creating a special Russian way of avoiding the impersonal patterns of European development, re-emerged after the Revolution in the guise of the Marxist utopia propagated by Lenin and his successors.

A further aspect of this is the concept of change. The built-in assumption in the European tradition is that the existing dispensation can be improved, so that change is to be welcomed, even if this does not mean that it is equally welcome to everyone. This has lent the European tradition a dynamism, that, while not excluding major upheavals, has tended towards a linear concept of change within the framework of the legacy of the past. Orderly transformation with due respect to the past are the guarantees that change will be for the better. This necessarily governs individual and group attitudes to change, to the expectation that change will occur, as well as to the limits of legitimate change. It further follows from this that the European cultural value system is open to experimentation and innovation and does not regard error as intolerable.

In all these areas, Russian culture gives rise to different perceptions of what is acceptable. Change tends to be viewed in a more cataclysmic fashion, the limits of acceptable change are qualitatively narrower and society's grasp of what is changed is much more tenuous, so that change becomes a source of fear. The experience of Russia and the Soviet Union in the twentieth century has only accentuated this perception. In essence, Europeans view change with a mixture of approbation, irritation (if it runs counter to their interests) and an expectation that they will have some control over it. This is not the case in Soviet Russia.

THE UNITED STATES AND 'AMERICA'

The bulk of the argument so far has concerned the relationship between Europe and Soviet Russia, but it should be understood that the European tradition differs from that of the United States as well. Indeed while it has tended very largely to turn its back on Russia, it has viewed, if uneasily at times, the United States as a yardstick by which to measure itself. European attitudes towards America are highly complex for reasons which are not obvious at first sight. In the first place, the whole of Europe participated in the shared experience of emigration to America. There are probably relatively few Europeans who do not have some kind of direct of indirect personal experience of this, through family or friends or communal memories; what is more, this is a continuing experience.

However, America as the target of emigration also functions at less obvious levels, not just the level of material improvement. It is equally the land to which people choose to emigrate and must thereby become something desired and thus enveloped in myth. A part of this myth is that America (not the United States, but 'America') is a kind of super-Europe, a land where all the petty frustrations and constraints to which the individual is subjected in Europe will disappear, where freedom and opportunity and choice are limitless. Hence European expectations of America are the highest, as they must be if America embodies the dream of an alternative Europe. This is, of course, an impossible role for the United States to play. America, the mythical land, can do so, but the United States, a real state with political and other similar interests, cannot, because politics requires compromises and deals, and myth cannot tolerate this. Europe in this sense is doubly parasitical on the United States – it has claims on it both as the United States, which gives it protection against the Soviet Union and as America, the myth-land, where all the things that Europeans have been unable to create for themselves at home become possible.

The myth creates a standard of behaviour to which Europeans not altogether consciously expect Americans to adhere. What results, therefore, is a relationship which is exacerbated by the unrecognized differences between European and American culture. One example of this is the Americans' different use of rhetoric, of their couching their public discourse in terms which Europeans interpret as 'moralistic', even though Americans do not necessarily do so. By this criterion, the United States will always be found wanting, it will never be able to measure up to Europeans' expectations, because Europeans have fused 'America' and United States and impose the duties and the obligations of the United States that are in reality appropriate to the myth-land.

This has never really been a problem with Russia (the Soviet Union is different), for Russia was not the myth-land of mass emigration (regardless of the fact that considerable numbers of Germans did go there in the eighteenth century). Particular European cultures have, of course, been well disposed towards Russia – Bulgaria being the best example, though until 1968 the Czechs too were very Russophile – but Europe as a whole has never had the same high expectations of it as of America. Obviously, it could not have, seeing that it was a state much like other European states, but less known and felt to be worse. The significant exception to this was the European left after the Revolution, though here it was the Soviet Union, the political entity, that was invested with the myth value that the rest of Europe imposed on America. When myth and reality diverged too obviously, the gaze of the Western left, which it seems cannot live without a myth-land any more than can the rest of Europe, shifted elsewhere, to China, Cambodia, Cuba, Nicaragua, etc.[16]

However, at the level of mass consciousness, the myth of the Soviet Union survived in an attenuated form, in that it is still vaguely seen as some kind of socialist state, so that the Soviet Union receives the benefit of the doubt attracted by those thought to be engaged in 'creating a better world'. This becomes more pronounced when Europe feels itself particularly disappointed by a United States that has acted entirely out of the 'American' character that Europe has imposed on it – the bombing of Libya in 1986 is a good example of this. At these times, the disappointed lover can turn towards the Soviet Union and flirt a little, and look for some good in it. This is all linked to the legacy of Marxism claimed by the Soviet Union and thus vaguely asserting a claim that it is somehow engaged in the quest of looking for the best in man, whereas the United States in the European perspective is capitalism writ large and capitalism, as every schoolboy knows, is about accepting that man is driven by the basest instincts. It is another question why acquisitiveness is conventionally regarded as 'base' whereas co-operation is thought to be 'high-minded'.

There is one final factor deriving from the foregoing which deserves special stress. My argument has not been that Soviet Russia is necessarily inferior, but that it is unquestionably different. To measure Soviet Russia by European criteria, therefore, becomes an attempt to impose those criteria on an alien world, something that we would seldom do with, say, China or Cambodia. We accept their differentness. We should extend the same tolerance to Soviet Russia. What is more, there are certain implications here for Western policy making. If we proceed from the assumption that Russia is European, then we are entering on a process with unrealistic expectations. It is only when we recognize that Russian culture has given rise to a very different system, that the rules accepted as universal in Europe do not apply to it on a one-for-one basis that we can take the basic differences into account and evaluate the similarities in their proper context.

What I have argued about the Soviet Union is not to be taken as applicable to Central and Eastern Europe, however. Here the problem is of a different order, for Central and Eastern Europe is an organic part of Europe as a whole, and its detachment from the mainstream of European development has been highly deleterious for all the peoples of the area who have to live with socio-political systems which work against rather than with the grain of tradition and the aspirations derived from those traditions. This is not to be interpreted as meaning that Central and Eastern Europe are as central to the

European tradition as France or the Netherlands. There are crucial factors of historical experience which diluted the impact of that tradition and resulted in a significantly weaker expression of Europeanness. Nevertheless, it is a distortion of the argument that the patterns of Central and Eastern Europe can be understood when detached from its broad European context. The remainder of this chapter will discuss these and related questions.

THE CENTRAL EUROPE DEBATE: THE (RE-)EMERGENCE OF AN OLD IDEA

It is against this background, then, that the European credentials of the recent Central European debate should be evaluated. The concept raises numerous difficulties and has its opponents or sceptics. But all the same, it has acquired a viability and even an authenticity of its own that place its existence beyond immediate challenge. The starting point for analysis must be to examine the nature of identity as such. Evidently all identities are to an extent constructed, but an entirely invented identity, one without any kind of roots at all, incapable of eliciting resonance from those whom it is supposed to define and serving no positive function, will hardly be a great success. Furthermore, because identities exist at different levels, with different functions, each person is perfectly capable of possessing several; indeed, he or she usually does, except in highly prescriptive, circumscribed and simple societies. This allows different identities, including overlapping or conflicting ones to be called on wherever the individuals concerned choose to do so. The claim by nationalists, for example, that each individual has one and only one identity is reductionist and antagonistic to choice, it inhibits innovation and is, in reality, a normative postulate. More often than not it is coupled with an attempt to legitimate an extension of some group's power over others. In this sense, every identity – beyond strictly impersonal ones bounded spatially by, say, the village – has imagined elements in it.

The argument that follows here is that the Central European identity is a classic example of this kind, in that the discussion of the first half of the 1980s takes a putative Central Europeanness as its launching pad, seeks to define it in terms most favourable to its unstated though evident goals and insists that the whole concept is apodictic, that it is up to its opponents to prove it false. Yet it would be wrong to see Central Europeanness in exclusively artificial terms. Its protagonists have tried to build their case on genuine factors and have reached back to a past that is at least as authentic as the Marxist or nationalist or liberal-democratic variants of it. Obviously, one of my assumptions here is that there is and can be more than one version of history – given that total history is impossible – and that any selection involves distortion by someone's criteria. Thus there is nothing inherently dishonest in what the Central Europeanists are attempting to do. Their objective in broad terms is to construct or reconstruct a consciousness which emphasizes values other than those propagated by the existing system, for this latter is seen as intellectually and morally bankrupt. The content of the Central European identity remains inchoate, though an attempt will be made in what follows to sketch its political outlines, but it must be understood as existing alike in the political, cultural, historiographical spheres and in their reciprocal interactions.

The first striking aspect of this newly emergent Central Europeanism is the way in which its protagonists insist on its uniqueness by differentiating it both from the broader European mainstream and, even more importantly, from the Soviet Russian tradition, together with the political systems imposed on Central Europe in the name of the latter. It is hard to avoid the conclusion that this second differentiation is the driving force behind the idea as it is currently understood. Certainly, when the debate was launched by Milan Kundera, it was given this quality which has served since to structure the debate.

The same differentiation is present in Czesław Miłosz's much more culturally argued definition, in which he makes the point of Central Europe's liminality to Europe as a whole. His starting point is: 'I was born and grew up on the very borderline between Rome and Byzantium.' Thus only from the outer edge of Europe, which is Central Europe or, in his case, Wilno, can one properly understand the true qualities of Europeanness. This is quite logical – after all, one does have a clearer perspective of one's identity when that identity is regularly tested against other identities. While this does raise the more or less geographical and semantic question that if Central Europe constitutes the outer edge of Europe, where is Eastern Europe to be found, it also points towards an important strand in the argument of the Central Europeanists, viz. that Europe is better appreciated from its periphery than its centre. Where the European identity is secure, as, say, in Paris or London or Amsterdam, the need to define it is much less acutely felt.[17]

RELIGION ON THE FRONTIER

This argument can be taken further.[18] Central Europeanness appears in a number of broader fields. Thus the fact that Central Europe is a frontier between East and West has left its stamp on its character and it derives many of its qualities from this. As concerns this frontier quality of Central Europe, reference may be made to the intermediate and transmittory nature of the area as between Latin and Orthodox lands. This implies that the cultures of the region have undergone the repeated experience of having had to absorb the values of whichever external power was stronger and of having developed an antemurale value system (seeing themselves as the eastern-most bastions of the West).[19] At the same time, it has also tended to point towards insecurity *vis-a-vis* value systems, in that they appear to be subject to change by seemingly uncontrolled and uncontrollable external forces. While the enracination of these values has taken place, it arrived later than in the West and the Church was to a far greater extent associated with the state. There were no Canossas in Central Europe. If anything, conflicts between secular and religious power tended to be settled in favour of the former, as with the case of St Stanisław Kostka or St John Nepomuk. This marks a difference, inasmuch as the division between God and Caesar, together with the processes of legitimation discussed in the foregoing, were less fully established. All the same, these lands were a part of Western Christianity and this has located Central Europe firmly in association with the West.

At the same time, in the realm of formal adherence and observation something of the centuries-long association with Eastern Christianity and Islam did not leave it untouched. Central Europe, given that it was a frontier area, lived closer to and was frequently subordinated to the Caesaropapist or Islamic imperium, which diluted its Western value system and introduced new elements into it. What is also relevant here is that the area was absorbed into the Western cultural sphere relatively late and it received Western institutions in a more or less fully-fledged form.

Native Central European input existed, but was smaller than the import. The founding of universities in Prague and Cracow illustrate this. Although they were both among the earliest such foundations north of the Alps, the concept of the university as a centre of specialization was developed elsewhere and, to an extent, these foundations were a kind of cultural colony. They were not, of course, entirely alien, but they were never as fully nostrified as, say, Bologna or Paris or Oxford. Similar patterns can be seen in the reception of, say, the Gothic or the introduction of feudal institutions, etc. Essentially, the political, economic and cultural matrix into which these Western institutions were placed never fully approximated to their places of origin. Therefore, either these institutions and technologies underwent some transformation or they remained alien to the region. Usually, they had features of both. It is in this sense, that Central Europe is transitional, transmittory and liminal.

Nor can it escape attention that Central Europe remained a frontier area quite literally until a much more recent period than did Western Europe.[20] The Polish eastern marches – the Kresy – the Pannonian plain, not to mention the Balkans, were the untamed Wild East of Europe, in some cases until well into the nineteenth century. In the military frontier that ran through Croatia, Slavonia and into the Banat, the tradition of adult male arms bearing survived into this century.

THE THREAT OF REDUCTIONISM

For Miłosz, much of Europeaness was bound up with the cultural eradiation of Paris, something which has almost died away and, by implication, has not been replaced by a functional equivalent. Indeed, the alternatives (again, this is as much implicit as explicit) are much more dangerous. Whereas there was once a common style in literature, a similarity of approaches, a shared cultural fund of ideas, images, values, these are under pressure from the processes of homogenization engendered by the march of science and technological change.[21] There are real dangers from a reductionism to so-called scientific principles, even in areas where these have little or no validity. At first sight, this might seem to have only marginal political relevance, but it is possible to interpret what Miłosz said (and the context, the Charles Eliot Norton lectures at Harvard, was literary rather than political which might explain why Miłosz himself left this unclear) as pointing the finger towards Sovietization, albeit there is no doubt of his intention to give his reproofs universal applicability. All the same, the all-exclusive emphasis on 'scientific socialism' and the threat of reductionism in the name of this principle is one that Central Europe has been exposed to for four decades. Equally, there is another thread in Miłosz's argument that is more universal – the danger that all processes, in West and East alike, are to be subordinated to the homogenization of so-called scientific principles.

The insistence on the need to reject reductionism in the name of Europeanism underlines both the multiple, varied quality of the European tradition, and the proposition that Central Europe shares in this. Underlying this point is the implication once again, that those coming from the edge of Europe have a better view of what it is than those who live in its centre. In this sense, Central Europeanism potentially has something wider to offer than a locally useful political device. Csaba G. Kiss points to a kind of Central European early warning system, which has acted as a sensor pointing towards phenomena later to become familiar to the whole of Europe. These include the soullessness and impenetrability of the modern state counterposed to the powerlessness of the individual.[22]

Central Europeanism can thus become an instrument for interpreting traits in all parts of Europe and can be a way of recognizing the main sources of the threats to Europeanness. This definition of reductionism appears to be far-reaching and covers any doctrine or proposition that claims to be able to understand all phenomena by a single overarching criterion and from which all others are to be derived. This can be Marxism, that seeks to reduce everything to economics, or religious or mathematical or what you will. The entire point about Europe is that it is a broad tradition which accepts conflicting and overlapping ultimate criteria, with none of them accepted as overarching.

Miłosz has not been the only one to insist on the strength of the European tradition and the place of Central Europe within it. Kundera, in his essay 'The Tragedy of Central Europe' took an analogous position, though from a more overtly political standpoint. In a way, Kundera's essay was a fortuitous and intuitive sense of a debate that was awaiting a particular focus to raise to to the surface. It was not a particularly scientific essay, but much more of a polemic; all the same, Kundera undoubtedly crystallized a set of ideas congenial to many in Central Europe, even if his writing elicited a good deal of scepticism elsewhere.

In his article he argues that Central Europe has been kidnapped by Russia; that Europe as a whole is the poorer for it; that as a result European culture has been subjected to a process of erosion, of the decomposition of its values and that creativity in Central Europe has largely ceased. This may be too pessimistic. It is hard to disagree with Kundera that artistic creativity – especially the broad, all-encompassing artistic works that gave meaning to social and political reality – has lost its sweeping quality. The idea that a major novel can distil a particular wide experience and give access to it by reinterpreting it, has lost its persuasiveness as society has grown in complexity. The problem is, rather, that the author (novelist, poet, dramatist) is no longer capable of seizing the totality of society and reflecting it through his/her own imagination because it has become too convoluted. Certainly, this has meant that the traditional role of the literary/creative intellectual has declined by comparison with the past and his/her stature has declined with it. But this does not mean, as Kundera seems to suggest, that creativity has deteriorated or ceased or has become impoverished. Instead the creativity that he finds lacking has shifted away from the traditional creative-cultural intelligentsia towards the social-scientific intelligentsia (historians, economists, lawyers and others). Indeed, the fact that the debate has been taking place testifies to the viability of Central Europeanness and to the need for an identity that would replace the straitjacket into which the area was constrained politically by the Soviet Union.

HISTORY AS AN ACTOR

Attempts to give Central Europeanness a sharper focus take up certain themes, sometimes overlapping with, sometimes cross-cutting other arguments, in an endeavour to locate this identity in a broad matrix. A second essay by Miłosz[23] ranges widely over the Central European past and present, in order to distil from literature what he considers to be some of the key features of the region and to offer answers to the question, what is specific to Central Europe. His first point concerns awareness of history. He argues that history is an actor in the present, possibly as a surrogate for it. Whereas in

Western culture, 'time is neutral, colourless, weightless ... [in Central Europe it] is intense, spasmodic, full of surprises, indeed practically an active participant in the story.' His explanation is that time flow is associated with change, often violent change, over which neither individuals or collectivities appear to have much control and is the more menacing. Consequently, they attribute an autonomy to it.

It is hard to disagree with Miłosz that the Central European tradition does have a very different attitude to history from what is found further West. Obviously all communities must have a sense of a shared past to be deserving of the name, but in Central Europe perceptions of history, its public roles and functions, are marked by a historicism, a propensity to project the present onto the past, to see history as a weight on the present that precludes choice and to seek legitimation for the present by often obscure and, prima facie, inappropriate historical precedents and to assume that answers to the present will be found in the past, that the present is best understood through the past.[24] One contemporary example of his may be seen in the Rumanian claim that by reason of Daco-Roman continuity, the Rumanian national imperative of creating an ethnically homogeneous state is justified through primacy of settlement. It is open to question whether ethnic rights (in the political realm) are most usefully determined by arguments over ethnogenesis.

The second proposition put by Miłosz is that irony, by reason of dislocated history and national humiliation giving rise to self-pity, a propensity to sentimentalize history and national identity, plays a far more salient role in the Central European mind-set. So, by way of example, Central Europeans might ask how it comes about that they have to cope with the irony of being colonies in an age of decolonization and, even worse, their colonial overlords insist that their rule be proclaimed just. What is to be the response to this Russian demand for self-worship? Hence, in this context, irony can help a community to come to terms with a fate over which it has no control and against which it feels itself to be helpless.

Miłosz's argument may be extended in seeing a broader and deeper function for irony. Irony is a way of understanding and structuring all processes in Central Europe, not just historical. In Central Europe, political power and the exercise of that power have operated according to a formally proclaimed set of regularities (even rules), which has become ossified and are not open to questioning by public opinion. Irony can therefore channel grief, anger, frustration – other politically unacceptable emotions – into something less destructive. In this respect, irony functions as a survival strategy, as a conventionally acceptable mode of structuring experience which establishes space between the individual and his sense of powerlessness. Švejk may have been a Czech, but his obdurate obedience to superior orders as a way of acting out humiliation and distancing himself from it through irony, is recognizable throughout the area.

THE POST-WAR EXPERIENCE

To all the foregoing must be added the determining experience of the wartime and post-1945 period. This has shaped central European perceptions in ways that are radically different from those of Western Europe. In the first place there was the experience of war and mass slaughter in Europe's twentieth century civil war of 1914–45.[25] This enhanced a sense of helplessness, of being caught up in events over which individuals have no control, where even bare survival is conditional, something which must have been exacerbated by its having come after the tranquillity of their grandfather's experience. In this situation, death and destruction were immediately experienced, as opposed to something which had become mythical or fantastical, as something outside the everyday range. The mass slaughter of 1914–45 also brought with it the experience of revulsion and quiescence – not least through the slaughter of the most active and the traumatization of the survivors. To this must be added demographic displacement. In the main, the Central European region was far more deeply affected by this than the West. It resulted in the destruction of continuity of residence, the evolution of which in the area was in any case late because of delayed urbanization. Thereby the growth of informal networks was held back, the broadening out of the individual view from family to something wider was hindered, and with it the slow, organic emergence of a widening number of networks to which individuals belong, thereby impoverishing their range of choice and impeding the patterns of lateral and vertical loyalties. The rootlessness of which several Central European writers complain has certainly been enhanced by the wartime experience in this respect.

Even more destructive, however, was the experience of an alien, totalizing revolution. The Stalinist period left deep marks on the area which mark it off from the West. The particular aspects that have to be stressed in this connection include the concentration of power in the hands of the communist party, which imposed its rule in the name of an ideology that was far from having attracted consensual support, and the concomitants of the revolution – rapid industrialization, the destruction of pre-existing rural patterns through collectivization, the brutalization of society by the engendering of fear, the enforcement of new and indigestible patterns of behaviour, the destruction of the language of public discourse and its replacement by alien codes and thoroughgoing atomization.

This has added immeasurably to the already well-established uncertainty and insecurity that was so characteristic of the region even before the communist revolution. In this context, by an irony which Central Europeans will relish, there has been a major divergence between the two halves of Europe concerning attitudes towards the Marxian legacy. Although the 1980s have seen a distinct waning of the erstwhile enthusiasm for the etatist solution of substituting the state for society in the West, there are still strong and influential currents that remain attracted to Marxian approaches. In the main, much of the political centre, not to mention the democratic left, is prepared to accept that while the Marxist answer as such may be mistaken, on the whole Marxism is about finding what is good in man. In Central Europe this attitude has been almost wholly eradicated by the actual experience of being ruled by self-professedly Marxist ideals. The depth of scepticism, disbelief, if not actual detestation of the Marxist legacy in Central Europe has no parallel in the West, where the welfare state experience of the immediate post-war era elicited a rather milder reaction in the form of anti-etatist, free market currents. As far as Central Europe is concerned, it has taken well into the 1980s before the sterile Marxist – anti-Marxist dichotomy has come to be replaced by a more wide-ranging debate.

The question of the language of public discourse requires further exploration, but it is hard to avoid the preliminary conclusion that in Central Europe there is something of a problem for anyone attempting to escape the all-enveloping, stultifying official language of Marxism-Leninism, which has been voided of meaning and is employed primarily as an instrument of censorship and as a self-sustaining ritual.[26] Occasionally, it is true, 'real language' – the language actually used in private discourse – breaks through. One noteworthy illustration of this came in August 1980 in Poland, when suddenly after weeks of industrial unrest – the wave of strikes which were to debouch into the founding of Solidarity – the official media stopped using euphemisms like 'unauthorized stoppages of labour' and referred to 'strikes'. But this is rare. In the Polish case, it was indeed the precursor of the irruption of the articulation of social autonomy that the system had denied by all the power at its disposal and was quick to re-establish after Martial Law. It is instructive that the invasion of the private sphere by the language of officialdom has left its legacy. Even *samizdat*, which has the express purpose of emancipating language from the fetters of the Marxist – Leninist meta-language, has been at times so imbued with the latter as to be near impenetrable. An egregious example of this last is the document prepared in 1986 by 22 Hungarian journalists and others in support of emancipating the public sphere from official control. Some of this document, which calls for openness and clarity, is practically unintelligible.[27] The distinction between the different halves of Europe is very deep in this area. While the bureaucratic, jargon-loaded forms of public expression, that rely on the passive, on impersonal forms, on mindless and meaningless abstractions, are not unfamiliar in the West, there have always been countervailing forms of expressions that stress clarity, easiness of access (e.g. newspapers) and intelligibility.

Underlying the problem of language is the fear particular to the area that the loss of language will be followed by the ineluctable loss of nationhood, culture, identity and eventually of self. The consciousness that this has political origins only makes matters worse, because it underlines the sense of helplessness felt in the face of Soviet power. This helps to explain the seemingly irrational refusal by Central Europeans to learn Russian. There is a near universal conspiracy that Russian, which is compulsory throughout the area (except Rumania), is not to be learned. This applies as much to the Slavonic Poles and Czechs, for whom learning Russian presents no major technical problem, as it does to the Hungarians.

THE STATE AND THE INDIVIDUAL

The defensive strategies developed in the different regions differ too, and predictably so. Given that the powerlessness of the individual in Western Europe has at no stage been as intense as in post-war Central Europe, strategies of dealing with the intrusiveness of the state have differed as well. In the latter, the most noteworthy have been irony, detachment, a readiness to invest unrelated events with symbolic significance, a propensity to historicism, a distrust of the state and officialdom as 'inauthentic' and a corresponding quest for control over one's life, all of which – as argued in the foregoing – already had well-established antecedents. But this has gone hand-in-hand with the search for new – old values as well. These include a revival of religiousness on a much wider basis than in the West, most obviously in Poland, but elsewhere too.

Politically and culturally rather more significant, however, is the problematic of the nation, nationhood and nationalism. In the Central European arena, nationalism has acquired a bad name. Many of the sins of the region have been attributed to it, perhaps not always justly. On the one hand, there is no doubt whatever that by emphasizing exclusivity and factors of divisiveness as a way of protecting the nation, Central Europeans have contributed to the instability of the region and thus the insecurity of their existence. On the other hand, the reception of nationalism was successful in infusing these societies with a new sense of purposiveness and in energizing them to construct more modern societies than the backward, archaic and segmented formations that existed in the pre-modern period. Nationalism will not go away in Central Europe, not least because it was the original mass political ideology of the region. But this legacy has received a new twist in the communist period. By effectively rooting out all other political traditions and values, which the communists effected during their externally imposed revolution, they left the field clear for the one which proved resistant to them – nationalism.[28]

The difficulty here is that nationalism is effective only in a certain limited range – broadly, those associated with the sustaining of identity. In many respects, this has been an overriding necessity in the region, but beyond that, nationalism has little to offer. Indeed, in its relentless emphasis on inward-looking, mildly or assertively xenophobic characteristics, its preference for organic rather than individualistic approaches, it promotes values which are not entirely incompatible with a modified communist authoritarianism. Ceausescu's Rumania is the best illustration of this. In this sense, the clean sweep of other values by the communists has resulted in a new reductionism – the pre-eminence of nationalism, which again threatens to differentiate Central Europe from the West. As against this, given the origins of nationalism as a political doctrine derived from culture, the peoples of the region are in an inescapable dilemma as long as the existing system subsists. They must defend their cultures, even if the price of this is high in terms of entrenching divisions and ignoring their neighbours facing near identical problems.

This is why the emergence of the Central Europe debate and the slow, halting (re)construction of a Central European identity have such a significance. Not only does this identity offer a way out of Soviet-type homogenization in emphasizing the European qualities of the local cultures, including above all those of pluralism and democracy, but by offering individuals a second, higher tier of identity, it can help them to escape the threat of reductionism encapsulated in political nationalism. By the same token, despite all the major and minor variations that differentiate Central Europe from the West, the Central Europe project is potentially a viable way of re-Europeanizing the area, of recovering some of the values, ideals, aspirations, solutions and practices that were eliminated by Soviet-type systems.

This is the sense in which the revival of the Central European idea is much more than a passing fancy, more than k.u.k. nostalgia, more than a backward glance at Kakania, Kaffee mit Schlagsahn und Sachertorte, an attempt to escape from the unpleasantness of contemporary realities into a misty and romanticized past. The whole thrust of the Central European debate has been to give it meaning under current political conditions and to forge it into an identity which is authentic enough to act as an organizing principle for those seeking something other than Soviet-type reality. How far this will work, or indeed, whether it will work at all, is something that only the people affected can decide. In the late 1980s, all the evidence suggests that the identity of Central Europeanness is attractive enough to a sufficiently wide range of people to give it a good head of steam.

NOTES

1 Vernon Bogdanor, 'Drawing the Lines', *Encounter*, September-October 1986, pp. 52–7.

28   George Schöpflin

2   Analysis of the Russian tradition has a sizeable literature, including Richard
    Pipes, *Russia under the Old Regime* (Weidenfeld, 1974); Roger Pethybridge, *The
    Social Preclude to Stalinism* (Macmillan, 1974); Tibor Szamuely, *The Russian
    Tradition* (Secker & Warburg, 1974); Teodor Shanin, *Russia as a 'Developing
    Society', Vol 1 The Roots of Otherness: Russia's Turn of the Century*
    (Macmillan, 1985), as well as Isaiah Berlin, *Russian Thinkers* (Penguin, 1979).
    The question has also arisen in connection with the 'Europeanness' debate and
    the status of Central/Eastern Europe launched by Milan Kundera's essay 'The
    Tragedy of Central Europe', *New York Review of Books*, 26 April 1984. This
    was also published under the title 'A Kidnapped West or a Culture Bows Out', in
    Granta, No. 11 (1984), and the responses to it, notably by Milan Šimečka,
    'Another Civilization? An Other Civilization?', *East European Reporter*, 1:2;
    Mihály Vajda, 'Who Excluded Russia from Europe?', ibid., 1:4; and Jane
    Mellor, 'Is the Russian Intelligentsia European? A Reply to Šimečka', ibid. The
    last three articles are included in this volume, see pp. 159–77.
3   Vernon Bogdanor, ibid.
4   John A. Armstrong, *Nations before Nationalism* (Chapel Hill, 1981).
5   Pipes, op.cit., p. 8.
6   This idea is taken from Julian A. Pitt-Rivers, *The People of the Sierra* (University
    of Chicago Press, 1971).
7   George Steiner, *In Bluebeard's Castle* (Faber, 1971), pp. 13–27.
8   Alain Finkielkraut, 'What is Europe?', *New York Review of Books*, 5 December
    1985 further mentions colonialism as a factor that militated against the
    acceptance of the European idea as positive on the part of the post-1945 left,
    inasmuch as Europe was viewed in negative terms as colonialist and imperialist.
9   The existence of a separate set of Church courts administering Canon law was an
    important source of alternative power to secular rulers.
10 Jenö Szücs, *Vázlat Európa három történeti régiójáról* (Magvetö, 1983); there is a
    somewhat idiosyncratic translation of this excellent essay, as 'The Three
    Historical Regions of Europe', in *Acta Historica* (Budapest), 29:2–4 (1983), pp.
    131–84 and sections, in a different translation appear in John Keane, (ed.) *Civil
    Society and the State* (Verso, 1988).
11 William H. McNeill, *The Pursuit of Power* (Blackwell, 1982), pp. 102–17.
12 Ibid, passim.
13 Stavro Skendi, 'Crypto-Christianity under the Ottomans', *Balkan Cultural
    Studies* (Columbia University Press, 1980), pp. 233–57, discusses some concrete
    instances of externalization.
14 Czesław Miłosz, *The Captive Mind* (1953) remains the classic account.
15 Mihály Vajda, 'Kelet-közép-európai perspektívák' (East-Central European
    Perspectives), *Hirmondó* (Budapest, *samizdat*), No. 8 (1984), pp. 4–23. There is
    a complete translation of this highly persuasive article in John Keane (ed.) *Civil
    Society and the State*, ibid.
16 Paul Hollander, *Political Pilgrims: Travels of Western Intellectuals to the Soviet
    Union, China and Cuba* (1981).
17 Czesław Miłosz, *The Witness of Poetry* (1983), p. 4.
18 Csaba G. Kiss, 'Közép-európai irók – Közép-Európáról: Bevezetö egy nem létezö
    olvasókönyvhöz', *Valóság*, 30:5 (May 1987), pp. 56–63. And see pp. 127–38 in

this volume for a translation in full.
19 Armstrong discusses this in op.cit.
20 W. H. NcNeill, *Europe's Steppe Frontier* (1964).
21 Armstrong, op.cit., p. 104.
22 See pp. 127–38 in this volume.
23 Czesław Miłosz, 'Central European Attitudes', *Cross-Currents: A Yearbook of Central European Culture*, No. 5 (1986), pp. 101–8 and see pp. 118–26 in this volume.
24 Numerous examples of this are detailed in Walter Kolarz, *Myths and Realities in Eastern Europe* (London 1946).
25 Naturally, this was also shared by Russia, if anything even more acutely, but was integrated into a different cognitive framework in which helplessness on the macro level is accepted, and the individual's horizons are restricted to the micro level.
26 Václav Havel, *The Power of the Powerless* (1985), pp. 23–96.
27 The full text of this appeared in *East European Reporter*, Vol. 3, No. 1, pp. 58–61.
28 Jan Józef Lipski, 'Two Fatherlands – Two Patriotisms', *Survey*, Vol. 26, No. 4 (117), Autumn 1982, pp. 158–75.

2
What Is Europe, Where Is Europe?
From Mystique to Politique
Hugh Seton-Watson

Nowadays, the idea of 'Europe' is equated in most West European minds with the economic institution of the EEC, the shared political-military commitments of NATO'S member-states, and with a vague notion of common – if frequently conflicting – interests, mediated by bodies like the European Parliament.

In the following chapter, Hugh Seton-Watson contrasts this formal and impoverished notion of Europe with the rich spiritual legacy of the 'European idea' dating from Christendom and the allegiance to a common cultural community which it spawned. Seton-Watson suggests that we need to revive once again a mystique *of Europe in order to resist both the reduction of the European idea to a* politique *dictated by 'Eurocrats', and the appropriation of European identity by Western Europe at the expense of the citizens of East-Central Europe.*

The way in which I have phrased my title is derived from a famous statement by Charles Péguy: *'Tout commence par la mystique, et finit par la politique.'* These words are virtually untranslatable, but perhaps a fair paraphrase would be: Every great enterprise starts off with enthusiasm for an exalted aim, and ends up being bogged down in petty politics.

How far does Péguy's proposition apply to what has been called 'the European idea' or 'the idea of Europe'? Let me first look to the *mystique*.

The word 'Europe' has been used and misused, interpreted and misinterpreted, in as many different meanings as almost any word in any language. There have been and are many Europes: the Europe of Greek mythology; the Europe of the geographers – the two extreme western peninsulas of the Asian land mass; the Europe of the Carolingian empire and its successor the EEC; the Europe of Byzantium; industrial Europe and agrarian Europe; 'capitalist' Europe and 'socialist' Europe; the Europe of the great powers and the Europe of Woodrow Wilsonian self-determination; the Europe of self-styled national states and of disaffected national minorities. That is not an exhaustive list.

Nearly all these Europes that I have mentioned come from the past, and some from the very distant past; but all to some extent belong also to the present. I must frankly admit my conviction – based on over 50 years of efforts to understand both numerous periods of history, and current politics as I have lived through them – that past and present are inextricably intermixed; and I make no apology for jumping to and fro in time in what I have to say.

Europe is more than a geographical expression. The growth of an increasingly homogeneous European culture, and also a belief among thinking men and women that they belong to a single, even if diverse, European cultural community, are facts of history and facts of this present time. The notion of a European cultural community, allegiance to which transcended, but did not normally contradict allegiance to a more precise regional or national sovereignty, is derived, I think, from an earlier allegiance to Christendom, and this in turn has its antecedents. Let me look briefly at these.

The notion of Christendom – a community of peoples, and a geographical area, as distinct from 'Christianity' which is a religious faith, or a variety of faiths of a common origin – goes back to the grant by Emperor Constantine to Christians of equal rights with other religions, which developed into an exclusive status for Christianity as the religion of the empire. Thereafter the Roman Empire was the land of the true faith, and the outside world was the land of infidels. This dichotomy became still sharper after the Muslim conquests of the seventh century, when Christendom became almost confined to Europe – and not all Europe, since it lost most of Spain for more than 500 years: and before Spain had been recovered, most of Russia, all the Balkans and the remnant of Asia Minor had been lost. The allegiance to Christendom as a higher ideal transcending narrower territorial and feudal loyalties was maintained by the reality of conflict, on sea and land, with Islam. It inspired the Crusades, which were of course also motivated by all sorts of ambitions, political intrigues, and lust for plunder. Its equivalent was the Muslim division of the world into the House of Islam and the House of War which – similarly combined with ambitions, intrigues and lust for plunder – inspired the numerous Arab or Tartar or Ottoman invasions of Europe, the last being the 1683 Siege of Vienna, after which there was a rapid decline in the fear of Islam and in the lip-service paid by monarchs to the defence of Christendom.

The dichotomy between Christendom and infidel was thus a reality for more than a millenium. But it too was related to something still more ancient, which we are too often inclined to forget in thinking about the origins of Europe. This is the dichotomy between the civilized world and barbarians. At the other end of the world the Chinese have long thought in these terms, but their concepts and ours hardly touched each other before the nineteenth century. In our part of the world this dichotomy was first clearly expressed in the two familiar contrasts of Jew and Gentile, and of Hellene and barbarian. The Jews were a small compact community with their own territory, something not so very different from the modern concept of a nation. But the Hellenes were divided between dozens of sovereignties, little states which fought each other, often savagely. Nevertheless, they were aware of being Hellenes and as such different from barbarians. The notion of barbarian soon came to mean not only people of foreign land and foreign speech, but also people living at a lower level of humanity, what we today would call 'uncivilized'. This was how the Hellenes and at a later period the Romans, heirs to Hellas, saw it. Today we may perhaps dispute their judgement: the greatest adversaries of Hellas, and later of Rome, the Persians, were certainly not uncivilized, and I suspect that the debt to them of Rome, and of ourselves as descendants of Rome, may be quite considerable.

The two dichotomies – civilization and barbarism, and true faith and infidel – were fused in the later Roman Empire. The one word which combined true faith with civilization was 'Christendom'. The Roman Empire disappeared, the barbarian Teutons and Slavs were brought into the true faith, and Christendom became coextensive with Europe – a geographical, not a cultural term. Across the Mediterranean a new religion and a new civilization flourished. Neither the Muslim world of the Abbasids nor the Europe of Charlemagne or Empress Irene was uncivilized, but this did not stop fanatics on either side from seeing them as such. And the general public image, or traditional stereotype, which emerged through the centuries was closer to the outlook of the fanatics than of the enlightened few on either side.

Already at the dawn of the Middle Ages a division, more important than the boundaries of local sovereignties, was beginning to appear within Christendom. Rome became a provincial city, while Constantinople remained the centre of a still powerful empire and of a sophisticated system of government, and the seat of a Patriarch whose missionaries went out to convert numerous pagan peoples, meeting and competing with the emissaries of the Bishop of Rome.

The contrast between Rome and Constantinople was deepened when a Pope crowned Charlemagne as Holy Roman Emperor on Christmas Day 800 AD. The authority of this revived Empire received at least verbal recognition from rulers in an area of Western Europe, whose boundaries coincided to a remarkable degree with those of the original EEC. Doctrinal disagreements between the two Churches grew fiercer, and led in the eleventh century to a rejection by Constantinople of the supremacy of Rome. Since then we have had a Roman Catholic Church and an Orthodox Church, hierarchically and dogmatically separate from each other. Even so, the notion of a single common Christendom survived, and was perhaps increased by the common experience of the early Crusades. It took a very heavy blow in the so-called Fourth Crusade of 1204, which consisted of the seizure of Constantinople by the western Crusaders at the instigation of the Venetians. This crime created a profound distrust of the West by the Greeks, traces of which survive to the present day.

Still more important, I think, were two great conquests of European lands from the east: first, of Russia by the Mongols, whose successors the Tartar Khans became Muslim, and second, of the Orthodox Slav states of the Balkans, and of Constantinople itself, by the Ottoman Turks. For roughly 200 years, from 1250 to 1450, the frontier of the lands of civilization and the true faith lay along the eastern borders of Poland and the north of what is today Rumania, and for the next 250 years the frontier swung round westwards through Hungary and down to the Adriatic. Beyond this line, to the east and south, were infidels and barbarians. Beyond it also were Christians, but these were almost all Orthodox, not Catholic; and so the rulers and thinkers of unconquered Christendom gradually, if not explicitly at least implicitly, wrote them off. Christendom became coextensive with Catholic Europe west of the Tartar and Ottoman borders.

The Balkan Orthodox mostly remained under the Turks for 400 years, but the Russians re-emerged sooner. Already in the sixteenth century there was a Principality of Moscow which was rapidly growing into a serious military power. The Poles, accustomed to seeing their border as the border of Christendom, found it difficult to see in the Muscovites fellow-members of Christendom. In the Polish view of Russians even today, apart from the traditional hostility to dangerous neighbours, and long memories of injustice and suffering in the past 200 years, there remains, I think, an element of contempt for the barbarian which goes back to a more distant past. There is something there which is not present in the long historical rivalries of western peoples, French and Germans, French and English, even English and Scots.

Equally important, and less appreciated, is how the Muscovites then saw the rest of the world. In the Orthodox view, the Catholics were schismatics who had seceded from the true faith – and of course the Protestants after the Reformation were schismatics from schismatics. Once Muscovy had shaken off the Tartar yoke, its ruler – Great Prince, later Czar (a Slavicization of the word Caesar) – was the only independent Orthodox ruler in the world, which meant the only truly Christian ruler. Christendom, the land ruled by a Christian monarch, *was* Muscovy: nothing else was. Muscovy faced to the west and north the schismatics whose vanguards were the Romanist Poles and the Protestant Swedes; and in the east and south the infidels – Tartars and Ottomans.

In the seventeenth and still more in the eighteenth centuries the idea of

Europe began to replace the idea of Christendom in the west. This was the result of various processes which made themselves felt at the end of the Middle Ages: the rise of secular sovereign states, expansion across the oceans, scientific discoveries, and above all the religious wars of the Reformation, which tore Christendom to pieces and created in thinking minds a profound disillusionment with the idea that religion could be the main unifying force in human communities.

The overarching unity of medieval Christendom had been expressed in the basic similarity, side by side with regional variety, of religious painting, church architecture, and literature in the common Latin language. In the secularizing Europe of the eighteenth century, styles of painting and architecture were no less interrelated; this was still more true of the flowering art of music; and though the growing secular literature was expressed in diverse languages its content was increasingly similar from country to country. This new secular European culture began to get a hold on the minds not just of a tiny vanguard of advanced thinkers, scholars and jurists, but of a much wider educated class, not excluding rulers and their officials.

If Europe was replacing Christendom in both Catholic and Protestant lands, this was not at first visible in Russia. Muscovy was coextensive with Christendom, and Europe was something foreign and odious, dominated by Romano-German schism. Certainly, there were individual Russians to whom Polish, Swedish, or German models were attractive, and such influences were not unknown at the court of Czar Aleksei Mikhailovich (1645–76), but they were very much a minor trend. This changed with the advent of Peter the Great. Though the effectiveness of his policies is arguable, and his motivation debatable, his reign was still a turning-point and he is assured of his place in history as the great prototype of the artificial modernizer of the underdeveloped society: the number of his would-be imitators in the twentieth century is legion. The myth of Peter, the creation of the new capital, and the symbolism of Pushkin's great poem 'The Bronze Horseman' have done their work in human history, and are doing it still, and no amount of burrowing by irreverent historians into the history of the real Peter will undo it, for better or worse.

Peter decided that Russia must become part of Europe, and his successors never abandoned that purpose, even if they ignored or reversed some of his policies. The Russian elite succumbed to the charms of secular European culture and of the French language. The Russian court modelled itself on European courts, the Russian dynasty intermarried with European dynasties and was welcomed by them. More important, Russian armies proved a match for the best European armies. Apraksin entered Berlin in 1760, and Suvorov beat armies of the French Revolution on Italian soil in 1799.

The age of St Petersburg, from 1702 to 1918, was the age of Russian membership of Europe, but it had its limitations. The growth of European unity in the eighteenth century was shaken by the first of the three great modern European civil wars, from 1793 to 1815, which Russian did little to bring about, but from which Russia was one of the chief sufferers. The invading army of Napoleon, which included contingents from most parts of Europe, aroused in the whole Russian people an implacable patriotic resistance, in which priests and peasants saw the enemy as the hordes of the Antichrist, and many more sophisticated Russians decried the forces of Romano-Germanic schismatic Europe, spearheaded once more by Poles (Napoleon had about 90,000 Polish soldiers, one in seven in his total). Nevertheless, after it was over, Europeanization became once more the aim both of Czars and of the social elite, although different schools of thought in Russian looked to different Europes, from the Prussia of Frederick II to the England of Gladstone or to the France of the Paris Commune. And below the educated elite – no less European than the French or German of its day – the cultural permafrost in which the peasantry was buried remained.

And now we come to the successive paradoxes of my parents' lifetime and my own. The cultural unity of Europe, the allegiance of educated persons all over this continent to an overarching idea of Europe, grew all through the nineteenth century, and especially in its last decades and in the first of this century. And side by side with it grew its negation: healthy natural devotion to individual national cultures, variant flowerings of an overall European culture, became perverted into nationalist fanaticisms: defence and self-defence of the disinherited and the oppressed became perverted into the fanaticism of unlimited class hatred; and boredom with routines of civilian life and yearning for the heroic was perverted into dreams of purifying blood-baths. And the dreams came true; nightmares were surpassed by real life. And the nightmares are still with us.

Russia, as a European great power, made its contribution to the launching of the second great European civil war, but was its chief victim. Russia's was not the highest casualty rate: that was the fate of Serbia, which lost a quarter of its population. But the successive disasters of war, civil war, famine, more famine and purges which overtook Russia surely surpass the record of any other country in modern times. Perhaps China could compete in ghastly rivalry.

And here is the paradox most relevant to my theme. The revolution made by one small political party against the parties which thought they had taken power when Czardom collapsed in war, was made in the name of what was then thought to be the most progressive body of thought in modern Europe – revolutionary Marxist socialism. But the effect of the Bolshevik victory was to destroy or drive into exile the greater part of the Europeanized section of Russian society – at least a million people. It is true that the Bolshevik party itself contained Europeanized Russians, not least Lenin himself, and that others found scope for their talents in the service of the new Soviet régime.

But these survivors did not last long: Stalin's purge in the 1930s finished them off, and political mores returned to the age of the Tartar yoke.

The transfer of the Bolshevik capital from St Petersburg back to Moscow had a perfectly practical immediate cause: the old capital was further away from the enemy, an essential point in 1918. However, it proved to be highly symbolic. Bolshevism turned its back on Europe. This of course is not how Soviet Communists see it. Russia, they would argue, belongs to Europe no less than it ever did, but this is for them of minor importance. The division that matters today is not between Europe and the rest of the world, but between socialism and capitalism. The Soviet Union is the leader of the forces of socialism, which are destined to prevail for the whole human race. The world is divided into two camps. On the one hand are the lands of socialism, or those struggling to build socialism. On the other hand there are three types: the capitalist countries; the developing countries in different degrees of dependence on the capitalists, varying from neo-colonial subjection to relative independence; and finally the countries ruled by renegades from socialism who falsely claim to be true socialists.

Now this picture does to some extent correspond to the reality of today — even if we may reject the labels which Soviet spokesmen would attach to us — and it is different from the past. Nevertheless, there is a remarkable similarity to an earlier stage of Russian history, that of sixteenth century Muscovy under Ivan the Terrible. The Muscovy was considered to be the only land with a Christian ruler. Muscovy *was* Christendom. It faced a hostile world, on the one hand schismatic Romano-German Europe, on the other hand the infidels. Today the Soviet Union is the land of socialism. Socialism *is* the Soviet system; no other system is. Some of the neighbours of the Soviet Union, and a few more distant lands, under Soviet tutelage, have made great progress towards socialism, but still lag behind the Soviet model. The outside world is hostile. On the one hand are the infidel exponents of unregenerate capitalism. On the other hand is the realm of the renegades to socialism, the Chinese Maoists. The main difference between the situation of the Soviet Union today and of Muscovy then is that then the schismatics were in the west and the infidels in the east, and today the positions are reversed.

Does a belief in the existence of a single European culture require the creation of a single European state, or federation of states? This was not the expectation of European intellectuals of the eighteenth and nineteenth centuries. After 1918, in search of thinking minds for drastic measures to prevent a repetition of the recent blood-bath, a few voices were heard in favour of the abolition of state sovereignty. But this was not prevalent in the heyday of the League of Nations, of Briand and Stresemann, whose outlook could well have been described by the slogan of a later generation: '*l'Europe des patries*'. In the 1930s, of course, Europeanism of any sort became remote. In the mid-1940s, during the third and worst European civil war, which was also truly a world war, the only unity offered to Europeans had as its spokesman Dr Joseph Goebbels and his weekly paper with cultural pretensions, *Das Reich*, to some extent an echo of the mythology of European unity favoured by Napoleon Bonaparte, and directed against the same two powers at opposite margins of the continent, Britain and Russia.

In the movement for greater European unity which developed after 1945, the nostalgic memory of a lost cultural unity was certainly a factor, but it was less prominent than a number of others which must be briefly mentioned.

One was the awareness of a common peril. Europe was threatened by Soviet power, as Christendom had once been threatened by Muslim power, first Arab then Turkish. One European, or partly European, power controlled half the continent beyond its borders, and the rest was in no position to resist its pressures from its own resources. It was not a question of an imminent danger of a Soviet military advance to the Atlantic. Rather, the danger came from economic exhaustion in Britain, internal disruption in France and Italy by indigenous forces linked to the Soviet Union, and the complete collapse and destitution of Germany. This rather complex but urgent danger was well understood by some Western statesmen, especially by Ernest Bevin and Dean Acheson. Together, in the face of great obstacles, not least from within their own countries, they set in motion the reconstruction of the economy of Western Europe. Then, political leaders began to think of ways of getting Europeans not only to live beside each other, but to work together.

A second force was the reaction of millions of Europeans against the destructive nationalism of the Age of Fascism. This was especially evident amongst French and Germans. The mutual fear and bitterness between these two had threatened the peace of Europe for hundreds of years, and especially for the past 80 years, and had greatly contributed to the making of both world wars. In the second of these both French and Germans had been utterly crushed and humiliated. As they scrambled painfully out of the pit, some of them resolved to put an end to this sterile enmity, and in the next two decades this aim was largely achieved. This has been seen by some British commentators as a misfortune for Britain, and the two men who did most to bring it about, General de Gaulle and Dr Konrad Adenauer, as unfriendly to this country. For my own part, I can only say that, having grown up in a time when reconciliation between these two great nations was more desirable, and more attainable, than almost anything, I watched the process with joy, and remain moved by the result, and do not believe that it can be to Britain's disadvantage.

The reaction against nationalism went naturally together with the notion of European solidarity. Especially for the defeated Germans and Italians, Europe was a replacement for the fatherland, the claims of which had been so long and so monstrously exploited and perverted by Hitler and Mussolini. A similar tendency was also to be seen further east, especially among the

Austrians, Czechs, and Hungarians. In the last two decades there has, I think, been some change. Generations born since the war have to some extent rediscovered a pride in and a devotion to their own national sub-cultures, without the xenophobia and arrogance of the Age of Fascism. My impression is that this is true of Germans and Italians, and certainly of Poles, Rumanians, and Hungarians. I would not, of course, claim that xenophobia has disappeared in those lands but it seems to me that it is far less than when I first visited them, and in general that the national patriotism of today is blended with European consciousness in a way that was not visible in the 1930s.

The French case is rather special. A sceptic may suggest that French enthusiasm for Europe is to some extent based on an identification of Europe with France, that European culture is French culture, that the appropriate language of European discourse is French and that the horrid patois of the Anglo-Saxons should be banished. There is something in this, but we must not exaggerate.

A third force which needs mention is American pressure for European unity. Certain deeply rooted American myths have to be borne in mind. There is the contrast between the numerous squabbling nations of Europe, with their endless entangling alliances and counter-alliances, and the great peaceful American nation, spread across a land about the size of the whole of Europe (including Russia to the Urals). It is true that America experienced a fairly frightful war 120 years ago with half a million dead, but it ended in victory for unity, and the generosity of the victors to vanquished ensure, so it is said, peaceful progress ever since. The secret of all this progress was the federal Constitution, strong enough and flexible enough to hold this great nation together already for almost 200 years. Why then can't the Europeans federate?

This, of course, has never been an official American demand, and the makers of American foreign policy have mostly known too much about Europe to think like this. But millions of Americans have thought and still do think this way, and a few words of explanation of the differences between Europe and America may be useful.

The American republic was populated from the beginning predominantly by people of one language – English – derived from mainly one country. Europe by contrast is the home of something like 50 language-groups which have existed as compact entities for a millenium or longer. Secondly, America was an almost empty land, full of splendid resources, and the Americans became, in David Potter's memorable phrase, a people of plenty. Europe, too, was and is extremely rich in resources, but they were divided between the numerous peoples: there has never been a time, as there was in American history, when this rich continent lay open to occupation and development by a newly arrived people. Thirdly, though the immigration of the nineteenth and twentieth centuries brought the United States millions of new citizens, at any particular moment the immigrants were but a small proportion of the total population. Uprooted from their homelands, they arrived in a country which already had its predominant language, its constitution, and its culture. They were also eager to be absorbed into this new culture, and if they themselves found it difficult, their children achieved it. In Europe, their kinsmen lived in solid compact populations in lands in which their ancestors had lived for generations or centuries, were attached to their distinct subcultures, and were being urged, by their politically conscious educated elites, to think of themselves as nations. Attempts either by pre-nationalist dynastic regimes or by proselytizing alien nationalist rulers to suppress their growing national consciousness caused them to follow extreme nationalist movements among their own peoples and this contributed as much as any other single cause to the unleashing of two world wars.

These differences between the American and European historical and social realities made the simple application of American federalist formulae to Europe quite unreal. But American exhortations to Europeans to unite undoubtedly had their effects.

Lastly I mention the economic forces for the creation of a West European common market, not because I think them less important than the forces which I have mentioned, but partly because my own economic knowledge is minimal, and still more because they are rather well known, and are constantly in the public mind, whereas the things which I have been stressing seem to me often to be forgotten. Moreover, it is, I think, true that the motives of the founding fathers of the EEC were not primarily economic, but that it seemed to them – no doubt rightly – that initial progress would come more easily and quickly in the economic than in other fields.

I come now to the question, what connection is there, or should there be, between a movement for European economic and political unity, and a sense of a European cultural community? The second can exist without the first: it did for more than 200 years. Can the first exist without the second? It can, but at great cost, and perhaps not for very long. Let us not underrate the need for a positive common cause, for something more exciting than the price of butter, more constructive than the allocation of defence contracts, a need for a European *mystique*. This was understood by the founders of the EEC, men well aware of the European cultural heritage, deeply marked by it. But when a *mystique* gets into the hands of the bureaucrats, there is apt to be trouble. Remember Péguy's aphorism, '*Tout commence par la mystique, et finit par la politique*'. The Brussels Eurocrats' *politique* may have much to be said for it, but it is a long way away from the *mystique* of Europe. The basic EEC territory was the former Holy Roman Empire of Charlemagne: even the border between the Federal Republic and the DDR is not very different from the line of Charlemagne's advance into Germany. Gradually this neo-

Carolingian empire has been extended, but with increasing pontifications as each new recruit was added.

Europe, whether it be a geographical, a cultural or a moral concept, has never been, and is not now, coterminous with the Carolingian empire. Attitudes to the concept of Europe today have striking similarities to those of the distant past. In particular, the two dichotomies of lands of civilization and barbarism, and lands of the true believers and the infidels reappear under new names on both sides of the Lübeck-Trieste line.

Of the dichotomies as seen from the Soviet side, and of the strange similarities in the Muscovite *'mentalités'* of late twentieth and late sixteenth centuries, I have already spoken. The two dichotomies apply also, though in different form, on the western side of the line. The spokemen of the EEC and NATO readily seek to appropriate the mystique of Europe, implying, even if not categorically asserting, that those beyond the line are sunk in a lower level of civilization, in fact in barbarism. They also see something which they call alternately 'the West' or 'Europe' as the protagonist of a true faith which most of them publicly identify with an abstraction called 'Western democracy,' while some still think in terms of the older contrast between Christendom and infidel or heathen. Their attitude recalls that of the leaders of late medieval and early modern Christendom who increasingly and implicitly wrote off the Christians living under Muslim rule.

But the truth is that nowhere in the world is there so widespread a belief in the reality, and the importance, of a European cultural community, as in the countries lying between the EEC territory and the Soviet Union. It is true that this belief is complicated by political considerations. The peoples of this region feel a certain resentment against the West Europeans for having done, as they see it, so little to help them; and at the same time, in terms of world power, they see the counterweight to their own imperial master not in Western Europe but in the United States. It might be argued that what they long for is membership of a Western community rather than of a European community. But these two concepts overlap in their imaginations, and the cultural community which they remember, or their parents remember and have told them of, is essentially European.

To these peoples, the idea of Europe is of a community of cultures to which the specific culture, or subculture, of each belongs. None of them can survive without Europe, or Europe without them. This is of course, a myth – by which I mean a sort of chemical compound of truth and fantasy. The absurdities of the fantasy need not obscure the truth; and whether admirable or not, any complex of ideas which gets a powerful hold over whole peoples is historically and politically important. Every modern nation has its historical mythology – including even the English, even if the most sophisticated among them turn their backs on it. For the western colonial subjects of the Soviet empire an historical mythology of Europe is added to their own individual national historical mythologies.

How many of them bother about these things? A minority of the population of course do, but a much higher proportion than among Western peoples whose national culture and identity has not been in danger for centuries. A large minority care deeply, and this includes working men and women in factory and field; and even of the majority, ill-fed peasants and all, I should hesitate to assume that allegiance, either to their own nation or to Europe is meaningless. 'The masses care for none of these silly ideas, only for material interests' (the comfortable patronizing cliche of progressive intellectuals) may or may not be true in England or Sweden. Maybe if it were universally true, the world would be a more comfortable place. But it is not, and least of all in the eastern half of Europe. The division of Europe and the forcible subjection of their national cultures to manipulation by conquerors whom they despise, is something to which they will not in the predictable future reconcile themselves.

My last sentence probably suffices to damn me in many minds as 'a cold warrior'. But all that I have done is to state in simple words the basic fact of which 40 years of study have convinced me. Yet such has been the impact of propaganda, counter-propaganda and disinformation that in the minds of hundreds of thousands of enlightened Western men and women, firmly devoted to freedom in their own countries, the present division of Europe has acquired a sanctity which they will fanatically justify; and to say that this division is permanently unacceptable for more than a hundred million Europeans, and will not last, is seen by them as tantamount to preaching nuclear war.

Now it is true that the emergence of Europe from the political ice age associated with the names of Metternich and Czar Nicholas I was brought about by revolutions (all revolutions of those years were crushed, just as all four revolutions since 1945 have been crushed), but by a series of what we may perhaps call medium-sized wars; and that the emergence of the new states in Eastern Europe was a result of a world war. It is also true that in a nuclear age, medium-sized wars in Europe are virtually inconceivable, and that a nuclear world war, whatever it did, would not liberate and reunite Europe. But do these truths give permanence and sanctity to today's division? There is just one statement that historians can safely make about history; that in history nothing is permanent. How change will come, historians are poorly qualified to predict; those who have tried have not added to human wisdom.

Let us stop thinking of the Soviet colonial empire as permanent, and stop speaking of the EEC's neo-Carolingian empire as Europe. There is nothing war-mongering or sacrilegious about these small changes in vocabulary.

The European cultural community includes the peoples living beyond Germany and Italy; and this is something which we should never forget, something in no way annulled by the fact that they cannot today belong to an all-European economic or political community. This is all the more reason for promoting, and for making the best possible use of, every sort of cultural contact with them that offers itself, and to show constantly that we recognize them as fellow-Europeans.

But do the British belong too? The belief that Britain has turned its back on Europe ever since the beginning of the British overseas empire, is widely accepted both within and outside Britain, but is at most a half-truth. It is easily forgotten that the English came rather late to overseas expansion, arriving after the Portuguese, Spaniards, and Dutch, and about the same time as the French. All these had strong links overseas, yet all took part in the cultural and scientific trends, as well as in the political and military conflicts of Europe, and so did the English, not to mention the Scots, Irish and Welsh.

While the metropolitan countries continued to be involved in Europe, from the overseas communities there emerged, in some cases through wars of independence and in others by mutual agreement, new states and new nations. Between the new states and the old not only trade but cultural links persisted and are still strong. However certain differences should be noted. Firstly, the total population of both France and the Netherlands is larger than that of persons overseas whose mother tongue is French or Dutch, whereas in the case of Portugal, Spain and Britain, the reverse is true. Secondly, whereas the numerous Spanish-speaking nations with few exceptions remain economically undeveloped, and all of them, as also the sole overseas Portuguese-speaking nation, are militarily weak, in the case of the English-speaking nations the reverse is true. Canada, New Zealand and Australia are advanced industrial urbanized states, and the United States is both economically and militarily the most powerful state in the world. If, then, the English have since the late nineteenth century been drawn away from Europe more than other nations of the west coast of the continent, this is because of the peculiar character of membership of the English-speaking world.

Not so long ago, it used to be argued that, for the British, membership of the Commonwealth was more important that membership of Europe. But though there are of course still many links with the former colonies, the expectation that the Commonwealth would be a signficant political unit has been proved to be fantasy. What has remained a reality is the English-speaking world, consisting of the United States, Britain, and three of the Old Dominions. When de Gaulle inveighed against *'les anglo-saxons'* he was speaking of something real. I do not see how any citizen of this country who knows something of international affairs and is concerned for the future of Britain can doubt that Britain belongs both to Europe and to the English-speaking world. For my own part, I know that my roots are in both, that I cannot give up either, that I cannot cut my mind or brain in two. The task that has lain before the British for the last three decades, and which regrettably their rulers have not discharged, is to be a strong binding force between the two, not to stand shivering on the brink of the Channel and the Atlantic, sneering in turn at those on each of the opposite shores, indulging alternatively in self-reproach and self-pity, doomed to the fate of the donkey which could not decide from which pile of hay to eat, ending up as prey for carrion feeders.

There is not much sign at present of an awareness of a European cultural heritage, a *mystique* of Europe, in Britain, or of any effort on the part of any political or cultural authorities to develop one. This may be partly due to the prevalence in a large part of our cultural elite of a hangover from empire in the form of a guilt complex towards the peoples of Asia and Africa. For a long time the word 'European' was associated with arrogant assertions of cultural, and racial, superiority. But if 'Europe' is associated with this arrogance in Asian and African minds, does this mean that Europeans should reject their own heritage? And if the history, arts, and literature of Europe are richer than those of sub-Saharan Africa, do we have to pretend it is not so? Can we not simply study honestly the African cultures, and help Africans to study their own? This I know well has been the practice in some parts at least of the British academic world, and one must hope that it will develop further. But it need not cause the British intelligentsia to shudder with guilt at the thought that the British is one sub-culture of a European cultural community.

This brings me to another confused but important question, the cultural relationship between Europe and America. 'European culture' is often said to be under attack from 'American mass culture'. It is easy enough to see what is meant by this, but rather difficult to formulate it in words. Could one say that contemporary mass culture is based on an ethos of short-term material hedonism: that the overriding purpose of all human endeavour should be to maximize material comfort? The larger the number for whom comfort is provided, the larger will be the profit for those who provide the relevant goods and services. Commercial profitability and mass consumer satisfaction go together. The best brief label for this that I know was designed by someone for whose memory I have little affection, but who was always better at words than deeds: Mussolini. His phrase was 'pluto-democracy'.

It is not my aim now either to denounce or to defend a culture or a society dominated by these principles, the practical results of which we all enjoy in our daily lives. The question which does concern me is, 'is this culture specifically American?' I think only to a rather small extent. It is American in so far as the United States is the most populous society of mass culture, and the first society to achieve it. The reasons for this lie in its history: partly in the great natural wealth of North America which the pioneers and subsequent immigrants had the great good luck to find there; and partly in the fact that the American republic was founded and developed by men consciously striving to create a new society and a new social ethos, no longer limited by traditional obligations and hierarchies. In Europe until about the middle of this century the commercial-hedonist values of capitalism had not won complete victory over the earlier values of service to the state, of classical humanism and of the City of God, whose origins go back through the Renaissance to the Middle Ages. In Europe the public ethos was an amalgam of these values, piled up on top of each other through the centuries, the relative strength of each constituent varying from country to country. This was especially true of the country which was the pioneer of capitalist enterprise, and also the country from which the ancestors of the American founding fathers had come, England.

But we would be wrong to see this contrast in absolute terms. The influence of the old traditions of Christianity, of Enlightenment and even of State service, were present in the minds of the Founding Fathers, and their influence can be traced in American history. Equally, the desire for material comfort was present in the minds of European men and women, and became a force as soon as most people began to feel that they could, or that they were entitled to, ask for a better life. This of course is neither a quick nor a simple process: it does not follow immediately from the introduction of universal suffrage, or the secret ballot, or even proportional representation. But by the 1960s it had become pretty widespread in Western Europe, enormously accelerated by television; and it had gone a long way in Eastern Europe too, and even in Russia itself, where material hedonism is in theory part of official doctrine, but long-term rather than short-term ('jam tomorrow'), and inhibited by politically-motivated economic scarcity and by well-organized coercion; and even in the Third World it had spread at least to a large part of the urban population. Consumerism, then, is not something inherently American. It is useless, as well as unhistorical, to make America the scapegoat for our troubled feelings. In so far as consumerism threatens the older values of what we may think of as European culture, this threat comes primarily not from America (even if some of its wares have American labels) but from within European society, and indeed from within the minds of almost all of us. The existence of consumerism does not prove the irrelevance of European culture; if European culture is a reality, it can accommodate consumerism, can come to terms with it as it has come to terms with more than one preceding ethos.

One final point I must make. I argued that the European idea replaced the idea of Christendom largely as a result of disillusionment with religious persecutions and wars. But this does not mean that religion ceased to be an important force in Europe, or that those who believed in a European cultural community did not believe in Christianity. Far from it. Christendom, the area within which Christianity has its believers, is worldwide, no longer coextensive with Europe. In today's world, allegiance to Christendom, the land of the true faith, can have no meaning. But Christianity is a powerful force still in Western Europe, and still more so in Eastern Europe. Any intelligent reader of the daily press must be aware of the strength of the Catholic Church in Poland. More difficult to estimate is the undoubted survival, inward renewal and expansion of the Orthodox Church in Russia.

The interweaving of the notions of Europe and of Christendom is a fact of history which even the most brilliant sophistry cannot undo. But it is no less true that there are strands in European culture which are not Christian: the Roman, the Hellenic, arguably the Persian, and (in modern centuries) the Jewish. Whether there is also a Muslim strand is more difficult to say. Medieval Muslim Spain was a channel by which European classical learning passed, through Romance versions of Arabic translations of Greek texts, into Western Europe. In the age of Ottoman greatness and decline, cultural interchange was less evident than commercial or military. In Europe today, even leaving out European Russia, there are many million Muslims, living in lands where many generations of their ancestors have lived. Modern Turks, of whom five million live in geographical Europe, and two million Bosnian Muslims in Yugoslavia certainly feel themselves Europeans, accept the European heritage as theirs. Whether this is true of the four million Albanians, with the highest birth rate in Europe, I would not risk a guess, still less of Muslim *Gastarbeiter* or immigrants from overseas. The apparently growing upsurge of Muslim militancy, in Muslim lands from Morocco to Malaysia, is perhaps above all anti-modernizing and anti-secular, but that it contains anti-Christian and anti-European elements can hardly be questioned.

However we may estimate the Muslim contribution, it is clear that the main strands in European culture have come through Christendom, from Hellas, Rome, Persia and the Germanic north, as well as from Christianity itself. To these were added the influences of the successive waves of invaders from the east as well as of the diverse cultures overseas which Europeans explored and exploited. The resultant compound, whose individual sources no one can unscramble, is the foundation on which the whole structure of modern science, industry and technology was built. These imposing structures fill the landscape, but the foundation is unseen and unremembered. There is still a European culture, and it is one embracing the people of the north-west peninsula of Asia and their offshore islands, and also many individuals outside it, in the Russian land mass and beyond the oceans.

It exists, but it comprehends only those who can see and feel it, and for this certain conditions must be fulfilled. In order fully to belong to European culture one must be aware of other Europeans, know some history, know another language or several, take some pleasure in literature or painting or old buildings. Those who have such awareness have always been minorities, everywhere. But in recent times some minorities have grown and some have shrunk. In most Continental countries there seems to be growth. Even the once invincibly unilingual Gallocentric French are learning their neighbours' speech as never before. In the Soviet empire there is a vigorous demand for foreign-language teaching, though there is some disagreement between rulers and ruled as to which language should be learned. Only in one country has the teaching of foreign languages – all of them, whether ancient or modern – the desire of pupils for them, and the belief by the authorities that they deserve study, strikingly slumped: in Britain. Nowadays foreigners are all learning English, so there is no need, some argue, for the English to learn theirs. Mass-produced translated texts will give us all we need, and with more and better computers, language learning not to mention literature and history, will be irrelevant.

Will they? How far is it possible to understand the thinking of persons of other lands without knowing either their language or their past? Even in hard-headed export trade the bilingual, or trilingual sales person has an advantage over the unilingual. As for history and literature, it is precisely the ability to remember, to imagine, and to record both memory and fantasy which differentiates man from ape.

Governments will continue to quarrel; conflicts of interest will persist, with changing shape and intensity, between nations and between classes; and the two ancient dichotomies of civilization against barbarism, and true faith against infidels, will reassert themselves from time to time.

But the unity of European culture is independent of these things. It is not an instrument of capitalism or socialism; it is not a monopoly possession of EEC Eurocrats or anyone else. To own allegiance to it is not to claim superiority to other cultures – not to the Chinese and Japanese, which today would be manifestly ridiculous; not to Muslim, even when its spokesmen proclaim their hatred of us; not to African, an injustice which is mercifully less widespread than it used to be; and not to American, though this is still quite fashionable among some who fancy themselves as European intellectuals. Nor should allegiance to it be incompatible with the aspiration to create in time a wider Western culture or still more distantly a world-wide culture of humanity. These admirable aspirations will not be advanced by ignoring or even erasing what is shared between all the peoples of Europe, or what is peculiar to each individual people. The unity of European culture is simply the end-product of 3,000 years of labour by our diverse ancestors. It is a heritage which we spurn at our peril, and of which it would be a crime to deprive younger and future generations. Rather it is our task to preserve and renew it.

3
The Meaning of the Social Evolution of Europe
István Bibó

The question of the location of Central Europe has preoccupied Hungarian historians, both in the geographical and in the political sense. While insisting on their European credentials, Hungarians have sought to differentiate between what was evidently their own different heritage and that of Western Europe, while firmly identifying themselves with it as a model to be emulated. This was the background against which a number of historians offered their definitions of Central Europeanness. They recognized that Hungary had much in common with Poland and Czechoslovakia, and shared certain features with Austria, some with Germany and the northern areas of Yugoslavia. On the other hand, there were marked differences between this Central European tradition and the Eastern one, to which Russia unquestionably belonged. The officially dominant line in Hungary had been that Europe was divided into two broad regions – eastern and western – with Hungary falling firmly in the former. This was widely interpreted as legitimating Hungary's inclusion into the Soviet sphere of influence. The difference was quintessentially about the make-up of Europeanness itself.

István Bibó first wrote on this topic in the immediate post-war period; it served as an early marker for the resurgence of the Central European idea.[1] He returned to this theme in the 1970s in his magisterial study of European history and traditions, an extract from which appears below. Here István Bibó considers the impact of the French Revolution, and especially its legacy of revolutionary violence, on subsequent concepts and forms of social change in Europe as a whole.

Bibó's essay was followed by Jenő Szűcs's much praised 'The Three Historic Regions of Europe', which directly argued that Central Europe constituted a specific region of Europe, with its own characteristics.[2] Péter Hanák's essay takes up the story where Szűcs left off and continues it into the modern period.

[...] The French Revolution was at the same time the most and the least successful revolution in European history, the most successful because it made possible a rational organization of society of a scope not achieved by earlier revolutions, and the least successful because it gave rise to a fear that has still not been outlived by the western world. What justifies and vindicates revolutionary violence? If we take into account that all violence, all hate springs essentially from the fear-distorted psychic state of man, we have to reject the idea that violence in and of itself has a liberating, creative effect, and that some kinds of social progress cannot be envisaged without violence. The basis of every productive attempt at organizing society is the realization that there are no irreducible conflicts of interest among people, only entrenched fears, perhaps built on fossilized social situations, but not real conflicts of interest, only conflicts of interest arising from such situations. Revolutionary violence is useful and fruitful if – and only if – it appears necessary to bring about the rapid dissolution of a fossilized power situation. In such a case, the role of the revolutionary violence is to show, with one or several violent gestures, that a power centre which looks invincible, intimidating, all-powerful and authoritative (but has in reality lost its function), has neither purpose nor strength left. This produces an immense feeling of liberation – psychological and actual liberation – among its subjects and opens up the way to the unfolding of their creative forces. Such revolutionary violence is fruitful only if it is momentary and, having accomplished its task, it ceases.

If this momentary revolutionary violence inspires in the victors a desire for permanence, and the pursuit of goals which can be realized only with the aid of a constant violence directed not only against the powerful but against the whole of society, and which cannot even in this way be made lasting, from that moment onwards revolutionary violence does not represent revolution but prepares for a new tyranny. It is not productive but instead fills society with incalculable fears.

The liberating effect of the French Revolution consisted of revealing to society from one day to the next that neither the monarchy nor the aristocracy were able to resist an uprising of the whole of French society, and thus it was possible to achieve quickly and easily the eradication of aristocratic privileges, and the jettisoning of most of its historical ballast. However, since this revolution was not controlled by the cautious bourgeoisie, which participated but was not alone in doing so, and had no decisive influence, the reins were handed over to rational social reformer intellectuals. They were motivated by ideology, subject to the terrible temptation of not stopping at the achieved results, but proceeding to further reforms based on abstract ideas not as easily realizable as had been the limitation of the monarchy and the abolition of aristocratic prerogatives. In a climate of anticlericalism generated by the ossification of the Catholic church during the counter-reformation, these enlightened intellectuals adopted the goal of destroying the church's spiritual power. Even though this goal seemed very modern and timely, its acceptance was the first step down a road where much more formidable and greater resistance was to be encountered than had been anticipated, and it became clear that the struggle no longer concerned the overthrow of a purely fictive power by the mere snap of the fingers. Rather, this was the path of an interminable and ultimately unwinnable combat which alienated the greater part of the country from the cause of the revolution; it meant the abandonment of the course of concrete social reforms for the sake of the unattainable goal of abolishing or transforming the religious feelings of the people.

The resistance of the monarchy, and of the otherwise helpless king became indomitably, or at least irrevocably, obstinate at this point. This was the complex of issues which eventually induced the monarchy to turn fully and openly against the revolution. The king turned against the Constituent Assembly primarily on the matter of the civil status of the clergy. This in turn provoked the attempted flight of the king, then the attempt of the Central European powers to intervene, and in the end it produced the revolutionary terror, the complete collapse of the monarchy and a perpetuation of violence in comparison with which the reign of Louis XVI appeared as a very mild form of rule. The Terror, for the justification of which an immeasurable amount of ink has been spilt, represented in essence a blind alley and the bankruptcy of the revolution.

It is not true that the maintenance of a revolution requires such terror; terror is necessary for the preservation of a revolution only if it adopts goals unattainable by sensible means. The revolution, received at first with general sympathy all over Europe, later aroused fear and in many respects hatred on account of the Terror. [...]

The unparalleled success and failure of this revolution and its lapse into terror created two unproductive human types. One is the revolutionary for whom the revolution is of such importance that he will do anything to justify the sterile, terroristic period of the French Revolution by recourse to such pretexts as national defence and domestic internal politics. In reality it was an outbreak of horrific mass hysteria which did not defend the French Revolution from those against whom it was meant to constitute a defence, but instead compromised it world-wide and caused the internal destruction of its brilliant personnel who were to be survived only by cynics and unscrupulous turncoats. The revolutionary is the kind of person who studies and elaborates the techniques of making revolution, the technique of perpetuating revolution, and devotes his life to this, although the most creative revolutionaries are those who choose this occupation under the impact of the given needs of a given moment and have not prepared for it, either professionally or technically, over a lifetime.

The other no less unproductive human type is the reactionary who, from a state of consternation over the Terror of the French Revolution, and pointing to the general upset and dismay generated by this period, rigidly opposes any revolutionary measure. He persecutes any manifestation of a revolutionary attitude, as well as of a reforming or critical one, and induces an ossified attitude in various institutions of power which discredits even the positive elements. The dangers of such a reactionary attitude are particularly great in that part of the world which considers itself to be the guardian of the achievements of the bourgeois revolution, and which in part does indeed preserve these achievements – let us call it the capitalist world – where a constricted fear of revolutionary developments can discredit the great historical merits of bourgeois democracy.

The next timely step in the social evolution of Europe, socialism, was formulated in this atmosphere of an extreme cult of revolution on the one hand, and of the wholesale rejection of revolution as holy horror on the other. This fact imposed an extremely heavy, initial burden upon socialism. In essence, the programme of socialism is only the logical continuation of the great step forward represented by the bourgeois democratic revolution. The bourgeois democratic revolution can be summed up as the gaining of ascendency of the consciously creative type of human being over the vainglorious, bellicose, aristocratic type.

In its time, the feudal and aristocratic system of Europe was a manifestation of the great social enterprise of Christianity aimed at the taming of violence, but this effort was obliged to come to a far-reaching and comprehensive compromise with that quarrelsome and barbaric aristocracy which had founded and organized the state of Europe. The more the endeavour to organize peace progressed, the more the loss of function by this aristocracy became evident. [...]

The bourgeois revolution was in a certain sense a logical continuation of the system of fedual liberties. However, this continuation was a relatively smooth one only in England, the Netherlands and northern Europe. In France it involved a great upheaval, and there is no doubt that there has been more connection and identity of tasks between the bourgeois and socialist revolutions than between either of these and Christian feudalism, with its aim of reducing violence. In essence the socialist revolution says that, as the social function of hereditary status has become obsolete and should therefore be abolished – as was done in the bourgeois revolution – so the social function of inherited wealth is also becoming anachronistic [...] and everybody should enjoy the fruits of labour in proportion to his real creative contribution.

This is the essence of socialism. However, by the time its concept was formulated, the great crisis in Europe concerning the interpretation of the French Revolution was at its climax. The revolution had substantially reversed itself, ended in Restoration, and was unable to complete its tasks. It was at this time that revolutionaries and reactionaries confronted each other most sharply, and in consequence the formulation of the agenda of socialism went hand-in-hand with the designation of revolution as its central category. Rather than defining in the first instance the social conditions deemed desirable, the path leading to them was described, stressing the inevitable necessity of revolution and its omnigenerative, creative magnificence. This is a fundamentally false ideology. Revolution cannot be willed; a revolution can only be accepted and pursued in a certain historical situation. To convert into an ideology the assertion that some changes are possible only through revolution is a completely distorted view, which would never have occurred to sober-minded people without the essentially romantic cult of revolution [...]

Whereas the nineteenth century followers of democratic French revolutionary activity, from Garibaldi to Petőfi, wished to justify the period of terror of the French Revolution, they were in no hurry to repeat it. They were men who fundamentally believed in freedom, in the institution of liberty and in humanity, and they attempted to put their beliefs into practice. By contrast the programme of socialist revolution formulated in the nineteenth century accepted in advance the inevitability and redemptive magnificence of revolution, but at the same time it deemed necessary the perpetuation of violence, modelled on the French Revolution. Such violence followed upon the truly productive reforms (fruits of the momentary application of violence) and changes enforced by continuous violence, changes arising from its own ideological vision and not from the genuine needs of society. This cult of violence attached to the pursuit of revolution for its own sake produced baneful consequences by the end of the nineteenth century and the beginning of the twentieth. By that time, social forces had assembled the positions of which had been shaken or rendered precarious by the democratic revolution, as had those forces which the threatening stance of the impending socialist revolution impelled to all-out self-defence. The groups shaken by the bourgeois revolution comprised in the first instance the aristocracy, which in the larger part of Europe had not completely disappeared, but whose position had been greatly weakened, as well as a substantial part of the petty bourgeoisie, relegated by large capital. In addition, they included employees and functionaries living on a fixed salary who felt themselves to be deprived in comparison with bourgeois wealth and, finally, broad segments of the peasantry which, confronted with capitalist practices, managed to adapt or to defend themselves only with great uncertainty and confusion. In contrast to the proletariat, which in its state of deprivation opted for complete antagonism, the above groups did not adopt a fully revolutionary attitude but rather evolved for themselves a new ideology turned towards an idolized past, but one which took over from the revolutionaries the cult of unrestrained violence. Essentially these social components generated what is today called Fascism. I shall not dicuss here what other, national problems contributed to Fascism in Europe. The point is that Fascism is one of the most terrible by-products of the partial failure of the French Revolution.

The other, not much less terrible by-product is what can perhaps be described by the word Stalinism, which was essentially a further consequence of the perpetuation of violence. Stalinism recognized, on the pattern of the French Jacobins, that violence which the founders of the revolution employed as a matter of course against the determined enemies of the revolution, against defenders of the *ancien régime*, could be applied not only against forces of the old order but also against dissident, recalcitrant, or simply rival groups of its own organization. Thus they let loose on their society the hysterics of unending violence, fatefully compromised the cause of the revolution and handed over the direction of affairs to administrators of power, to clever manipulators and to complicit survivors of the Terror, essentially in the same way as had happened during the French Revolution. The most extreme forms of Fascism were annihilated in the Second World War but the world is still living in the trap of that terrible, spurious and artifical contradiction which is centred on the interpretation of the French Revolution, and by now we can add the Russian Revolution, and which has pushed into prominence the two unproductive human types: the revolutionary and the reactionary, and the products of their further deformation, the Stalinist and Fascist, or to use the more modern word, the 'McCarthyist'. One can say that these adversarial human types are living off each other: each has a desperate need of the other, because each justifies with reference to the other what he himself commits. They would be in great trouble if the other did not exist, and from time to time they themselves produce the other in the form of conspiracies, so as to justify their own behaviour. [...]

Where the conditions of a revolution exist, one should return to the classic democratic forms of revolution. It is not by chance that the classical democratic forms of revolution remain the most attractive. These take as their model the great initial period of the French Revolution, the destruction of the Bastille, the Hungarian Revolution of 1848 or other, similar so-called bourgeois revolutions. This happens in spite of the fact that according to every paper-theory of revolution they represent an obsolete revolutionary form. Nevertheless these classic revolutionary traditions, with their claim to universality, absence of class belligerency, universal humanistic goals and intellectual protagonists are more attractive to youth even today. And indeed they are more appropriate exemplars than are prescribed, systematically organized revolutions prepared according to a so-called science of revolution and implemented in this way.

Social reality has time and again compelled socialist revolutions, including the October 1917 Russian Revolution which started the chain, to conclude an alliance with all democratic forces – among them the forces of bourgeois democracy committed to the totality of civic liberties, that is, to pursue a so-called popular front policy. On the other hand, the dogmatic standpoint which regards the dictatorship of the proletariat as the only possible and truly socialist programme has again and again induced the representatives of socialist revolutions to treat this policy of a popular front as mere short-term tactics that should be kicked aside as soon as practicable. Essentially, the initiation and then blocking of popular front experiments is a characteristic feature of the history of socialist revolutionary activity. In reality, this history would take a straight course if it were realized at last that the formula of a popular front is not a transitional tactical experiment, but the only feasible and fruitful way of social reform in a Europe in which there is no practical prospect of the popular masses carrying out a revolution in supreme desperation.

The suppression of the Hungarian revolution of 1956 and of the Czechoslovak transformation of 1968 meant the end of such experiments to return to a policy of a popular front, and in both cases the justification given was the danger of a restoration of a reactionary, capitalist order. In reality, one can assert with rather strong probability that the liquidation of large capital and of the large estates had produced fundamental and irreversible changes in these countries which in practice no change of regime could have abolished, and the chance of a serious reactionary or restorative danger emerging in either country was exceedingly small. Very extreme fluctuations could have occurred, but a lasting installation of reaction or restoration was most unlikely. By contrast, and in opposition to the above view, I have to say that in the socialist countries the currently prevailing one-party system and the non-application – indeed the vehement defamation and repudiation – of the evolved Western technique of civil liberties not only deprive the inhabitants of these countries (including the Soviet Union) of these techniques, which are branded as bourgeois but which in fact enhance liberty in any social system, but also gravely impair the international reputation of the socialism prevalent in these countries.

The evolved Western technique of civil liberties, branded as bourgeois but in reality of universal validity – the combined system of parliamentarism, plurality of parties, freedom of the press, judicial protection of rights, independent courts, judicial redress against arbitrary administrative acts – is one of the greatest, most enduring and most successful achievements in social organization of the whole of Western culture. It is at the same time, with its distant Christian roots, the only real and lastingly effective reflection in social organization of the Christian programme of freedom from violence. To declare this to be a speciality of capitalism, of the bourgeoisie, is nothing but a justification of the maleficent cult of violence left behind by the French Revolution, a justification of political power structures which can only be maintained by the application of a greater quantity of perpetuated violence than is used in so-called bourgeois democracy, even if the form of this violence is sometimes more and sometimes less acute.

If in the majority or the totality of socialist countries a political team could be found which would dare to take that step, regarded today as very risky, of plunging headlong into civil liberties of the Western type, it would experience to its surprise, possibly after minor convulutions, that the achievements of socialism were not threatened by any serious danger. It would become clear that an unheard-of quantity of creative energy had been liberated and the influence of the socialist countries on a Western world beset by a moral, political and spiritual crisis would be enhanced. It is only a one-party bureaucracy which would have to be eradicated in some form – for example, by merging it partially into the state bureaucracy. It would have to be admitted that modern society, which has in large part jettisoned the ballast of a hereditary aristocracy and has partly discarded, and wishes to discard entirely, the ballast of an hereditary aristocracy of wealth does not want to fill the place of these with a political aristocracy based on a different kind of selection, another ruling class, because it requires no ruling class at all.

The reduction and abolition of violence means at the same time the reduction and abolition of domination. Modern society needs only a certain freely mobile elite of achievement, but not an aristocracy, no ruling class and no groups claiming the right to lead society by right of office. Yet on the criticism voiced by the Chinese Communists and by the most extreme Western student movements against revolutionary rule of the Soviet type, considered to have become bureaucratized, one can say that *medicina peius morbo*, that is to say the medicine is worse than the illness as these movements do not escape the vicious circle of the revolutionary cult of violence; they only wish to replace bureaucratized violence with anarchic violence. This could only have one of two possible outcomes: either the regime of violence brought about in this way would itself become bureaucratized and ossified sooner or later in some form, or the anarchy created would in some way benefit a retrograde reaction. Any social reform which does not aim at realization but turns the process of reform, the revolution, into a permanent state, one which has no vision of a system balanced in some way, is a contradiction in terms and can lead only to insanity. By contrast, in a realized system there is only one remedy against the known phenomena of bureaucratization and ossification, and this is the reduction of the quantity of violence to a minimum, a bold augmentation of the quantity of liberty. The only factor able to exert a real, living, permanently functioning and at the same time institutionalized effect against the bureaucratic and oppressive social and political position of what is, by a fashionable word called the establishment, is constituted by the forms of liberty itself, forms institutionalized, but at the same time filled with a vital breath and spirit of freedom.

At this point I should like to refer back to what I have said earlier and, to some extent as a digression, consider the European system of civil liberties. In essence, this was elaborated jointly by English political practice and by the ideological practice of the French Revolution. Its decisive elements are: the separation of powers, a parliament of popular representation constituted by general elections, an executive power either responsible to parliament or in some way designated and revocable by the people, or, if not revocable, then subject to a time limit on its mandate, a judiciary independent of the executive power and competent to pronounce in some form on the acts of this power; making the control of all these institutions possible, a free press, freedom of thought, assembly, and so on, and extensive local autonomy. These elements make up a cohesive system; they mutually support each other like the links of a chain and none of them can be removed without the whole system, the whole chain suffering damage. This system cannot be identified with such short-term transitional phenomena as capitalism and the rule of the *haute bourgeoisie*, or bourgeois ideology, but is rooted much further back in the past and stretches, it is to be hoped, far ahead into the future. The whole system can be regarded as one of the least controversial, the most enduring, most creditable, most humane, least perilous and overall the greatest achievement of Western culture. Although the final elaboration of the system occurred in the context of many anticlerical sentiments, its ultimate roots lie in the organization of society begun by Christianity in Western Europe. More precisely its ultimate roots sprang from Graeco-Roman political practice, but this was built by the organization of society under Christian inspiration, and in this sense the system of civil liberties is perhaps the single genuinely successful realization of the moral programme of Christianity advocating freedom from violence. History knows no other system that would have liberated to the same extent the world of politics, and through this the life of the entire society, from domination and from violence practised by others, one that would have made it possible for the possessors of power to give up their place to others who, at a given moment, appear more fit to occupy it, without risking violent death and the scaffold, and to enable the people, at the decisive moment, to rid itself of unpopular power-holders. Naturally, this system of civil liberties and of democracy does not mean in any way that through the institution of democracy, the people is acting directly. Democracy based on civil liberties does not prevent the minority in power from carrying through by way of skilful manipulation, many things which the people had not directly adopted as goals, but it can and does prevent those in power from implementing things that are plainly contrary to the manifest will of the people. [...]

NOTES

1 István Bibó, 'A kelet-európai kisállamok nyomorúsága', (The Plight of the Small States of Eastern Europe), *Összegyűjött munkái* (Bern, 1984), Vol. 1, pp. 202–51.
2 Jenő Szűcs, 'The Three Historic Regions of Europe', *Acta Historica* (Budapest, 1983, vol. 29, pp. 2–4), and sections, in a different translation, appear in John Keane (ed.) *Civil Society and the State* (Verso, 1988).

4
Central Europe: A Historical Region in Modern Times
A Contribution to the Debate about the Regions of Europe
Péter Hanák

Did the shift in the sixteenth and seventeenth centuries that affected Prussia, the countries of the Habsburg monarchy and Poland (until then belonging to the Occident) result in such thoroughgoing structural changes that henceforward they had to be considered East European lands? This is one of the crucial questions raised in the debate about the regionality in Europe. To rephrase the question, should we accept that, owing to this shift, these countries – previously the Eastern zone of the West – became the Western 'rim' of the East ... or did they turn into an intermediate region having its own specific characteristics?

Theoretical arguments supporting the switchover into the East are based largely on Marx's conclusions about the feudal backwardness of the area beyond the Elbe, Engel's writing on the 'second serfdom' and on Lenin's statements about the 'Prussian way'. All these conclusions however, are comparisons with the classic – English – type of rising capitalism, or with the 'American way' of agrarian capitalism; they do not claim to be comprehensive definitions of the historical region as such. In order to define properly this historical region, we must unravel a bundle of quite complex factors. It is also important to establish to what extent may these areas beyond the Elbe, Engels's writing on the 'second serfdom' and on Lenin's view of economics and of social history.

Our historians tend to see the factors and characteristics of this shift towards an East European type of region in features like the growing dominance of the seigneurial domestic economy based on socage; the decline of towns; a strongly similar structure and practice of Absolutism; and a parallel development of nascent capitalism.

In my opinion, this convergence of regional features in fact disguises two, typologically different, regions whose developmental tendencies sometimes coincide, at other times diverge. A closer examination of economic and social history, of state structures, of political and cultural characteristics, supplies proof enough for us to observe that the idea of a unified East European region does not take into acount the existence of two genetically, structurally and developmentally different regional entities: the Central European and the East European.

My arguments in support of this view are:

1. *Genetically*, Central Europe – up to the sixteenth century an integral part of the Occident – did lag behind, indeed regressed in contrast to early Western capitalism, sometimes even became subordinated to it. Its areas under Turkish domination sank into decay in an absolute sense. Instead of a gradual loosening up of feudal relationships, the seigneural type of economy based on socage became dominant; capital accumulation and early modernization in cities and towns faltered; centralization by the state weakened and got distorted. In Eastern Europe proper, by which I mean largely Russia, however, we can speak of *readjustment*, almost of *reintegration* into the European economic, political and cultural system. Nevertheless, there was no question of a 'second serfdom': the burden on the serfs may have increased or lessened from time to time, but there was no effective change in their subordination or in their rent-charges. Trade revived in the towns, craft industries developed – the recognition of cities as one of the estates came about in the eighteenth century (the 1785 statutes of Catherine II); the centralizing tendency and bureaucratization of the state progressed without a break from Ivan IV to Peter the Great and then to Catherine the Great.

In my view, therefore, Central Europe did to some extent diverge from the West in the sixteenth and seventeenth centuries, but this decline turned into an increasingly fast process of catching up, from the end of the eighteenth century onwards. In contrast, Russia, which to some extent had readjusted itself to Europe in the sixteenth and seventeenth centuries, developing apace throughout the eighteenth, slowed down during the nineteenth century, lagging behind European modernization and 'bourgeois' development.

2. The crucial difference between Western and Eastern agrarian development lies in the increasing dominance of money-rent (even within feudal conditions) in the West; following the dissolution of the feudal system, in England a capital-based tenancy became the rule, whilst in France a free peasantry became predominant; in contrast, in the East, 'it was not money-rent but socage (*corvée*), that became the preponderant form of feudal rent, and it was this economy, based on the extraction of labour by landowners, that grew into ... a capitalist economy.'[1] It should be noted that the author

speaks of the transformation of the landowning economy, not of that of socage, in the context of an Eastern model. That is to say, the immanent tendency of the Western feudal money-rent system was towards a transformation into capitalism, whereas the intrinsic tendency of socage is self-maintenance and self-aggrandisement. There is no *direct* route from socage to wage labour. Abolition of socage may be the result of revolution or of structural reforms; but, in the ensuing period, depending on the general economic situation, many aspects of serfdom may survive (like payoff in labour) and the changeover towards the employment of wage labourers may take a longer or a shorter time.

3. What was the process of transformation, from seigneurial economy based on socage to capitalism, like in Hungary?

From the legal point of view, socage was abolished by the revolution in 1848. This was brought into effect by an Imperial Patent in 1853. Thus the socage system, the manorial economy, had been the dominant form of the agrarian system in Hungary up to 1848; this had remained an important factor even on those large estates that were making great strides in modernization. However, our historians have pointed out that the fruits of socage decayed in this period not only qualitatively but quantitatively too, and other forms of cultivation emerged in the course of time.

One narrow but important transitional form of progress towards a capitalistic development was 'manumission'. Before 1848 in Hungary, apart from free towns and privileged areas, peasant communities, or indeed individuals, redeemed over 260,000 *morgen* (approx. 130,000 acres), about 2 per cent of all land, according to János Varga. This meant that socage or any other obligation was paid off in one lump sum or in instalments. These were converted now into *money-rent*.

We may well ask, where did the money come from, in the case of peasant communities in villages or rural settlements? (It was Peter Takács who has recently cast some light on the money-making possibilities of serfs, by an ingenious analysis of the 1772 *Investigationes*.) It turned out that, in the final third of the eighteenth century, in the very backward Nyírség (the North Eastern corner of the Great Plains), the serfs' chances of earning money had increased quite considerably, mainly by growing tobacco, rearing sheep, bee-keeping, cartage and day labouring in the Tokay vineyards. It is true that these were somewhat exceptional in that almost immobile backyard of the country, but peasant production and trade showed an upward trend throughout the land. Already in 1741, there were four Greek *quaestors* (petty-traders), nine Jewish rag-and-bone men or leaseholders and three noble-men traders in Kisvárda (a small market town in the Nyírség); in Nagyhalász (a large village) two Greek *quaestors* and one Jew were active. And these data cannot be considered exceptional.

There is a very strong presumption that there was a *demonstrable correlation between the settlement of Greek-Serb-Jewish traders and the upturn in peasant production.*

In the first decades of the nineteenth century, this picture becomes even more vivid. The 1828 census lists quite a number of free peasants engaged in animal husbandry, serfs practising road haulage or growing produce. We must therefore note the fact that, from the end of the eighteenth century onwards, there is a *clear tendency in the decline of labouring obligations and an increase in money-rent.* This was a decisive factor in the transition to a capitalistic economy in Hungary, resembling, but not too closely, the 'Prussian model'.

This decline in labour obligations or in rent-in-kind was reinforced by the process of increasing conversion of serfs into *zsellér* (manumitted serfs) becoming free but largely indigent peasants (*inquilincus*). between 1780 and 1848. Whilst the number of serfs tied to the land grew by only 25 per cent in this period, the number of *zsellér* almost quadrupled, from 215,000 to 827,000. Taking the peasantry as a whole, the ratio of serfs tied to the land fell from 66.6 per cent to 39.5 per cent whilst the percentage of *zsellér* increased from 33.3 per cent to 60.5 per cent.

The category of *zsellér* in that time comprised a very heterogeneous group: there were among them labourers attached to a manor, perhaps rendering labour for a plot of land; tenants of outlying fallow land; leaseholders of vineyards; and, significantly, more and more *wage labourers*. With the fruits of socage diminishing all the time, it became imperative for landowners and serfs alike for the latter to become tenured or to undertake wage labour. The area rented by *zsellér* in the 1840s was almost 1 million *morgen* (½ million acres), 7.8 per cent of all land. To this should be added another 10 per cent by serfs or by town-dwellers. Admittedly, we do not know very well the conditions and actual positions of the *zsellér* in terms of labour relationships and nature of tenure, in animal husbandry, viniculture, and so on. Certainly these were contractual relationships, the tight framework of feudal subordination having been left behind. In any case, the tendency is clear: beyond feudalism, we can see 'embourgeoisement' on the one hand, proletarization on the other.

This process was being reinforced throughout the first half of the nineteenth century by the increase in the number of many different kinds of wage-earners, farm hands, seasonal workers, day labourers, harvest-hands and so on. It is true that the forms of payment, the legal-contractual position and the terms of service were still burdened by various feudal vestiges, but the bulk of wage-earners were already outside the feudal order. Their mere existence, however precarious, was a sure sign of the dissolution of feudalism.

Last but not least, mention should be made of the fact that, already by the second half of the eighteenth century, we find examples of capitalist *tenure* and this phenomenon increased throughout the next hundred years. This mostly took a somewhat disguised form in what was called *arenda*, tenancy

A Historical Region in Modern Times 61

granted for a specific activity. But there are plenty of data proving that next to tenancies granted mostly to Jewish citizens for inns or butchers shops, covert forms of land tenure were also appearing. These tenants contributed quite considerably to capital accumulation and to the modernization of agriculture and infrastructure.

4. I think that, on the whole, we can safely state that the trend of commercialization in agriculture faltered in the seigneurial economy based on socage (until now considered to be the main line of development), and the true rise in the trend came from manumission and peasant tenure of a contractural nature on the one hand, and from capitalist tenure and the accompanying forms of wage labour (open or disguised) on the other. The feudal order was already in the final stages of dissolution in the first half of the nineteenth century. Károly Vörös has proved this very ably, through his careful and convincing analysis of the 1828 census.[2] We find that in 1828 only one half of the non-noble population found its way into the census; what is more, only one half of the 5 million people thus accounted for were subject to socage or belonged to the category of *zsellér*. The network of traditional feudal relationships was already in terminal decline. These millions of people were already in turmoil, their links with the feudal social order had already been broken, or only very loosely maintained. We do find some *zsellérs* who were obliged to do 18 days' or 12 days' socage, but their economic position, indeed their whole existence, was defined by such links less and less. All those who broke free from the structure of feudalism found a new existence in tenancies or in straightforward wage-earning (albeit still burdened by feudal elements). Thus they became parties increasingly interested in a bourgeois transformation.

5. From all this we may draw the conclusion, with some caution, that by the early period of the transition to capitalism in Hungary, new features had already appeared in the dominant 'second serfdom', in the manorial economy based on socage. On the one hand, the manor turned into a 'mixed economy' unit, granting tenancies based on contract, and hiring *zsellérs* or wage labourers. On the other hand, capitalistic enterprises cropped up next to them, peasant tenancies and the like, with the corresponding growth of ground rent in money. Within the 'Prussian type' of development – complementary to it or in contrast to it – the English or French types of agrarian practices also gained ground. In this period of gradually decaying feudalism in Hungary, we find a distinctly regional form of development (that may have shown variances according to different areas or to the nature of economic units), a combination of the Prussian, the English and the French prototypes. (Looking further ahead, the mixed character of capitalist agriculture is even more evident: around 1900, large and medium-sized estates made up 40 per cent of all land, peasant property the same percentage, and smallholders owned 18 per cent. In the management of large estates, capitalist

tenancy was ever more popular: one quarter of all estates above 1,000 *morgen* were managed by capitalist tenants.)

These tendencies towards embourgeoisement may not have been strong enough in themselves to do away with feudal relationships in a swift and thorough-going manner, had they not been supported by the general trend towards capitalism working its way not only through Hungary but through most lands of the Habsburg monarchy, and spurred on by Western European industrialization. Uplifted by the waves of the 1848 Revolution, the leading elite of liberal noblemen and their allies could liquidate the economic, social and political *ancien régime* in a revolutionary manner.

In Central Europe, especially at its Eastern edge, that is in Hungary, the nobility never succeeded in tying the serfs to the glebe fully and permanently. The 1785 Edict of Joseph II granted freedom of movement to the serfs. The 1848 Revolution in Hungary can be placed halfway between French Jacobinism and the 1861 Russian reform. In the context of our area, the serfs were liberated in a radical manner.

6. By this, we do not imply some sort of arithmetic mean. There was a great difference between the policies applied in Hungary and in Russia. In Hungary, redemption was carried out partly by the State (for example, the distribution of common land), partly by individual peasants; in Russia, the land allocated to liberated serfs had to bear a very heavy burden of redemption. The decisive difference between the development of agrarian capitalism in Central Europe and in the Eastern parts goes further than this: in Hungary, capitalistic *private property* had already appeared in the last stages of feudalism, openly in the form of redemption, covertly in the various forms of tenure, the latter having been based on contract. This state of affairs was then legalized by the Revolution and consolidated in the following period of upswing in agricultural prosperity. In the Eastern region this kind of private property with clear title was very scarce as liberation did not turn the serfs into outright owners. Heavy obligations of a feudal character remained: the burden of redemption, of pay-off in labour and other forms of indemnity. The great majority of liberated Russian serfs remained in village communities, having joint ownership of common land. The decade preceding the 1917 Revolution was too short to allow the emergence of widespread individual ownership and of a capitalist economy in agriculture.

The liberal slogan of the great reform period in Hungary: 'Property and Freedom' became a fact in 1848, then after the 1867 settlement, even if not in the clear form of the Western model, having been burdened by many traditional features and restrictions. In Eastern Europe, as far as the bulk of peasantry was concerned, individual property did not become preponderant; neither did freedom for society as a whole, in terms of local self-government, freedom of organization or civic rights.

7. The system and structure of feudalism was radically different in the

Central and in the Eastern regions of Europe.

In the Eastern part of Central Europe – in Hungary and Poland – the nobility was more numerous, better organized and more independent than in Russia, where Tsarist autocracy, from Ivan IV onwards, turned 'service nobility' and boyars alike into state employees, direct subjects of the Tsar.

Even in the latter stages of feudalism, the Russian peasantry showed a much more heterogeneous picture than serfdom in Central Europe. In Russia, free peasant communities in the outlying areas made up a considerable part of the whole. For a time, they remained free from overlords, perhaps paying taxes to the state and doing military duty. In Hungary, feudalism came to full fruition in the sixteenth century; its shackles were somewhat later partially shaken off by the martial order of *Hajdu* (free soldier-settlers) and by the inhabitants of free boroughs.

In Russia, a considerable number of the *Holop* (virtual slaves) remained in existence up to the seventeenth century. In the course of the sixteenth-seventeenth century Settlement, the (until then) somewhat better placed serfdom also became subjected to the semi-slavery of the *Holop*. Following the 1649 decree establishing perpetual serfdom, the landlord was free to sell his serfs on the market, had the right to banish them or to punish them at will. In the seventeenth and eighteenth centuries the burdens of serfs only multiplied and became more and more onerous, and the only means of protest was rebellion. The defeat of peasant revolts led to further diminution of peasant production, let alone tenure or similar forms of loosening up. Later on, some opportunities did arise in primitive industries or in petty trading. These, however, tore the peasant out of the framework of the feudal village.

In Central Europe, the serfs struggled for freedom of movement, for personal liberty, then, having achieved these, for free ownership of the land. In Russia, the first concern of serfs was a guaranteed adherence to the land (as a defence against their being sold or purchased like slaves), and the next one a lightening of the burdens of socage.

8. There were quite considerable differences in the development, legal position and economy of towns as well, if we look at both Central Europe and Eastern Europe.

To begin with numbers, there were proportionally many more towns – and town dwellers – in the Habsburg Monarchy than in Russia. In the Monarchy, the ratio of town dwellers was 8 per cent in 1735, 8.6 per cent in 1840 (in Hungary, 5.3 per cent and 6 per cent respectively) whilst in Russia excluding Poland it was 2.96 per cent in 1782, and 3.8 per cent in 1811.

In the Monarchy, the cities and the free royal boroughs had enjoyed the autonomy and the rights of European *civitas* ever since the Middle Ages. The rural boroughs under the jurisdiction of squires exercised a limited self-government. Many of these towns were not royal foundations: Vienna up to the sixteenth century, or Budapest in the eighteenth and nineteenth centuries, developed without royal sponsorship, sometimes even in opposition to royal wishes. It is true that the development of towns had been halted in the sixteenth and seventeenth centuries, particularly in the parts of Hungary under Turkish occupation, but, from the middle of the eighteenth century onwards, they made up for the decline of the previous two centuries. Major centres of trade and communications, mainly along the rivers Danube, Tisza and Drava, developed rapidly. In the course of their growth and development, the towns succeeded in affirming – or indeed in acquiring – civic liberties.

The development of towns in Russia, following the subjection of free merchant cities by Muscovite centralization, took a different direction from the Western model. The citizenry in the pre-industrial period was weak and heterogeneous; if not created by Tsarist power, it was completely dependent on it. The Tsarist rule tried to knead the settlers (*posadkie*), mostly artisans emerging from serfdom, itinerant traders or erstwhile peasants, into some sort of citizenry. For instance, the 'citizen estate' was separated from the serfs; Peter the Great and then Catherine the Great granted them certain privileges, even a limited autonomy. In spite of all these moves, the Russian towns and their citizenry remained organizations wholly dependent on the rule of central power – it may be said that they belonged to some extent to the 'oriental' type of town defined by Weber (O. Brunner). The Russian town and the Russian citizen remained units of a servicing community fully integrated into the hierarchical order of Tsarist autocracy (Hildermeier).

9. The scrutiny of the modernizing role of towns leads us to the much debated question of the genesis of capitalism. The American historian Gerschenkron considers the development of Russian towns as the model; in his view, it was the State, and foreign capital, that played the most significant part in the origins and growth of capitalism in Eastern Europe (where he includes the easternmost areas of the Habsburg Monarchy too). (Admittedly, Gerschenkron did not survey the genesis of capitalism as such, and concentrated his attention on the upswing in the second half of the nineteenth century. Nevertheless this does not excuse the erroneous features of his conception.) Approaching the question from a different direction, certain neo-conservative historians and some populist writers and sociologists also consider capitalism to be an importation, introduced from above and from the outside. In their view, capitalism was not the result of an organic development in our region. In its intitial stages, Marxist historiography also overemphasized the generative role of foreign capital penetration and the role of midwife played by the State. (This view may have been a contributory factor to the treatment of the two regions as one unit.)

It is quite true, of course, that neither in Russia, nor in a great part of the Habsburg Monarchy, were the traditional, walled-in, secluded cities or towns (or their citizenry) the hot-beds of capitalist modernization. The real trading centres and industrial enterprises emerged largely in manorial establishments, in rural boroughs or in village markets. The central figure of capitalist development is not the traditional guild merchant with his town shop and warehouse, the *mercator*, but the itinerant trader, the buyer (*quaestor*) or the tenant innkeeper or shopkeeper (*educillator*).

In my region, this itinerant purchasing agent, in contrast to Western Europe and Russia alike, was not a scion of the 'autochtonous' local citizenry; most of them were immigrants, Germans and Jews in Poland, Greeks, Serbs, Armenians – and later, Jews – in Hungary.

In what way were these immigrant traders superior to traditional urban merchants, or rather, why was it that these people implemented the accumulation of commercial capital? How did it come about that they became the capitalist entrepreneurs?

First of all, these seventeenth and eighteenth century immigrants concentrated their activities on areas of trade somewhat neglected by traditional merchants. They turned their attention to home-grown agricultural produce first and foremost. The Greeks and others soon dominated the livestock trade, the purchase and sale of corn, wine, wool and hides. These traders visited not only the well-known markets in towns or the large estates, they made an appearance in the smallest villages too. The development of an internal commercial infrastructure was the result of their efforts.

The humblest link in this chain was the petty trader (*circumforaneus*), with his sack or box on his back (hence *dorsarius*), the next one a carter who called on villages and isolated manors. The central link was the trader-innkeeper; his store was the point of collection, storage and transfer. He also sold beer, wine and spirits (often brewing his own brandy) but usually kept a general store as well. The *quaestor* from the town may have had an agent (factor) dealing with these tenant traders and the larger estates. Transportation was mainly the job of the 'factor'. At the upper end of the chain stood the wholesaler residing in the bigger towns, maybe as far away as Vienna. He stored and brokered the bulk of produce, like wool, tobacco, wine, hides and feathers, often for the export trade.

All these traders played a very important part in the development of transportation, both on land and on the rivers. They were the creators of the mobility of accumulated capital: it was the Greeks who introduced the bill of exchange, the bond and the use of collateral security.

These middlemen were also pioneers in increasing and speeding up capital accumulation by turning traditional trading patterns into two-way trade. On their trips for collecting rags, feathers and hides, they also took with them merchandise in demand in the villages. The buyer often made an advance payment for standing crops in the spring, on newborn lambs, on the grape harvest, collecting in the autumn with a hefty interest. The capitalist trader was thus a money-lender too, thereby additionally increasing his efficiency, his funds and capital accumulation in general.

The main difference between the travelling buyer and the traditional merchant (to be more precise, between the Jewish tradesman and the rest, including even the Greeks and Armenians) lay not only in making good use of the levers of accumulation or in the methods thereof, but in concentrating on the direction of investment – in current usage, on his *investment strategies*. The Greeks, Germans and Armenians, becoming affluent, strove to gain citizenship, they became part and parcel of the traditional civic order, and in some cases achieved noble rank. Up to the 1840s, these avenues remained closed for the Jews. Their accumulated capital was turned therefore into further commerce, means of transport and, eventually, into the prospering food industry.

This somewhat sketchy typology may lead us to two important conclusions. First of all, this arc of ascent from itinerant trader to buying agent, to storekeeper, then to capitalist entrepreneur differs quite considerably from the Western model, and perhaps even more from the Russian one. In Russia, this middleman function was to some extent performed by petty traders risen from the peasantry, but largely without capital, in conditions of poor infrastructure and lacking a proper commercial network, altogether without a supporting environment. Secondly, the progress of accumulation in commercial capital and the nature of its reinvestment refutes the conventional views on imported capitalism, on the generational character of foreign capital and on the supporting role of the state. Habsburg Absolutism did devote its attention to the development of Austrian and Bohemian industry, although less and less ardently after 1815. From the point of view of the Hungarian economy, its policies affecting capital accumulation and enterprise were largely negative. In fact, the economic policy of Vienna and the state of affairs ruling in Hungary discouraged foreign capital investment for quite a long time in a country offering hardly any safeguards.

It was not the capital that was of foreign origin at the birth of capitalism, up to the 1850s, but the enterprising trader. In the end, however, most of them settled down, became Hungarian subjects and underwent the process of assimilation. These people cannot be considered to have been the agents of *foreign* capital. The genesis of capitalism in Hungary was by no means an inorganic development, thrust upon the people from outside. It was the most fruitful route for the organic development of capitalism, not only in Hungary but in the whole East-Central region of Europe.

10. As a last item in my summary analysis of interregionality, I should like to point out a few characteristics of state structures and of political systems in this area. Admittedly, there are many similarities between East-Central Europe and Russia – bureaucratism, militarism and the primacy of the state apparatus in all social and power relationships. On the surface, the triumphant rule of Absolutism in the second half of the eighteenth century paraded in the guise of the same sort of Enlightenment. (Frederick the Great,

Joseph II and Catherine the Great are sometimes depicted as members of the self-same masonic lodge). In fact, quite considerable differences already separated the two regions by that time; these became even more pronounced in the course of the nineteenth century.

Taking into account economic progress, the level of modernization and the strength of the burgher element, in the period of Absolutism the Habsburg Empire greatly surpassed the Russia of Catherine. If only for this reason, attempts at on-going modernization were more realistic and the results more effective in the Habsburg domains than the plans for reform of Catherine's court.

In the Habsburg Empire, there already existed an emergent middle class, made up partly by lesser nobles, partly by learned elements of humbler origin; this was a suitable basis for the rise of a professional bureaucracy. The rulers deliberately nurtured this class of civil servants. The bureaucracy built a structure, and gave stability, to the functioning of the Austrian state apparatus. In Russia, recruitment and training of a similar bureaucracy was more of a hit-and-miss affair, its functioning more like that of a set of cabals.

The overwhelming power of Austrian Absolutism was always restrained (sometimes more forcefully, sometimes less so) by the existence of the Hungarian Estates. At times, for instance, against Joseph II, even the slumbering Austrian and Czech Estates rose up in protest.

In Austria, the separation of the *Hausmacht* (the powers of the royal house) and the powers of the state was enshrined in law. Imperial possessions and state treasury, court officials and civil servants were kept aloof. Legislative and executive powers were not separate, it is true: laws were promulgated by the Emperor, but he too was subject to them. (In Josef Sonnenfels's[3] definition, a country with laws in common, with a legally established government, all subjects being equal before the law: these things make up what can be called the 'motherland'.)

This principle *rex sub lege*, prevailing in the constitutional system of imperial Absolutism, brought the countries of the middle region more into propinquity with the West, fairly sharply dividing them from the Russian East, where, even at a time of flirting with ideas of reform inspired by the Enlightenment, the ruling model was one of autocracy, coloured by many features of outright despotism.

11. Enlightenment giving birth to liberalism, tolerance (religious and otherwise) growing into constitutional rule, finally modernization: these ideas became governing principles of statecraft in the nineteenth century in Central Europe. It may also be worthwhile to carry forward the parallels beyond the revolutionary period of 1848.

Even after the reform of 1861, Tsarist rule remained an autocracy, not overly constrained by the principles and institutions of constitutionalism. Meanwhile the Habsburg Empire became a constitutional monarchy following the 1867 compromise. The supreme power did jealously guard the unity of the dual monarchy, had a hand in maintaining the social order, reserved for itself the unfettered control of the Army – these features of Absolutism did not disappear completely. The lower grades of executive power did have considerable discretionary jurisdiction. The Habsburg Monarchy was a peculiar mixture of the 'authoritative' state and the constitutional state (*Obrigkeitsstaat* and *Rechtsstaat*).

Nevertheless constitutional rule was a living reality in the monarchy. The various institutions of constitutional nature did keep a check on the ruler and his governments. Parliament may have been a pretty weak body (in Austria in particular) but it still offered a forum to the opposition, especially to the representatives of national minorities.

Governments (apart from the opposition) were also kept under scrutiny by various national and social interest groups and organizations. Socialist trades unions could operate legally, Socialist parties and the whole working-class movement grew, from modest beginnings, into powerful organs. There may have been limitations, but the basic freedoms did prevail, first and foremost the freedom of the press. The authoritative ruler and his executive arm may have hankered after some sort of Absolutistic behaviour, but they had to operate under the scrutiny of widespread public opinion. Furthermore, quite considerable bodies of communal or local autonomy were allowed to be established – in contrast to the East – and these were also capable of counteracting the executive branch.

It is true that at the turn of the century militarism gained ground in the monarchy, but the constitutional bodies, Parliament and social organizations also gained in strength at the same time. The Austro-Hungarian Monarchy was the Eastern frontier of liberal constitutional rule up to the First World War. This political system (in spite of its limitations and transgressions) carried forward and upheld the heritage of European humanism, enlightenment and liberalism: pluralism and tolerance.

The Monarchy (including Hungary) as a system of state powers and of politics, stood in the middle between the fully-fledged parliamentary democracy in the West and autocracy in the East. This is precisely the meaning of the term: Central Europe.

Finally, I should like to add, in lieu of an epilogue, two comments.

1. The fact that the concept of Central Europe was made use of by German imperialism, and became discredited by Hitler, does not do away with the historical reality of this region as an entity. To paraphrase the nineteenth century Czech historian František Palacký: the peoples of the region were here before Hitler and will remain here long after him.

2. The fact that the peoples of this region, next to deep-seated links and fraternal contacts, have often been at loggerheads, riven by conflicts and hatreds, is no argument against the historical existence of the entity. On the

contrary, this is proof of its existence: it is neighbours who are mostly cursed by anger, hatred and strife.

The historical existence of such an entity does not necessarily imply the perception of regional indentity.

NOTES

1 Z. P. Pach, *Magyarország története*, 1526-1687 (The History of Hungary, 1526-1687), Introduction.
2 Károly Vörös, *Magyarország története*, 1790-1848 (The History of Hungary, 1790-1848).
3 Josef von Sonnenfels (1732-1817) was an influential theoretician and reformer under Maria Theresa and Joseph II.

5
Intellectuals in East-Central Europe: Continuity and Change
Zygmunt Bauman

Since the Enlightenment, Western intellectuals have defined as one of their main tasks the jealous guarding of the autonomy of intellectual activity from social pressures and political influence. However illusory this autonomy may in fact be, it has none the less provided the 'intellectual idiom' by which Western intellectuals have sought to cultivate spheres of moral authority resistant to state interference.

In contrast to this model of intellectual autonomy, Zygmunt Bauman traces the multiple lines of penetration which have historically governed the relationship between the intelligentsia of East-Central Europe and structures of officialdom. Bauman shows how today's educated elite in East-Central Europe continues to be an integral feature of the political system, even if its status and function is more narrowly circumscribed by party injunctives.

Shortly after the Polish October of 1956, C. Wright Mills came to Warsaw to learn from the experience of Polish intellectuals then fresh from the battlefields of the revolution they first spurred and later helped to contain. A few days after his arrival the new political leader, Władysław Gomułka, went on the radio to criticize, in no uncertain terms, the views of the undisputed intellectual leader, the philosopher Leszek Kołakowski. The censured professor and his friends were nonplussed; they remembered only too well the times when names appeared in public speeches only to disappear from public life. But Mills was elated. 'However hard did I try to push and kick the American political establishment and spit in its face,' he reminisced, 'no one paid attention. In your country,' he went on, 'the word counts. And so the word can change things. What you, intellectuals, do,' he concluded, 'matters.'

One of the most brilliant social scientists among recent émigres from the Soviet Union had written and published a collection of short stories. His first literary venture had been warmly received by the critics. Still, he felt uneasy.

'Were I still in the Soviet Union,' he complained, 'I would know for sure who I am. If I became a member of the Union of Soviet Writers, I would be a writer. If not, I would not.' This was a joke, of course. But the voice was serious.

These two true anecdotes set the parameters for my theme. They provide the two axes against which intellectual life in communist regimes is plotted. First, there is the uniquely central location of intellectual activity and its products in the process of systematic and social integration which draws intellectuals into direct engagement and competition with political power. Second, there is a degree of regimentation of intellectual practices unknown in the West, and a continuous pressure to incorporate and assimilate centres of intellectual authority within the structure of officialdom.

Numerous writers in the West and East alike stress the essential similarity of intellectual work, whatever the systemic context in which it happens to be located. Intellectual pursuits are, so to speak, *jeux sans frontières*, deriving their crucial characteristics from their inner nature: the values they serve and the pragmatic rules of conduct such values unambiguously determine. The common nature of intellectual work casts the incumbents of intellectual roles in similar moulds, again with no regard to the political colouring of the society inside which the roles are to be played. Countries differ, of course, as to the conditions they create for intellectual role-playing. Countries may promote the kind of work and attitudes typical of intellectuals, they may merely tolerate it, or worse still, they may contain, hamper, or arrest it; but they hardly ever alter the nature of the intellectual vocation. Commitment to the universal character of intellectual work is likely to persist and be restated on both sides of the great divide because of the major role it plays in the defence of the identity and status of intellectuals against other kinds of power. Such a defence cannot be carried out in any but universalistic terms. Zhores A. Medvedev, one of the pioneers of the Soviet intellectuals' campaign for repossession of vocational rights, provided a telling example of the intimate link between the argument of universality and the claim to the uniqueness of status:

> There is only one social group of people in the world which, not only on account of its position in society but simply on account of the humane qualities inevitably inherent in it, on account of its selection of people for these qualities and on account of the character of its daily activity, is connected in a world-wide mutually dependent, mutually advantageous, a mutually respecting system of friendship independent of national frontiers, constantly sharing among itself all possible help and interested to the utmost in the progress of mankind, of which it is the standard-bearer and motive force. This group consists of the scholars, the scientists, the intelligentsia, in the sense of the scientific, technical and culturally creative intelligentsia, and not simply that class of people who have had a secondary or higher education.[1]

Not for the first time in history world authority is claimed in the name of a kingdom 'which is not of this world'.

More importantly for my theme, what hides behind the rhetoric of universality is the conception of a *soi-disant* 'extraterritoriality' of intellectual activity, its essential independence from social determination, or its ability to raise itself above the level of social pressures and necessities. This conception has been permanently present in the intellectual discourse since the self-constitution of the intellectual vocation in the Age of Enlightenment. It was expressed originally in the idea of the precedence of eternal and immutable Reason before transient and imperfect man-made laws and institutions. The idea is of an intellect fully formed and whole before the determining force of man-made realities is brought to bear. Reason, therefore, can be reached directly. The road can be obscured, but not blocked, by social obstacles erected on an entirely different level. Karl Mannheim gave the old conception its modern rendition, better attuned to an age of advanced sociological awareness, in the idea of the *frei schwebende* intelligentsia: a loosely knit aggregate of people who collectively and *ex post facto* attain independence from particularizing social determinants, as they draw liberally from all particularized and socially determined categories and hence are not 'at home' in any.

In order to understand the substance and the dynamics of intellectual life in the specific context of the East-Central European communist regimes, one must distance oneself from the rhetoric generated within the self-constituted concerns of intellectual tradition. However justifiable the claims to extraterritorial universality may or may not be (a question we deliberately leave open), our task demands that intellectuals and their unique role be repositioned in their specific historical and territorial context. We need to separate the conditions under which the intellectual mode, with its characteristic pursuit of universality, was brought into being, from the quite distinct conditions under which it was borrowed, absorbed and adapted far from the time and place of its origin. In the part of Europe we are scrutinizing, the latter conditions provide the key to the history and social location of intellectuals.

The word 'intellectual' is of quite recent usage – it became common during the course of the infamous Dreyfus affair. The concept behind it, however, can be traced further back. How far back depends on whether we are simply interested in the presence of a separate category of people assigned the role of manipulation and interpretation of the elusive but crucial factors of social integration called values, meanings and symbols. On the other hand, we might be looking for a distinct 'intellectual mode', 'idiom', or 'pattern' articulated, codified and practised by such manipulators and interpreters simultaneously as a tool of self-definition and as part of a bid for social power. In the first case, the ancestry of the modern intellectual would be as old as human society; it would include not just the millenia of clerisy, not just the scribes of ancient bureaucracies, but would reach the obscure beginnings of social life in the form of Mircea Eliade's 'shamans' or Paul Radin's 'primitive philosophers'. In the second case, the birth of intellectuals is well defined in historical space: it occurred during the Age of Enlightenment.[2]

The framework of this essay allows us only to note that the birth of an intellectual idiom was not a matter of spiritual discovery. It was a product of complex social and political development, which included among other processes the dissipation and progressive bankruptcy of the traditional mechanism of communal and parish social control, the gradual re-integration of society in the centralized form of an absolutist state, and the concomitant articulation of the problem of social control as an exercise in bodily and spiritual drill performed by professionals and calling for expert skills. These processes have been amply documented and illuminated in the writings of Michel Foucault and his followers.[3] On the other hand, the possibility generated by structural dislocations had been actualized and given shape by the gradual disengagement of the educated elite from its former administrative and economic functions, which led to the formation of *les sociétés de pensée* with their illusory autonomy of thought and independence of discourse, argument, and truth from political and economic power and influence – a process brilliantly analysed by François Furet.[4]

Once born, the intellectual idiom did in fact acquire an autonomy of sorts. Its birth would have been impossible had it not been for a unique complex of structural dislocations within a specific corpus of local West European tradition. Since its articulation, however, the idiom has become detachable, to a degree, from its original context and, in principle, transferable. It was subject to what anthropologists call the 'diffusion of stimulus', a process which takes place when a cultural concept, an ideal, a postulate, or a norm, travels without the corresponding structural transformations which had made it a functional possibility in the first place. Having travelled alone, as a stimulus, or as an ostensibly purely spiritual influence, cultural patterns are often grafted onto wholly uncorrelated structures. In the process, they undergo substantive and functional changes, sometimes of a truly radical nature, while preserving at least the visibility of original kinship bonds. Neither the affected structure nor the foreign graft emerge from the process unscathed, though the concealment of this fact is more often than not the very condition of successful transplantation.

Soon after its birth, the intellectual idiom embarked on an adventurous journey that remains unfinished to this day. From the very start, however, it travelled not merely as a pattern for contemplation or spiritual refinement. What really brought it into salience and rendered it an object of envious and hopeful emulation was its explosive and spectacular application in the French Revolution. The question of who was the true agent of the Revolution, which class was its principal actor, has been asked again recently and has yielded some surprising and unconventional answers.[5] But whatever answer might turn into the scholarly canon of the next decade or so, one thing can hardly be in doubt. A revolution (as distinct from a rebellion or a *coup d'état*) – a daring, perhaps audacious, intent to transform a total system of society through the sheer legislative effort and education of minds, an active attempt to impose a complete model conceived in the course of intellectual analysis upon a society different from it in virtually every detail, a stubborn insistence on treating every gap between the *a priori* approved model and recalcitrant reality as so much ignorance, superstition and moral evil – all this could derive its authority and self-confidence only from the phenomenon described above as the 'intellectual idiom'. By the very fact of offering such authority and confidence to the boldest, most shocking, and hence the most consequential event of the modern era, this idiom gained a wholly new dimension of significance and acquired an important, though contentious, place in the political thought and action of our times. Having culminated in the Revolution, the intellectual idiom, as pieced together and codified by successive generations of *les philosophes* and *les idéologues*, instilled in the European mind of the nineteenth century the belief that thought could be potent enough to destroy and create social realities. The more reluctant the local reality was to change, the keener and more radical this belief would tend to be – a connection which Marx spotted early, in a socially stagnant Germany as it gazed avidly at the breath-taking pace of social change across the Rhine.

The event described as 'the birth of the Russian intelligentsia', and the less studied rise of local (later to become national) intelligentsias throughout East-Central Europe in the second quarter of the nineteenth century, was the most poignant case of the early diffusion of the intellectual idiom. This part of Europe was well behind its western counterpart by all standards of economic and political development. It had neither crushed its peasantry nor politically dispossessed its aristocracy. The states that ruled this area were no more than urban-based bureaucratic systems imposed upon peasant communes, ruled by custom, and upon small to large, sometimes very large, local fiefs and baronies ruled by traditional landowners. Even the spreading market could be absorbed and adapted to the benefit of these landowners. The dynasties identified with the states wielded what Michel Foucault dubbed a 'sovereign power' (and Ernest Gellner, a 'dentist power' – extraction by torture ...); they confined their governing ambitions largely to revenue raising, and were essentially unconcerned with the administration of the daily lives or productive initiatives of their subjects. They had few, if any, moralizing and proselytizing aspirations. Cutting across many an ethnic and linguistic boundary, the dynasties also held uneasily together heterogeneous mixtures of otherwise unrelated ethnic groups, languages, cultures, and customs, which could hardly look toward vesting their group identities – either symbolically or politically – with the state. The latter appeared foreign to many, too noncommittal to most, distant and indifferent to all.

Two distinctive features of the East-Central European scene proved to be of particular relevance both to the urgency with which the stimulus of the intellectual idiom was embraced, and to the seminal transmogrification this idiom underwent in the course of its adoption and adaption.

The first was the absence of an absolutist state successfully undermining the autonomy of intermediate levels of systematic integration; the state could not seriously contemplate legislative initiatives genuinely affecting the conditions and conduct of its subjects. To employ Shils' terms, this meant the absence of a 'centre' powerful enough to transform the rest of the society into a 'periphery'. Hence, the well-nigh millennial ambitions inherent in the intellectual idiom lacked a vehicle. The budding intelligentsia of East-Central Europe was, from its inception, confronted with the task of constructing a political body capable of effective action instead of merely converting the already existing state machinery to its rationalizing purposes. Travelling east, the intellectual idiom grew in its political dimension. Having been always concerned with the state as the source and authority behind the law, and hence behind social change, in its eastbound journey the idiom gradually raised its aspirations from a mere advisory role to the level of legislation itself. Those who were to work out the shape of reason-dictated institutions had to shoulder simultaneously the responsibility for the construction and entrenchment of such institutions. The French Revolution offered a better pattern for such responsibility than the abstract explorations of *les philosophes*.

The second seminal distinction of the East-Central European scene was the complete lack of overlap between dynastic states and the motley collection of ethnic traditions and linguistic communities. The unrelatedness of the two effectively eliminated the possibility that the existing monarchies would ever combine political rule with cultural ascendancy; or, to put it differently, that they would be able to employ cultural domination as one of the key supports of their political rule. This circumstance put at the sole disposal of the intelligentsia the enormous realm of would-be national integration where it encountered no competitors. It became the peculiarly East-Central European pattern to find intellectuals functioning as national leaders and to treat enclaves of local languages or dialects – in the theatre, the press, parish churches, or in more fortunate cases in the schools and *belles-lettres* – as the true location of national homes. Thus political authority came to be seen as an emanation and supplement of cultural ascendancy, rather than vice versa.

Add the two together, and you will get a model which – unlike the pattern which inspired it – is absolutist, fundamentalist, and totalistic in its long-term aspirations and middle-range programme. The intellectual idiom as embraced in the East knew no division of labour between political and cultural leaders, between body politic and 'civil society', between rights of the legislator and the duties of spiritual leadership. The separation between intellectual work and professionalized politics, the retreat of intellectuals into distinctly cultural institutions, the growing preoccupations of intellectuals with the autonomy of culture (which meant simultaneously their unconnectedness with politics, or, to put it bluntly, their political irrelevance) – all these processes which had been set in motion in the West soon after the Napoleonic wars and by the end of the nineteenth century reached their completion encapsulated in Weber's idea of *Wertfreiheit* – made little progress in East-Central Europe before the fulfilment of national aspirations in the wake of the Great War, or, for that matter, ever since.

One factor was the continuing underdevelopment of the East, made all the more salient by the spectacular advances of the West. The two faces of underdevelopment were the persistence of a vast, primitive and ignorant peasantry, and the feebleness of the modern entrepreneurial class. Truly modern urban conditions were confined mostly to state and national capitals, while the countryside and small towns where the huge majority of population lived filled the hearts of the prophets of Reason with a mixture of compassion and horror. With the best of intentions they found it difficult to imagine a rational order or a new morality arising from this sea of squalor and superstition. Except for a romantic fringe, the recipes for social renewal all agreed on at least one point; that the enlightenment of the people should stem from the reform of state power, and not the other way around. Reform should be accomplished for the people, but hardly by the people.

In the East, there was no room for the vision of the deprived and the destitute as the carriers of the new order. Positing the proletariat in the role of the collective Messiah, Marx spoke of a society where 'everything solid melts into air' and 'everything sacred was profaned'. He sang the praises of the bourgeoisie for its unprecedented feat of destroying all the noxious loyalties constraining human individuality one by one: the bonds of community, regionalism, the parish, the family, guilds and corporations. In the process, the bourgeoisie spawned a class of people as unbound as Prometheus, unattached, atomized, already turned into individuals through the disappearance of all and any *pouvoirs intermédiaires* and of all the traditional forms of collective dependence and protection. The proletariat was thus to be that category of unattached, uncontrolled, and hence rebellious and militant people who, in the consensual opinion of post-Enlightenment thinkers, would call for the imposition of rational order through rational law. Rational law was a law setting conditions of liberty for free individuals; the kind of reformed law postulated in the West could address itself to this task, as there were free, or potentially free, individuals waiting to be so addressed. This was not the case in the East, however, where the preachers of reform through power and legislation faced a task of an entirely different order.

Serfs of the landowning gentry and dependents of *mir* or *zadruga* were generations away from the free and unattached Western producers who longed for legal liberty to affirm and confirm their freedom. The promoters of the rule of reason could not count on their active support, much less on their participation. Hence the curious phenomenon of an intelligentsia lukewarm about political democracy and universal representation, cautious and self-limiting in its propaganda of liberal ideas, and allowing little room among its concerns for the preaching of individual rights and their legal guarantees. Still more importantly perhaps, the intelligentsia of East-Central Europe, the more so the farther to the east and south, was to be irreparably split (between factions, and inside the soul and mind of virtually every member) between the *Zweckrazionalität* of the West and *Wertrazionalität* of indigenous 'collectivism'; between the idea of speeding up the destruction of the *ancien régime* and the need to build up the new and rational order directly on the foundations of the ancient institutions and in a form fairly different from the cold, competitive and atomized world of capitalism. The intellectuals' claim to power could be and was argued equally well in terms of both projections.

Performers of the professions and vocations to which the 'intellectual mode' (according to the patterns already established in the West) had been ascribed were recruited mostly from the gentry in the East. At a time when 'the first generation of Russian intelligentsia' came into being, and indeed almost half a century later, when the concept of intelligentsia and its peculiar mission became part of the vernacular, the urban middle classes of the western type were still relatively small and insignificant. Gentry, on the contrary, were numerous beyond any comparison with their western counterparts. The majority were small land owners, and by the nineteenth century most gentry families ceased to be capable of supporting their offspring on income from the land even before serfdom was legally abrogated. Many sons of the gentry, particularly the non-inheriting ones, had to look for alternative sources of living and status. The spectacular spread of new universities and other establishments of higher learning throughout East-Central Europe was to a considerable extent the product of pressure and demand from the gentry. The traditional elite, denied the possibility of reproducing its status through traditional means, made a bid for an alternative set of values and vehicles of status-reproduction which would render its leadership and privileges secure even as they further sapped the traditional basis of class continuity.

If the land available to gentry ownership was by nature limited (and modernization of agriculture would, if anything, further limit the number of landowners whose status could be supported by it), arts, sciences, professions, and learning in general seemed at first to have a virtually unlimited potential for status-generation. If limits of land-ownership appear 'natural' (in the sense that little can be done about the problem by methods available to humans, however eager and powerful), any limitation on the volume of learned and 'cultured' men society could absorb and offer a status matching their claims seemed 'artificial' (that is, brought about by unjust laws or faulty institutions), and hence called for social reform. In East-Central Europe the most conspicuous such artificial hurdle was the virtual monopoly of foreign elites in the state administration and judiciary system. This monopoly was guaranteed by law, or more insidiously achieved *de facto* because the language of a foreign elite was the official medium of communication in politics, administration, and the courts. These limitations therefore became the prime targets of the new educated elite's demands.

The obvious strategy in the ensuing struggle for change was to demand recognition for local languages, which were often no more than regional dialects, as legitimate languages of public life. This strategy proved to be particularly successful within the Habsburg Empire, perhaps due to the fine balance of power between German and Hungarian speaking elites. Until the Great War, little such progress was made inside the borders of the Russian Empire, and still less inside Germany. But all over East-Central Europe the new educated elites arrived on the historical stage carrying the banners of national languages, both the well established ones, like Polish, and others preserved only in the oral tradition by illiterate peasants and lesser townfolk. These languages became surrogate national homes and the seedbeds for future national states. Frantic efforts were made to codify 'uneducated' languages, to collect, in the absence of literary monuments, the oral lore of stories, myths, folk ballads and songs, to devise new alphabets fitting the phonetic peculiarities of peasant dialects and simultaneously manifesting their separateness and linguistic status, to work out dictionaries, and to encourage a vernacular press and theatre.

One crucially important side-effect of this strategy was the splitting of the 'public sphere' (brilliantly analysed by Jürgen Habermas in his study of *Öffentlichkeit*) into two loosely interconnected and largely autonomous areas: the political-administrative-juridical area, symbolically set apart by its usually foreign language, and the sphere of 'civil society', embracing popular arts and popular ideologies, again separated symbolically by the language it used. The latter was the language of 'the people' and at the same time incomprehensible to the political and administrative officials. The split by itself rendered relatively secure the independence of budding national intelligentsias from the interference of established political elites and offered the same intelligentsias a privileged access, through shared language, to their respective 'peoples'.

Thus, one of the most persistent effects of the peculiar circumstances of the birth of the intelligentsia in East-Central Europe is the tendency to view the relation between the political state and civil society as one of conflict and competition rather than of consensus and mutual support. There also remains the remarkably elevated status of the intellectual profession and of the educated elite in general. Their forefathers, after all, enjoyed a virtual monopoly of spiritual leadership, elsewhere shared with political elites; moreover, for a long period in national history they played the role of a substitute for the absent national state and thereby gained acute political significance through their cultural, ideological, and generally symbolic activities. Nowhere else in modern times has there developed such a deep belief in the well-nigh magical power of the word and of cultural symbols in general; nowhere else have such far-reaching hopes and formidable fears surrounded their use.

The acquisition of uncontested leadership within their own autonomous section of the public sphere came to the new educated elites rather easily. The new elites simply 'slipped into' the position occupied by the land-owning gentry in an essentially unchanged social hierarchy, while interference by more powerful but foreign elites was limited and ineffective.

'The people', in whose following the educated elite sought its power bases and legitimization of status, had little tradition of independent action. Their subordination to the gentry was much older than the ascendancy of the current empires; it filled the whole of remembered history. The one constant factor behind the mobile and shifting political arrangement of this part of Europe was the patron – client relationship between the local gentry on the one hand and the peasants and townfolk on the other. Patronage meant economic exploitation, of course, but also an unchallenged moral leadership and cultural superiority. I say 'superiority' rather than 'hegemony'. The latter term, part and parcel of the intellectualist idea of culture as it emerged in the eighteenth century, presumes an educating action undertaken by the 'higher' culture in relation to the 'lower', and it takes for granted the proselytizing missionary nature of the higher culture. This was not the case with traditional gentry patronage. While patronage assumed that the superiors were better, there was no effort to remold the inferiors in their image. On the contrary, lasting differences were acknowledged and their perpetuation and reproduction, to keep each side of the relationship 'true to its kind', was one of the paramount motives and functions of this patronage.

Redefining cultural superiority as cultural hegemony, an act recognizing the inherent missionary nature of 'higher' culture and consequently of the state of war against the 'lower' ones – now redefined as backward, retarded, ignorant or superstitious – was a new element grafted onto the old institution of patronage by the educated elite in its effort to replace the gentry patrons. Whether in its pre-modern form or in its new shape worked out by the educated heirs of the gentry, patronage meant an unquestionable asymmetry of power, the right of the patrons to command, and the duty of the clients to obey. Within the relationship of patronage, the split between the subjects and the objects of action was unequivocal and permanent.

Patronage is therefore an ambiguous affair, eluding facile appraisals. It is not a mere domination; it is a domination all right, but one suffused with rules of sympathy, a dogma of loyalty, and presumptions of gratitude. It is not mere subordination; it is indeed subordination, but one entered into and perpetuated in the expectation of benefits, material or spiritual, to ensue from it. It is not merely inequality; it is inequality, but one which assumes equivalence in the exchange of aid for obedience. To invoke Foucault once again, one can grasp the ambiguity of patronage by considering it as a variety or aspect of 'pastoral power', power which is not (at least in theory) exercised in the interest of the power-holders. Rather, the power-holders have a task (other- or inner-worldly) to perform for the benefit of the objects of their power. The objects of power are deemed to be imperfect and incomplete without this task being performed, and they are seen as incapable of performing the task on their own. The gentry's patronage certainly resembled this model closely. So too did the patronage of the educated elite, the 'intellectual idiom' adapted to the social hierarchy of East-Central Europe.

It is the contention of this chapter that the historical adventures of the intellectual idiom, once imported and appropriated by this part of the world, and in particular its institutional foster parentage, go a long way toward providing a frame of reference within which the paradoxes of the intellectuals' status and cultural life in today's communist Eastern Europe can best be understood.

The radical intelligentsia of East-Central Europe, the one which would not be absorbed by the *ancien régime*, and hence could not exercise the functions dictated by the patronage model, saw political revolution as a natural extension of its programme and as an indispensable vehicle of its fulfilment. In order to raise the practical opportunities for historical action to the level of its vast ambition, the radical intelligentsia (to paraphrase Marx, or rather to see through his self-deception) had to 'constitute *itself* into the state'. It needed powerful tools to reshape the society according to the precept of the reason-cum-morality which it alone carried.

Proselytism, moral mission, and cultural crusade, the universal features of the intellectual mode as born and shaped in the course of the 'civilizing process', were hence mingled in the East with the search not so much for an enlightened despot, but for the despotism of the enlightened. For quite a large section of the intelligentsia the takeover of state power (or the institution of states to provide new levers of power) came to be the paramount means to this end, but a means which usually turned into an end in itself. Some saw their historic function to be dependent on the creation of national statehood; others wished to replace the established elite of existing states in order to use extant power resources for remaking the social order in a way more suitable for a successful accomplishment of their intellectual mission. Some others still intended to collapse the two targets into one. However hotly debated at the time, however deep the splits they caused inside the educated elite, these differences seem relatively minor and secondary if seen against the apparently shared conviction that shouldering the burden of political rule was a condition of, and the natural consequence of, their legitimate concern with the proper performance of the intellectual role.

The most seminal of the intellectual camps in the East, the Marxist, the Bolshevik, the Communist, was certainly a most radical, but not necessarily an idiosyncratic or freak expression of this intellectual spirit. Its intense preoccupation with state power was widely shared in quarters far removed from, and hostile to, the Bolshevik political programme. For the intellectuals who made the Russian Revolution, the toppling of the Tsar and the institution of Bolshevik rule was a ground-clearing operation indispensable for the construction of a new society, dictated by the precepts of reason and/or the laws of history. It answered the true, if suppressed, human needs, visible only to the enlightened, who were able to lift themselves high enough above the level of the mundane and the particular. It was for this purpose that they constituted themselves into a party, aptly described by Antonio Gramsci as the 'collective intellectual'. Once the party reached its destination and constituted itself in turn into the state, no conflict was envisaged between the new political power and the mission of the intellectuals. Indeed, the former was welcomed as the fulfilment of the latter.

No wonder that one of the items conspicuously absent from the agenda of the revolutionary intelligentsia was the autonomy of intellectual work, and in particular its independence from the state. Indeed, what useful purposes could be served by any separation between the intellectuals and the political state, by setting apart the spokesmen of reason and its principal tool? Would it not be as regrettable as the separation between producers and the means of production, which the revolution was committed to rectify?

This omission is particularly striking as it occurred at a time when in the West the defence of the 'civil society' (the space in which ideas are conceived, debated, disseminated, absorbed, forged into attitudes and actions) from the state had been an established concern, or a solid attainment, of the intellectual professions. Ever since the rout of *les idéologues* by Napoleon after the abortive Malet conspiracy, the political interests of Western intellectuals focused on cultivating areas of authority immune to state interference. 'Freedom of thought' (one plank in the liberal platform betraying more than any other its affinity to intellectual interests) meant precisely that: the right of professional intellectual bodies to settle their own disputes and so to retain an unchallenged authority in deciding the matters of truth and cultural value. The spectacular success of the intellectuals in defending their own domain from political encroachments had, though, an unanticipated and hardly desired effect. The growing skill of the body politic to function without the kind of services the intellectuals were best at supplying also meant the growing irrelevance of intellectual work to the political process. Hence the envy felt by C. Wright Mills listening to the public chastisement of a Polish philosopher.

A similar divorce between the intellectuals and the state did not follow the Russian Revolution. Neither side thought seriously of emancipation from the other. The revolutionary intelligentsia embraced the revolutionary government as the supreme embodiment of the Kingdom of Reason. In this respect, their conduct was more akin to that of the first and the second generations of *les idéologues* in the French Revolution than to that of their twentieth century contemporaries in the West. The new political rulers, on the other hand, bore the indelible mark of their origins in an intellectual utopia. They did see themselves as a 'collective intellectual', they remained piously faithful to the divine powers of the Word, and for a considerable period of time they believed in education and the dissemination of ideas as the principal vehicle of historical action. Again it is Robespierre and St. Just who come to mind. It was this belief which supplied justification for the blunt dismissal of any thought of 'independence' of intellectual activity, and for the uncanny seriousness with which even ostensibly detached and noncommittal ideas and cultural artefacts were treated. The practical effect was the elevated position assigned to intellectual professions in the theory and function of officialdom in the communist state, resulting in a redefinition of the vaunted and glorified 'engineers of the soul' as an extension of the political organs of the state. Hence the discomfiture, reported tongue-in-cheek, by the Russian émigré faced with the absence of any institutional approval of his credentials as a writer.

The principal reason for which a large part of the intellectuals, and particularly the part which felt strongly about its own vocation as defined by the intellectual idiom, looked at communist revolutionary ambition with avid hope (all possible criticism notwithstanding, it could not just bring itself to wishing for an unqualified defeat) was that in a number of respects the communists seemed one of many fully legitimate offspring of this hardcore intellectual tradition. The communist revolution, itself the work of 'professional revolutionaries' drawn from the ranks of the intelligentsia and owing their missionary zeal to the ambitions cultivated within the intellectual tradition, proclaimed its intention of reshaping society according to the requirements of reason as fathomed and spelled out by scientific analysis. This revolution founded its legitimacy upon the distinction between the wants of the people, confused as they were by their limited experience and ignorance, and the sound knowledge of the true needs of society, known only to the educated elite. This distinction has always been the axis of the intellectual world-view. The revolution reproduced and put on a stronger foundation the essential asymmetry of historicity, with the majority of people cast in the role of the objects of historical action, and the minority 'in the know' holding firmly to the responsibilities and privileges bestowed by the role of instructors and guides. The communist revolution explicitly proclaimed and ostensibly practised the unity of power and knowledge, the innermost core of the intellectual idiom.

In East-Central Europe there was a continuity of pastoral power and patronage of sorts linking the moral and economic leadership of the gentry through the spiritual leadership of the intelligentsia to the political domination of the Communist Party. The elements of continuity were in no way minor or secondary; they related to quite central aspects of social structure and the deployment of power. It is these elements of continuity which account for the remarkably close mutual engagement between the ruling party and the intelligentsia. Both could claim to be in the same business, to bear the same responsibilities, to share the same duties; both had to invoke the same legitimation in their respective bids for influence and elevated social positions; both had to recognize in each other's work an activity which they could not refuse legitimacy without sapping the ideological foundations of their own practices. However bitter the conflict and the rivalry between the two, they were enacted, so to speak, within a joint scenario that in normal circumstances would not necessarily have led to a radical and irrevocable breach in communication.

The continuing conflict and the rivalry, however, stem from the same source which generated broad agreement. They are organic and ineradicable because of the lateral, rather than processual nature of the continuity of idiom. The party has neither eliminated nor 'devoured' the intelligentsia. The two exist side by side, as structurally separate social categories, whatever their personal or functional connections. The party cannot help but strengthen the grounds on which the intelligentsia may claim its autonomy by multiplying the ranks of the educated elite and by widening the scope of crucial tasks for the educated experts to perform. Perhaps most importantly, the services of the intellectuals must be engaged in the task of reproducing the party's own ranks as well as its governing and managerial skills. On the other hand the party voids the potential autonomy of the intelligentsia by expropriating its constitutive functions.

The party had assumed the sole right of initiative in the very same areas of social life that were originally the exclusive, well nigh definitional, domain of the intelligentsia. The selection and dissemination of cultural values, the formation of opinions and evaluation of social change, the critique of ideology, the articulation of the criteria of moral and aesthetic judgement, and decisions on the content of public education and the 'civilizing process' in general have become matters of party policy and action.[6] Such freedom of creation as may be offered to or won by the intellectuals themselves would have to be circumscribed by these strictly forbidden territories. It is this limitation which is experienced and articulated by the intellectuals as 'lack of freedom'. Other classes within Communist-ruled societies, however deprived or oppressed they might be in other respects, would seldom consider lack of access to decision making in cultural, moral or artistic matters as an act of expropriation, so that it is only the intelligentsia which decries this particular restriction. Seventy years after the October Revolution the party's regular, ritualized brawls with intellectuals signal little else than the party's real or imaginary fear that the intellectuals might be breaking out of their confinement and trespassing on turf reserved for the party's direct rule.

From the point of view of the logic of the Communist system, the usurpation by the party of the territory traditionally administered by the intellectuals is in no way arbitrary; it cannot be reversed, or even seriously reduced by a liberal-minded leadership as long as such a leadership is committed to the preservation of the system held together by party rule. An 'enlightened despot' inside a Communist state is a contradiction in terms. It is the essence of the Communist system that it cannot securely rely on a 'second line of trenches' in the form of a civil society, generating on its own, particularly when left alone, moral and cultural attitudes of the sort required for the reproduction and conservative adjustments of the existing structure of domination. Spontaneous social processes or tendencies of a kind which keep the capitalist structure of domination alive, no matter how unconstrained and radical the questioning of its political legitimation may be, have not yet been set in motion within the communist regimes. Inside the latter, domination still has a mainly political foundation. It has to be reproduced with the resources monopolized by the political sphere, namely a mixture of coercion and ideological indoctrination. The need to indoctrinate renders the intellectual tendency to dabble with values and ideas a direct threat to the very source of the system of domination. As long as it lasts, this systematic arrangement leaves no room for an autonomous civil society and hence no room for the autonomy of the intellectuals, except for strictly professional areas tightly confined within politically defined boundaries.

It follows from this structural setting that there must be conflict between the intellectuals and the party. The confrontation between the two may be seen as a competition between alternative elites trying to control the flow of history. But there is also another side to the competition. Those eager to explain behavioural tendencies in terms of material conflicts can show that the disagreement over the distribution of surplus product, particularly the intellectuals' share, exacerbates the ideological tension. In Communist societies the general lowering of living standards has dealt a particularly bitter blow to the intelligentsia. Before Communism, educational professionals boasted an elevated position on the income scale. Now, except for small privileged minorities inside each of these professions, this is no longer true. Communist industrialization has drastically downgraded the relative standing of the intelligentsia and redirected the available surplus product into areas of the economy seen as more 'productive'. The hundreds of thousands of newcomers who flooded into the hitherto restricted ranks of the educational professions found there a lingering memory of a comfortable standard of living but a reality without an equivalent income. In itself this could be a cause of dissatisfaction and a stimulus to rally under a banner of specifically 'intellectual' demands. Attaining greater control over 'cultural policy' and strategic decision making would then be an indirect path to a change in the pattern of surplus distribution.

A parenthetical note should be added here to avoid confusion. Though, by tradition, the term 'intelligentsia' is still treated by many students of Eastern Europe as if it consisted of the entire 'educated elite' of the society, this corresponds to a historical memory rather than to contemporary reality. The time when the two categories overlapped has long passed; it was confined to the very early stage of the history of modern intellectuals. In fact, one of the most crucial achievements of modern intellectuals which entrenched them in a strategically central position was the establishment of education as a major instrument for the reproduction of society and for the allocation of functional roles within it. In West and East education transformed culture into capital *sui generis* to be deployed by those benefiting from its distribution.

This means the intellectuals cannot reproduce themselves and their social role without maintaining the character of culture as capital, that is, making it desirable and accessible. It is the utility of culture as capital that continues to give intellectuals a social base. But distribution of this capital dilutes it and means that not all, or even most of its beneficiaries become intellectuals. An education system spawns specialties and fields of expertise that are ever more isolated from each other. The link between the 'original myth' and its remote eventual product becomes increasingly tenuous. Indeed, the educated specialists can no longer be called a 'group' in any sociological sense, only a catgory. The more 'occupationally oriented' they are, the more specialized, the less likely they are to see themselves as part of the intelligentsia which this essay has been discussing.

In Communist-ruled East-Central Europe the educated elite has been the most rapidly expanding part of the population for several decades. In most countries, practically all modern specialization came into being during the period of Communist rule and the specialists have no collective, institutionalized memory of professional life under any other conditions. What follows is that everywhere a considerable part of the educated elite has been made to the measure of the Communist regime from the beginning. Coping with the situation defined by the Communust bureaucracy has been an integral part of their occupational training and professional upbringing. Occupational skills and the bureaucratically shaped context of their employment have been, so to speak, geared to each other. To a great extent, therefore, the skilful performance of occupational roles is dependent on the perpetual presence of a bureaucratic context. Many a specialist develops a vested interest of sorts in bureaucratic stability. He would feel ill at ease if called, for instance, to exercise his professional acumen under conditions of free competition, or if he had to work in a less strictly organized context without instructions, directives and ubiquitous normative regimentation.

The political prerequisites of bureaucracy and the technical prerequisites of an occupation are easily distinguishable in theory, but in practice they often merge. The notorious (again theoretical) conflict between the two kinds of prerequisites does not necessarily breed an anti-systemic attitude. The threat of abandoning the specialist to his own resources through withdrawal of bureaucratic tutorship and surveillance may seem to many more sinister than the prospect of continuing daily frictions and squabbles with party bureaucrats, which has been seen from the start as an acceptable part of occupational risk.

The point I wish to make in light of the above considerations (necessarily very simplified) is that unlike in the case of 'the intellectuals', there are no systemic grounds for the conflict between the occupational roles of the educated elite in general and the Communist bureaucracy. One can understand the success of the party in mobilizing wide sectors of the educated elite against the intellectual opposition, without necessarily resorting to 'false consciousness' or the memory of terror. Most of the postulates the intellectual opposition may advance toward the system, postulates indispensable from the point of view of the 'intellectual mode', would leave wide sectors of the educated elite at best lukewarm, faintly suspicious, uneasy at most times, and occasionally ready to rally to the defence of the system. Nevertheless, within the sphere of the education and cultural establishment, within some professions, and of course on the fringes of these groups, there remain a considerable number of intellectuals who identify themselves as such and are recognized to be part of the important 'intelligentsia' of which I am speaking.

To return from the disgression, the question remains whether the true focus of the conflict between the intellectuals and the party is the control of historicity (as Touraine, for example, would insist), or the control over surplus (as Konrád and Szelényi would have us believe).[7] In either case, it remains to a large extent a 'domestic affair' of the dominant elite, without much affecting the structure of domination as such. For this reason, the conflict at most times leaves other classes of the society indifferent. The struggle does not affect them and its outcome is unlikely to alter their location at the 'receiving end' of the domination structure. That this is the case, the Russian intellectual dissidents, and the educated and artistic elites of Hungary in 1956, Czechoslovakia in 1968, and the Poland of the 1960s all learned the hard way. There are numerous accounts of the blank incomprehension, if not chilly suspicion, with which the workers greeted intellectuals' forays into factories and their attempts to stir commotion and discontent among 'the people' to prompt them to join ranks in defence of the intellectuals' demands.

Roman Zimand has looked recently again into the published evidence of the Polish intellectual response to the explosion of the Stalinist myth by Khrushchev. It has remained in our collective memory as a most audacious, uncompromising, radical, and profound attack upon the very foundations of the Communist suppression of freedom. In some respects, it was like that indeed; with the iron lid suddenly removed from the seething cauldron of national discontent, the intellectuals could not but ask searching new questions and offer heretical answers to the old ones. And yet one declared 'truth' escaped all questioning; it appeared to be shared by the communist authorities and their intellectual adversaries alike (at least, an overwhelming majority of the latter), and indeed served as a tacit, but unencroachable, outer parameter of the debate conducted under conditions of a well-nigh unconstrained freedom. This unquestioned truth was 'a profound conviction that the people are incapable of a self-rule, and that control over practically everything – a modified and reasonable control, to be sure – is indispensable'. Most of the participants of the debate considered areas vacated by state supervision as a void rather than as a space won for popular self-government or an autonomous civil society. Such participants feared the void no less than did the communist rulers of the country.[8]

There is, however, another aspect to the conflict between political and intellectual elites capable of lifting it above the level of mere 'sibling rivalry' in the higher regions of social hierarchy. This other aspect has slowly gained in significance over the years, though in a number of communist countries it is as yet difficult to evidence. This is the pressure exerted not just against the exclusivity of the party's rule, but against the scope of that rule itself. It is an attempt to fold back the extent of political domination over other areas of social life. The conflict may express itself in an effort to push back the boundaries of the state and thus liberate the territory of civil society from political supervision. At that point the conflict becomes more than a private affair between educated elites. Here the interests of the intellectuals coincide and overlap with the interests of the most numerous and most deprived classes of Communist society. They meet, in particular, with the drive of the workers towards trade-unionist rights and economic self-management, or the farmers' drive towards a less regimented market for agricultural products and equipment, both of which demand an exemption of vast sectors of economic and social relations from the command of the state. This is a ground on which a lasting alliance between otherwise distinct social groups can be forged and maintained, as argued convincingly by Krzysztof Zagorski.[9]

So far the only case when the potential of such unity had been brought to the political surface was the spectacular episode of Solidarity in Poland.

Diversity of sectional interests was overshadowed and reduced to a secondary role by the unity of practically all classes of society in their struggle for the emancipation of wide areas of economic, social, and cultural life from state control. It seems that the reluctance to aim for the replacement of the ruling elites, however pragmatically wrongheaded it might have been proved by the military restoration of the *ancien régime*, was an indispensable condition of this broad alliance. The Solidarity episode was therefore a challenge to a much older tradition.

'In the summer of 1980', wrote Andrzej Kijowski, 'the Polish intellectual accepted the superiority of the people'. This acceptance was, by all historical standards, a genuine, unprecedented novelty, as Kijowski explains:

> The Marxist – Leninist Party called the intellectuals into the ranks of the 'conscious minority', which according to the theory of dialectical materialism should guide the masses to the fulfilment of their historical task. For this party calling and mythology, the road was paved by past mythologies, which framed the successive self-definitions of the intellectuals: those of a philosopher counselling the King in the style of the Enlightenment, of the romantic prophet reaching for spiritual leadership by divine inspiration or the authority of history, of the teacher of the masses in the positivist mood – of the apostle of science and progress. ... The intellectual class has a 200-year long history, during which its self-image went through many changes; what did not change was its belief in its own superiority.[10]

There is a sense in which the Solidarity episode can be described as the first genuinely working-class revolution. This time, the mass movement accomplished more than to provide a powerful wave on the crest of which an alternative elite might ride to government power and pastoral authority. It questioned the very principle of such government and such an authority. The intellectuals found themselves, for the first time, reduced to the role of advisers, whose opinions could be solicited or rejected at will; a familiar experience, to be sure, but this time those demanding advice and using it at their discretion were 'the people' themselves, heretofore passive recipients of enlightenment, and docile objects of the civilizing drill. The authority of the intellectuals in the realm of civil society, stolen or severely truncated by the Communist Party (by itself an admission of entitlement), now has been denied as a matter of principle. The autonomy of civil society *vis-à-vis* the political state, so it transpired, is not necessarily tantamount to the restitution of the pastoral rule of the intellectuals. This was, indeed, a discovery.

The Solidarity episode was far too brief for the new structures to solidfy, much less to mature. It would be irresponsible to extrapolate a general tendency from what might have been an abortive, not viable situation. But there is little doubt that the experience sent shock waves throughout East-Central Europe. It will take some time for the full import of the event to sink in, to be measured, and to be absorbed. But in all likelihood it will exert a far-reaching influence on the self-definition, programme, and strategy of the educated elite.

The selectivity of historical memory is notorious. There is no way to say in advance what it will retain. Will it be the intoxication of a society once more becoming fluid and pliable, eager to be reshaped and redesigned, the exhilaration of 'making history' and believing that it can be made more rational, humane, and enjoyable? Will it be the heart-warming sight of the nation suddenly enthused by values, projects, and principles which the intellectuals always wished, in vain, to get it to adopt? Or, on the contrary, will it be the horror (even if kept subconscious at the time) of popular disenchantment with authority spreading to include disenchantment with the self-proclaimed intellectual alternative to the party's rule? Will the historical memory of the intellectuals retain the pleasures of life free of the stultifying control of the party bureaucracy, or the knowledge that such freedom is paid for by the insecurity of intellectual superiority?

I have tried to expose the inner ambiguity, the irremovable contradictions, and the dialectical interplay of opposition and mutual dependency, in the love – hate relationship between intellectuals and Communist rule. The historical experience of Solidarity may strengthen either of the two sides of the contradiction. It may deprive the communist state in Poland of all intellectual support. In this case the state will seek the ways of making its rule independent of the services intellectuals are capable of providing, and hence, in a truly 'Western' way, rendering intellectual work politically irrelevant. Or it may stimulate at least a part of those in the intellectual category to reclaim their legitimizing role and to turn wistfully back to a sheltered existence under the protective wings of the state. With the present pitiable condition of the Polish economy, the state is likely to depend for some time yet on ideological mobilization; therefore the claim may be granted at least until further notice.

In Poland, the Solidarity departure, however radical and novel, was a final stage in the long process of historical learning. Each successive stage from the Poznań riots through to the Polish October, to the March 1968 strike and the movements of 1970, 1974, and 1976, started at a somewhat higher level than the preceding stage. Some of the old mistakes were avoided and some of the old illusions shed. Such historical learning as a continuous and cumulative process was largely absent in other East European countries. The Polish product may still spread to other areas of the communist world through the diffusion of stimulus. But then, in the absence of local, indigenous traditions these Polish discoveries may exert an exactly opposite effect, alerting intellectual elites to the unsuspected radicalism of popular anti-authoritarianism. It seems that there is evidence pointing to the possibility of both effects.

NOTES

1. Zhores A. Medvedev, *The Medvedev Papers* (Macmillan, 1971), pp. 170-1.
2. I deal with the origins of modern intellectuals in my *Legislators and Interpreters* (Cambridge, Polity Press, 1987).
3. See Michel Foucault, *Power and Knowledge* (Brighton, Harvester Press, 1980).
4. François Furet, *Penser la révolution française* (Paris, Gallimard, 1978).
5. See Immanuel Wallerstein, 'The French Revolution and Capitalism: An Explanatory Schema', *Praxis International* 5 (April 1985), pp. 1-22.
6. See Stefan Żółkiewski, *O kulturze Polski Ludowej*, (Warszawa, Państwowe Wydawnictwo Naukowe, 1964), p. 38.
7. Alain Touraine, et al., *Solidarité: Analyse d'un mouvement social, Pologne 1980-1982* (Paris, Fayard, 1982); György Konrád and Iván Szelényi, *The Intellectuals on the Road to Class Power* (New York, Harcourt Brace Jovanovich, 1979).
8. See Romand Zimand, "Z mobilu," *Aneks* 38 (1985), pp. 74-87.
9. See Krzysztof Zagorski, *Society, Economy, and Class Relations* (Canberra, Australian National University, 1983).
10. See Andrzej Kijowski, "Co się zmieni to ...", *Arka* 1-9 (Kraków, 1983-4), pp. 131-42.

6
We, Central-European East Europeans
Miroslav Kusý

Central Europe's division into eastern and western halves following Yalta has tended to produce a binary form of thinking about Europe itself, as if these two geo-political entities were simple, mirror images of each other. Miroslav Kusý argues that there is no opposing symmetry in the terms 'Western Europe' and 'Eastern Europe' because the connotations attached to each are fundamentally different in character. While 'Western Europe' offers its inhabitants a supra-national identity based on the evolving, integrative process of the post-war period, a comparable integration in Eastern Europe has meant only the consolidation of the power bloc, rather than any genuine interpenetration of nations and cultures.

You call us 'Eastern Europe' and describe us as 'East Europeans', and all of us – from the 'East' Germans of the GDR to the Hungarians, Poles, Czechs and Estonians – feel slighted and reject the label.

We were all Central Europeans in the past. The trouble is that Hitler destroyed Central Europe for good and all, after which the post-war settlement fixed the status quo and the Iron Curtain finally divided it between West and East. Objectively speaking, in terms of political geography, many of its inhabitants became *de facto* East Europeans. So what are they complaining about?

They feel quite simply that the description is not only – or even primarily – geographical. However, the real misunderstanding arises when one leaves aside the geographical connotations, for straightaway, the concepts of 'Western' and 'Eastern' Europe lose their common *principium divisionis*. The term 'East European' was not coined to the same pattern as 'West European' and is not its logical counterpart on this side of the European divide. As a result, we end up talking at cross purposes.

When the expression 'West European' is used (frequently shortened –

though not altogether justifiably so – to 'European'), we think of people whose original homeland has widened to all intents and purposes to encompass the whole of Western Europe – people who feel at home there, as part of an economic, cultural and political entity which is already considerably integrated internally. In other words, this entity forms a single, higher territorial community in the sense that all those who live within its bounds already have a real awareness of 'West European identity'.

Such peoples as the French, Italians, Swiss or Dutch did not evolve such a 'European spirit' by shutting themselves in their own national backyards and dreaming about it, but by emerging from them. They became Europeans in the practical meaning of the word by effectively widening their common territory.

In many respects the post-war process of West European integration was spontaneous in the economic, cultural and political sense, as well as in terms of employment/migration and tourism. Furthermore its formal expressions such as the EEC, the European Parliament and even NATO are not its *spiritus agens* but rather its consequence. However such formal manifestations are not even held in the same sort of regard in all of the countries involved, and are actually the subject of numerous controversies. In this sense European integration preceded these formal arrangements and stands above them. Thus it is possible for Danes or Belgians, for instance, to have a feeling of West European identity without this necessarily implying anything about their attitudes or those of their governments towards the EEC or NATO.

But what do we 'East Europeans' have to hold us together?

West European integration occurred without us and without any regard for us. We do not belong to the supra-national community which was created, either physically or even spiritually. We are too cut off from it by now. We lost Central Europe as a living space and have not yet to managed to create anything adequate to replace it. On the contrary, what two world wars divided and set at loggerheads continues to be divided and mutually antagonistic.

So far, no spontaneous grassroots process of integration has happened since the war (in any sense comparable with the West European integration process) and each of us secretly hopes that it never will in the near future. Our mutual national antagonisms are still sufficiently alive as to push us in the opposite direction. Your average Slovak still finds the idea of a closer territorial union with Hungary unthinkable. Czechs and Poles are hardly going to form a community with the Germans, but then nor are the Czechs and Slovaks with the Poles, for that matter. Possibly only the Bulgarians retain some sort of affection for the Russians. The non-Slav nations regard all Slavs with deep suspicion and perhaps a certain degree of contempt, while the Rumanians, Hungarians and Germans would not seem to have very much in common either.

We have certainly not created any supra-national cultural, intellectual or moral community with which each of our countries might identify. Instead, we have remained shut in our national enclosures and cast hostile glances in each other's direction over the walls.

Are there really any of us who have a sense of 'East Europeanness'? I don't know of anyone. On the contrary, the idea of an East European identity is something we all shun as a calamity that could one day befall us. This is not just a question of relations between people who were once Central Europeans. No, what we all realize is that the only conceivable East European community that could be created and function in a situation of absolute Soviet hegemony would be a Russified one. However, doesn't something of that sort already exist, or if not, isn't it being created?

Even though it may appear that way to Western eyes, I believe it to be an optical illusion. 'Eastern Europe' is nothing more than a power-political bloc of the Comecon and Warsaw Pact states. An 'East European' is nothing but a Hungarian or a Pole living in a country which happens to belong to that bloc. And any sense of 'East Europeanness' that the Germans or Czechs might have is tantamount to the feelings shared by an eagle and a lion living alongside each other in a zoo from which there is no means of escape.

Let us assume, therefore, that so far no spontaneous 'East Europeanness' has come into being at the grassroots level. But what about further up? Isn't that precisely what the dominant power structures in this part of the world are trying to create?

We are all aware that direct sovietization has occurred only in a fraction of former central European territory, that is, in the annexed states on the fringes (the Baltic states, Sub-Carpathian Ukraine, Bessarabia, etc.). Similar attempts (which included Gustav Husák's concept of a 'Soviet Slovakia' from the period of the Slovak Uprising) were nipped in the bud. The point of sovietization of that type, however, was not to promote a sense of 'East Europeanness' but instead a statist consciousness of Soviet patriotism: the creation of a would-be Soviet man and the unity of the Soviet people. How much the Soviets have managed that is another matter entirely.

The most determined, indirect attempt at sovietizing the erstwhile Central European countries took place in the 1950s. This was the transplantation of the Soviet life-style, Soviet models, Soviet literature – Soviet everything, in fact. This was intended to constitute the unifying element for the entire bloc, with a view to creating a sense of belonging and a bloc indentity among the member countries.

By and large this attempt failed, not just because the underlying idea was unacceptable, not just because of the way it was carried out, but to a great degree merely because there was no concomitant *de facto* integration of the bloc countries in the form of mutual interpenetration of national economies and national cultures, nor any widespread cross-frontier contacts between the nation-states. On the contrary, its basic premise was the maintenance of mutual isolation wherever possible.

'Existing socialism' took note of the failure of that attempt. None the less, indirect sovietization left behind it many rituals (such as the grandiose celebration of the 'Great October Socialist Revolution', Lenin's birthday, the annual 'Month of Soviet Film', lip-service to Service models, etc.), though nobody takes them seriously any more. Participation at May Day demonstrations is ensured by means of rewards. Existing socialism has abandoned any ideas of an all-embracing intra-bloc integration at grassroots level among the countries concerned (that is, if it ever did take the idea seriously in the first place) and is instead going for a strictly limited top-level integration of the states involved as being the sole 'legal entities'. However the effect of such top-level integration is anything but the creation of a supposed 'East Europeanness'.

Admittedly, the basic forms of this integration from above have existed here since the founding of the Soviet bloc. In its original form, however, as it appeared in the 1950s, the function of this sort of integration was limited solely to that of keeping us in check by means of physical force.

The power bloc demands that maximum degree of integration of the top-level political, economic and military circles of the member countries, and in this respect we must admit that – apart from the odd discord – the Soviets achieve, in joint party consultations, the Comecon and the Warsaw Pact, a 'unity' and 'cohesion' beyond the wildest dreams of the other side: the European Parliament, the EEC or NATO.

However, such bloc integration remains at the summit of power and never descends any lower. It does not affect society and culture lower down in the countries concerned, nor does it seek to. In this sense, political integration involves solely top party officials, statesmen and diplomats. Likewise, military integration concerns only the chiefs of staff and not the actual armies themselves. It is typical that Soviet troops which are deployed throughout the majority of bloc member-states are kept in strict isolation from the 'fraternal' troops of the country in question – not to mention from the 'fraternal' local population.

And what about economic integration within the bloc? This is still in its infancy. The sort of economic co-operation that has existed so far in the form of trade, international division of labour, technological unification, etc., truly has little in common with genuine economic integration. Essentially it should be aimed at creating an East European common market (instead of mere bilateral export – import treaties) with a dynamic movement of capital, investments and labour within the framework of the bloc as a whole, and at building direct production relations as well as scientific and technological links between the firms and organizations of the countries concerned, not to mention setting up joint enterprises and international combines. In the light of these criteria, how does the present state of economic integration between Czechoslovakia and the Soviet Union measure up, for instance? The November 1986 agreement provides for the twinning of 17 enterprises on each side with a view to the creation of direct relations and notes the existence of three joint enterprises. And this is probably the highest achievement of which the two sides can boast in terms of bloc-level international economic integration.

So far, economic integration within the Soviet bloc has essentially taken place at such elevated levels that it does not affect daily life in the countries involved in such a way as to make all inhabitants directly aware of it, for it to influence their standard of living and life-style and generate in them a feeling of belonging to the bloc, of a shared sense of 'East Europeanness'.

The opposite is true, in fact. Even the economic factor tends to be more of a force for disunity in Eastern Europe than the reverse. At the macroeconomic level, for instance, the first major joint investment project by Hungary and Czechoslovakia – the Danube barrage at Gabčikovo – is the subject of ongoing controversy between the two partners; the Soviet Union is cutting back still further on contractual deliveries of crude oil to its bloc partners: Czechoslovakia's partners are reluctant to take up their contracts for nuclear power-stations, etc. At the microeconomic level, consumer goods which are commonplace in one country of the bloc can be scarce or unobtainable in another: there is a sense in which customs regulations between Czechoslovakia and the GDR or Hungary are stricter than between Czechoslovakia and Austria, for instance. Momentary economic prosperity in one country of the bloc is not in any way reflected in the economic situation of its bloc neighbours and is therefore regarded by the latter with envy and hostility. By the same token, the economic crises that erupt every so often somewhere in the bloc arouse a feeling of gloating satisfaction in the victim's neighbours of the 'serves you right!' variety. The popular view here in the early 1980s was that the Poles went bankrupt because of their never-ending strikes and maximalist demands, and the Rumanians because of their slovenly, lazy ways. Why do you think the average Hungarian or East German thinks we have hit rock bottom now? The explanation would not be very flattering for us, I'm sure.

But what about tourism within the bloc, both on an individual or mass basis – the universally accepted means for different nations to get to know each other?

Tourism here has never assumed the form of unrestricted travel, in other words, the form whereby West Europeans get to know their territory. It is restricted by various passport regulations, both on entry and exit, as well as by customs and exchange limitations. Such restrictions, which are periodically tightened and relaxed, are influenced by economic and political conditions. Honecker did not let his Germans visit Dubček's reform-communist

Czechoslovakia; Husák closed the doors to Poland for his Czechs and Slovaks at the time of Solidarity or the Pope's visit. Every country of the bloc employs various methods to impede what is the most widespread and popular form of tourism within the bloc: one which has its roots in basic economic scarcity and the influx of worthless currency from fraternal neighbours. In the 1960s, Czechoslovakia was 'kiss (little) Amerika' for the Hungarians who used to come here on shopping trips, and at that time the shops here would receive circulars with a list of those goods which were to be concealed from Hungarian tourists. The contrary is now the case, and Czechoslovaks scour Hungarian and East German department stores and shops, while impoverished Soviet tourists fight over goods in Czechoslovak stores. Special shops for hard-currency Western tourists inaccessible to the travelling East European plebs exist in possibly all the Soviet bloc countries. According to this principle the Rumanians have even started opening segregated snack-bars in their Black Sea coastal resorts: the one kind sells a wide selection of perfectly chilled imported drinks, while the other offers warm local beer and lemonade. In Slovakia's Tatra Mountains, West German or Italian tourists can drive their limousines in areas strictly barred to all other drivers: they have hard currency. This does not particularly bother the locals. What does rankle with them permanently is the influx of East German and Hungarian skiers and holiday-makers who book up all the cheaper chalets and hotels, elbow them out of the queue for ski-lifts and throng the mountain trails. By and large, foreign tourists from within the bloc are not welcomed as 'good news' for the development of a major branch of the national economy, but as a burden which makes things even more difficult for us here. Is it conceivable that such 'scarcity tourism' within the bloc could ever lead to closer ties between the populations of the different countries? The actual effect is the contrary: sharpened mutual hostility and the entrenchment of our division.

All this leads me to conclude that those in the West who currently regard Eastern Europe as the common territory of the peoples living there and believe that we share a feeling of 'East Europeanness' are barking up the wrong tree. The debate about pan-European detente is between two power blocs: on the one side there is Western Europe and on the other the Soviet bloc – not West Europeans and East Europeans, because the latter do not exist. The dialogue about an eventual all-European cultural identity is entirely a West European affair which so far does not address us in the 'East'. If we too are to take an effective part in it then we must first of all establish and assert our own identity in a practical way.

(*Translated by A. G. Brain*)

7
The European Ideal: Reality or Wishful Thinking in Eastern Central Europe?
Miklós Duray

While the category of Central Europe suggests an entity whose component parts share certain distinctive features, it is well known that Central Europe is also the site of long-standing ethnic, linguistic, religious and other differences. Moreover the conflicts arising from these differences have to a great extent determined the fate of Central Europe since the collapse of the Habsburg Empire.

Miklós Duray, a leading activist of the Hungarian minority in Slovakia, analyses the national and power-political interests of the Central European polity and argues that the absolutization of the national idea at the expense of minority nations has been a constant feature of political systems in the region – totalitarian and democratic alike.

The 'European idea' and 'Europeanness' are becoming fashionable concepts throughout the European continent. In the case of the West Europeans, it would seem to be an attempt to offset the influence of the United States on the old continent. Further east, however, deep in the heart of the continent, its significance is rather more as a counterbalance to the traumatizing outcome of Yalta, to the stifling presence of the Soviet Union. Obviously the idea can hardly make inroads in society so long as it is proclaimed for political reasons alone. It is conceivable, I admit, that as far as we Central Europeans – or more precisely Eastern Central Europeans – are concerned, Europe has never been as important as it is now and we have never before sought salvation in it so desperately as we have over the past 40 years, in other words, since the time when we came under the thumb of the Soviet Union to which our cultural and political traditions are alien, the moment when it became a habit to divide our continent into western and eastern halves. It is hard to imagine that anyone who used to be a friend of the Soviets could have conceived this 'friendship' in such terms.

At a time of revolutionary advances in communications and information, Europe has never been so remote from the eastern part of Central Europe as it is now. Moreover, the inhabitants of our part of Europe have the feeling that the West has turned its back on us for good, although it is a well-known fact that the Eastern part of Central Europe – which can be defined both territorially and politically – has lagged behind the West in terms of social development since the end of the Middle Ages. One reason for this is the fact that, for centuries, this geographical zone acted as a buffer between West and East. But there was no cross-fertilization of the two confronting cultures; instead the antagonistic power ambitions of the two sides cancelled each other out. In spite of this, Central Europe, including its eastern reaches, came under the influence of all the main European spiritual currents. Our common European continent saw the separation of secular and ecclesiastical power. Gothic cathedrals sprouted up almost at one and the same time – even if the spires in the east were of rather less spectacular dimensions – and they served to define categorically European culture's eastern boundary. We experienced the flowering of the Renaissance more or less at the same time, albeit at different levels of intensity. Western and Central Europe also shared the experience of the Reformation and Protestantism. Those innovatory movements did not give rise to new antagonistic churches and sects – as in the case of other religions – but led instead to a process of democratization. They gave birth to the idea of liberalism, pluralism, modern democracy, socialism and the defence of the human individual, all of which constitute the shared reality of the West at the present time. The common cradle of Western and Central European culture is Western Christianity and the Jewish spirituality from which it derived.

We were cut off from *that* Europe, when, with the assistance of the Communist parties of the different countries, we became dependent on a dictatorial power to which our common European cultural and historical traditions are alien. But was it really all Communism's fault? By no means. Communism, through the intermediary of the Leninist parties, was only the chosen instrument for reinforcing the totalitarian system and extending the power of the dictatorship. So are we to blame the West for having sold us down the river? That too is out of the question, even if they did help to push us towards our destiny. We cannot even blame our geographical situation, because the example of Finland obviously negates such a theory. No, the fact is that Central Europe slowly but surely surrendered to totalitarianism.

What is paradoxical about our situation is the fact that humanism, rationalism and the Enlightenment which had started to break down ossified social barriers and make education generally available, not only served to democratize cultural, social and political life, but also gave rise to a new concept: nationalism. They thereby created a new barrier between nations, one which has yet to be overcome in the eastern part of Central Europe. This barrier was created as a result of the absolutization of the national idea. And it gave rise not only to the emancipatory national language campaigns but also to totalitarian nationalism on the one hand, and national political struggles on the other, both of which result in different nations weakening each other and themselves.

At the time when the national idea took root, the ethnic and power relations in Central Europe were sufficiently balanced to prevent one nation or power from achieving exclusive domination easily or by the legitimate use of force. However, that state of equilibrium did not foster the idea of preserving balance through treaty, but on the contrary inspired thoughts of disrupting it. [...] The history of that period came to a final end in 1918, the year which marked the beginning of the new era in which we still live. It is therefore enough for us to recall its final phase: at the end of the eighteenth century, power within the Habsburg Monarchy started to polarize and, right up to 1918, decisions about the Empire's development were taken by two main centres: chiefly the dynasty (i.e. the Austro-German regime) and also (after 1867) to a certain extent by the political leadership of the Hungarian state. However, neither of those power centres proved capable of fulfilling their historical mission of modernizing the Empire and creating the conditions for preserving its unity. It should be pointed out, however, that the blame cannot be laid at their door alone. The failure was also assisted to a lesser extent by other nations and ethnic groups of the Monarchy, not to mention the international political situation. It is important to note, however, that the Czech lands took no part in that share-out of power. The chief reason for this was the presence of a large German population in Bohemia whose interests, both national and capitalist, were bound up with those of Austria, and who therefore did not support the Czechs' aspirations for self-government.

Historians generally attribute the break-up of the Austro-Hungarian Monarchy to the failure to solve the problem of national relations. This is not entirely true, however. The main reason was a clash of national and power interests among the individual countries of the Empire, even though these antagonisms were often artificially provoked. National policies merely ministered to those interests. This does not mean, of course, that I wish to make light of the national oppression which affected, to different degrees and at different times, all the component peoples, with the exception of the Austrian Germans and the Empire's German population as a whole.

The clash of national and power-political interests within the framework of the Empire can best be illustrated by reference to the history of the Hungarians and Czechs, two nations which became rivals in the second half of the nineteenth century. [...]

There was one factor in Hungarian history which was not present to such a degree in the history of the monarchy's other nations. I refer to the effort to regain the Hungarian nation's former glory and power. In the light of the circumstances of the time, this may be regarded as unrealistic and detrimental to peace in the region. At the end of the eighteenth century, the Magyars realized to their dismay that the ethnic ratios in the country had fatally altered since the time of the last 'glorious' national sovereign, Matthias Corvinus, at the end of the fifteenth century when their superiority was of the order of 80 per cent. Why it came as such a profound shock was partly because it was now clear that, whereas before the Turkish occupation of the country their power and the country's internal situation (including the ratio between ethnic groups in the population) was similar to that of contemporary France, by the time of the national revival there was almost no trace left of their superiority. Not only had their power and international authority disappeared in the meantime but, as a result of the considerable devastation, their backwardness could be reckoned in centuries. Hungarian politics was unable to rid itself of this complex until 1918, and from the time of the Austro-Hungarian settlement, efforts to shift the balance towards Magyar dominance repeatedly cropped up at the centre of state policy. Such a situation inevitably provoked the resistance of the country's non-Magyar inhabitants whose proportion of the population had increased many-fold. The Magyars' fear of ethnic inferiority can perhaps only be compared with the Czechs' traditional fear of the Germans. But the Magyars feared something else as well: the loss of their kingdom's territorial integrity whose area was then four times that of the present-day Hungarian republic. [...] This chiefly explains the harshness of Hungarian policies in 1848 towards the non-Magyar political movements. After all, the Rumanian, Serbian, Croatian and Slovak political endeavours, which were equally militant, represented a threat to the kingdom's newly restored territorial integrity. At that time, the policy of the Czechs was to call for the federalization of the monarchy, having moderated their original demands out of fear of expansionist Greater German plans for the restoration of the Holy Roman Empire. However, the Hungarians, because of the above-mentioned fears, were opposed to federalization and sought instead to shore up their own power. This moment may be regarded as the first major clash of Czech and Hungarian power interests within the framework of the Habsburg Empire. But both were to emerge defeated from their struggle against the dynasty. After all, not only was the Hungarian Empire crushed – with the assistance of the Russian Army – but even the Kroměříž [Kremsier] Constitution granted in 1848 fell far short of the expectations of the Czechs, not to mention the aspirations of the anti-Magyar movement in the Hungarian lands. [...]

With the Austro-Hungarian (Magyar) settlement of 1867 came the first open and serious signs of Hungary's intentions to preserve the unity of the Habsburg Empire. The oath of allegiance sworn to the House of Habsburg in 1688 and 1741 by the Hungarian estates could hardly be regarded as lasting.

The political developments in Bohemia after the settlement took an opposite course. [...] In the dualist system which we regard as a great success for Hungarian policies, the way was closed for the Czechs to follow the same course as the Hungarians. This was the second clash of interests and it turned out to be fatal since it ushered in a gradual reversal of Czech policies, with a strengthening of the currents opposed to imperial unity, as well as of anti-German tendencies. It is worth nothing here that this change came about precisely at the time when Czarist Russia's pan-Slavist agitation was beginning to exert a powerful influence on the individual Slav nations of the monarchy, which either succumbed to it or used it as a lever to advance their own political ends. [...]

The changes of attitude within Czech and Hungarian politics in the last third of the nineteenth century had a monumental influence on the future political settlement in Eastern Central Europe which came into being with the disintegration of the Austro-Hungarian Monarchy. On 28 October 1918, Czechoslovakia was created as the successful culmination of Czech political revanchism which had been provoked by the monarchy's previous dualist system. The fact is that Hungary had been proclaimed the arch-enemy of the Central European nations regardless of the fact that it it had acceded only to the second rung of the power structure after Austria, the Empire's symbolic and administrative centre.

We can most simply sum up the situation created in 1918 as follows: what suited the new states established at the expense of the Empire and accorded with their power interests was detrimental to the Austrian and German populations and ran directly counter to Hungarian interests. The interests of the Austrian and Hungarians clashed least of all.

However it was not merely a question of contradictions between the different powers. The national and power interests of the new states were actually conceived in opposition to the national, ethnic, historical and cultural traditions of the Austrian and other Germans, but they clashed most of all with those of the Hungarians. The disintegration of the Monarchy, despite the major political and economic transformations, engendered a state of shock – particularly spiritual and emotional – in the members of the defeated nations. It disrupted millions upon millions of families and family relationships, destroying livelihoods and undermining national identity. The causes are obvious. Within the political designs of the new states which had emerged as victorious on the historical stage, there was room only for their own power interests, for the interests of the ruling nation. There was no room for the national and cultural interests of the defeated nations of the former political system, nor was there any provision for protecting the interests and identity of the national minorities created by the fragmentation of national entities. The political character of Central Europe in the twentieth century was determined by this factor most of all. It was in this respect that Eastern

Central Europe most clearly divorced itself from the West. Emanuel Rádl wrote that the 1918 Constitution of the Czechoslovak Republic arose in an Absolutist fashion on the basis of military law, since it regarded the German and Hungarian populations as an enemy defeated in war who could simply be dictated to. A political investment like that by a nation of the region could expect a return only in the form of conflict.

The most important turning point in the modern history of the eastern areas of Central Europe came in 1918, with the collapse of the Habsburg Empire. That revolution gave free play to all the sentiments of hatred, revanchism, vengeance, separatism and irredentism which had been suppressed or only partially sublimated until then. There was no longer any need to worry about the interests of a larger entity, in other words, unity of a higher order. The Little Entente which came into being in the 1920-2 period did not in fact serve to protect the area but instead was a vehicle for the anti-Hungarian interests of the newly-created states. The interests of the wider geo-political area, in other words, the common interests of the nations living in that part of Europe, became lost amid the particular interests of the new states. [...]

Whereas under the Habsburg Empire the roots of political error sprang from the two main poles of power, after its collapse there were as many sources of error as there were new states. None of the Central European nations rose to the major challenge of defending the political region. In his radio broadcast on 6 October 1938, the day of his abdication, President Beneš spoke quite self-critically when he categorically identified the cause of the then political catastrophe as being the outcome of national antagonisms. He was ready to accept the possibility that as a result of the changed conditions, that is the revision of the frontiers approximately in accordance with ethnic principles, the conflicts between the neighbouring states would disappear. It is typical of today's official historiography that it regards this stand of Beneš as defeatist.

Nowadays, few people doubt that the causes of the Second World War should be sought in the collapse of the peace settlement that ended the first global conflict. The crucial element in the final crisis was the fact that the victorious powers and their satellites sought to take absolute advantage of the defeated nations. However, apart from satisfying the aspirations of the victors, the Versailles system also predetermined future developments. Regardless of the advantages they obtained after the First World War, the Central European states and nations became the playthings of Fascist power.

After the collapse of the Austro-Hungarian Monarchy, the German populations of the new states, especially Czechoslovakia, found themselves deprived of their former social status. Vienna or Austria, their natural metropolis until then and itself having difficulty coming to terms with its defeat, was unable to play its former role. And so some of those Germans (not

The European Ideal

to mention Austria now stripped of its imperial glory) felt the need for a powerful patron capable of fostering their self-assurance. This they found without difficulty in post-Hohenzollern Germany as it goose-stepped towards Fascist totalitarianism under the leadership of Chancellor Hitler. Such attempts at bolstering national positions were also the chief hallmark of the alliances which certain Central European countries – irrespective of whether their aspirations were just and justified or exaggerated and aggressive – were to strike with Hitler's Germany. The Slovaks did not ally themselves with Hitler out of anti-Czech or anti-Hungarian sentiment, nor, for that matter, in order to be the only ally to take part in the military invasion of Poland, but because their legitimate right as a nation to establish their own state could only be implemented within the Axis. Equally, Hungary did not enter into negotiations with the Italians and Germans according to the principle 'any enemy of my enemy is my friend', but in order to regain a part of that territory inhabited by three million Hungarians. The Rumanians did it in order to retain as much as possible of Transylvania (which they had not yet had time enough to Rumanize), to get back Bessarabia (which had been lost yet again) from the Soviet Union, to have the influence necessary to hold on to Dobruja which they had obtained in San Stefano in 1877 in return for Soviet-occupied Bessarabia, and finally, in the hopes of gaining still further territory (e.g. Transnistria). The Croatians did not enter into a pact with Hitler because of their dislike for the Serbs, but solely because this was the only way to achieve the independence they yearned for. In fact even the agreement between Germany and the Soviet Union signed by Hitler and Stalin in August 1939 was of this variety, because it gave the USSR the advantage over the Baltic states and Eastern Poland, which it was able to exploit after the Second World War without requiring the agreement of the other powers. As is known, the situation of the Czechs and Poles was rather different. However it was not only because it stood in the path of Hitler's Germany that Czechoslovakia was engulfed by the waves of the pre-war storm. The national ambitions of the neighbouring states which led to the dismemberment of the Czechoslovak Republic in 1938–9 reflected proportionately the extent to which Czechoslovakia had acted contrary to their interests when drawing its state frontiers in 1918. An exception to this was the creation of the Protectorate, the German occupation of post-Munich Czech territory on 15 March 1939, and the occupation of Poland by Hitler's Germany and the Soviet Union.

There was no way for Hitler's Central European allies to satisfy their territorial ambitions except to the detriment of their neighbours. [...]

Nationality policies and how they were formulated merit particularly close examination in view of the international tensions arising from the changes of regime of 1918–19, the consequent frontier revisions of 1938–40, the territorial reparations of 1945 and the retaliatory measures that continued up to 1949. The deepening of conflict within our region was caused especially by the fact that some ten million Germans and Hungarians found themselves in the situation of national minorities on the territories of three of the newly-created states: Czechoslovakia, Rumania and Yugoslavia. Poland was an exception in this respect.

It is widely accepted that, because they were drafted in circumstances of relative democracy, the first Czechoslovak Republic's policies on nationality differed from the nationality policies after the Second World War, i.e. those of the Third Republic. The reasons for this should not be sought in the first instance in the state's domestic political conditions, but in the international political situation. After all, the political system in Czechoslovakia in the 1945-8 period did not differ fundamentally from the pluralist system of the First Republic, but the international political situation was very different. Czechoslovakia's policies on its nationalities from 1919 onwards were heavily influenced by the existence of the Treaty of Saint Germain, but equally by the republic's efforts to win international prestige. In a certain sense this constituted positive pressure on the republic to reach a democratic settlement of the issue. As a new state, the Czechoslovak Republic was created in accordance with the proclamation of nations' rights to self-determination, so it could not afford to be criticized internationally as a suppressor of national minorities through its nationalities policy. After the Second World War, however, there were no such international political considerations to restrain the country's politicians – of whatever political affiliation – from seeking to take absolute advantage of the country's position as a victorious power. There was no need to take account of any extenuating factors in the international situation – almost to the contrary. The situation positively invited unrestrained behaviour because the concept of ethnic totality, no less alien to modern European traditions than Hitlerite or Stalinist ideas, had become the rule. It was an attempt to create a purely Slav state. Such an approach was no more in tune with European traditions than Hitler's racist national totalitarianism, over which the world was just celebrating its victory. In this connection, the Hungarian writer from Slovakia Zoltán Fábry wrote: 'Having jettisoned the moral ballast of anti-fascism, the victors could simply appropriate fascism – as the most refined form of the power principle – and put it to general use'.

Czechoslovakia was to receive considerable international support for its 'final' reorganization of ethnic relations in the Eastern part of Central Europe. At Potsdam, the victorious powers, chiefly under pressure from Czechoslovak politicians not only endorsed the expulsion of the Germans, they actually ordered it to be done. Admittedly, they did not determine *how* it should be carried out. However only the Soviet Union supported the total expulsion of Hungarians from Czechoslovakia. The USA and United Kingdom were opposed. This fact must be noted because the only ally

Czechoslovakia had in solving its nationality issue according to the principle of '*Endlösung*' was the Soviet Union, which was – apart from the passing phase of Hitlerism – the only totalitarian state on the European continent. In other words, a totalitarian solution could only win the support of a totalitarian regime. This is one of the possible explanations why, in December 1943, Czechoslovak politicians received support in principle from the Soviet Union for their plans to expel the Hungarians in the same way as the Germans, and why they did not obtain similar assurances from the other Great Powers. For whereas the USA and the United Kingdom also agreed in 1943 to a partial resettlement of the Germans from Czechoslovakia, their democratic principles made it difficult for them to accept even those limited proposals. Opinions were expressed among them that the resettlement and expulsion of populations from their homeland was a Nazi-style solution. In fact, President Beneš's chief fear throughout that period was that the Americans would come out against the idea of deportation and instead insist on the stabilization of the Munich frontiers. The Czechoslovak exile authorities were confronted with two alternatives: either to try to overcome those humanist reservations or to use force. But the second alternative could only be achieved with the help of the Soviet Union. [...]

It is inconceivable that the exiled Czechoslovak political circles, or even the Moscow leadership of the Communist Party, could have predicted the upshot of that Moscow-aligned policy. Support for Czechoslovak nationalism was to be given in return for unreserved recognition of the Soviet Union's hegemony and its consequences, i.e. including the military occupation of Czechoslovakia on 21 August 1968, when, as Kundera put it, the nation's identity-card – Czech culture – was torn up. [...]

The failure of various attempts to return to Europe, such as the murderous crushing of the Hungarian revolution by the Soviet army in 1956, the military and political destruction of the achievements of the Prague Spring, and the prolonged state of emergency in Poland after the Soviet-inspired military coup of 13 December 1981, which involved the suppression of the trade unions' revolutionary movement to restore the legal plurality of public life, serves to confirm above all that the defence of this part of Central Europe is impossible in terms of the present constellation. This is a warning to Western Europe too. The defensive potential represented by a community of Central European nations was acknowledged in the last century by both the Hungarians and the Czechs. [...]

After the Second World War the Czechoslovak government decided to settle the Hungarian and German question in Czechoslovakia in its own way, though not entirely without inspiration. It could look to at least two earlier examples: the Stalinist solution, such as the resettlement of the Crimean Tartars throughout the Soviet Union, or there was the fascist approach of K. H. Frank with his plans for securing German *Lebensraum* by expelling the non-Germanized Czech population. This latter plan may well have motivated the Czechs' anti-German policies. However, even the most objective reasons that are not actually motivated by self-defence but in fact are based on prevention and revenge, inevitably lead to brutality. What sort of state would the world be in if every victim of Hitler's concentration camps were to be avenged in similar fashion? After the Second World War, we had distanced ourselves too far from a potential political settlement of this region's problems and were striding away from Europe in seven-league boots.

Looked at in the light of the Czechoslovak solution to the German issue, the question of the Hungarians in Czechoslovakia has remained unsettled. However this is not solely due to the failure of the policy of total resettlement.

Later circumstances were also unconducive to solving the issue. In February 1948 the communists took power in a pro-Soviet putsch. Since the end of 1944, the Czechoslovak Communist Party had made the running in anti-Hungarian nationalist propaganda. At its conference in Košice on 28 February 1945, the Communist Party had proclaimed from Soviet-occupied territory a policy of Slovak *Lebensraum*. It was to entail the planned 'Slovakization' of areas with Hungarian populations, to be carried out on the grounds of historical rights and the hypothesis of original Slovak settlement of those lands which had supposedly been Hungarianized in the interim. The programme was outlined at the conference by Gustáv Husák who has been General Secretary of the Communist Party since 1969 and President of the Czechoslovak Republic since 1975.

After 1948, however, Communist dictatorships were also set up in the other countries of Eastern Central Europe, which created a new situation. Whereas during the three post-war years it had been impossible, because of the Western powers, to solve the Hungarian problem by means of resettlement, now, after the communist coup, it was just as impossible because of the Soviet Union which forbade its satellites to settle their mutual differences in public.

It should be stressed here that the attenuation of anti-Hungarian pressure in Czechoslovakia's nationalities policy after 1948 and the Communist putsch had nothing to do with any 'humanist' characteristics of the Leninist policy on nationalities or communist 'internationalism'. It was simply motivated by a need to demonstrate to the West the international unity of the Communist parties. Thus the Czechoslovak state's policy on nationalities evolved under the influence of international political circumstances, much as it had during the First Republic.

However the Communist take-over did not just eliminate the possibility of an aggressive solution; it also ruled out any other sensible political option, for reasons inherent in the country's political system as a single-party state run on totalitarian lines which did not allow society to evolve in a pluralist way. The fact is, though, that after the Communist take-over of 1948 the anti-Hungarian policies became noticeably milder. One cannot categorically reject the thesis of those who, in the light of the country's anti-Hungarian traditions, maintain that in spite of the anti-democratic nature of the Communist regime, the latter has afforded the Hungarians living in Czechoslovakia greater protection than would a freer and more democratic political system. It would be hard to prove this assertion but we do know that during the period of so-called 'national democratic revolution' of 1945–8, they were afforded no protection at all, more likely the contrary. A programme of overt persecution of the Hungarians and their total liquidation was launched. And the Communists of the time were possibly more aggressively anti-Hungarian than anyone else, but that was during the immediate post-war period, with its ballast of hatred and moral deformations. Rather more disturbing, therefore, was the wave of anti-Hungarian hysteria and agitation that washed over Slovakia during 1968's democratization process, when those who had witnessed the post-war persecution of Hungarians recognized with horror the similarity between them and their own previous unhappy experiences and suffering.

Can the Communist regime truly afford Czechoslovakia's Hungarian residents protection from the aggressive nationalism of the majority population? It certainly is capable of preventing open conflicts, not only in order to demonstrate forcibly its 'proletarian internationalism', but also because this system cannot abide conflict, except for the class struggle and other power struggles, of course. However it neither can nor does protect them against the national ambitions of the majority population, since the Hungarian minority stands in their way. The main reason it cannot do so is because it – the Party-cum-autocrat – is itself the guarantee of the majority's aspirations. This is the chief clause of the unwritten social consensus between the regime and the majority nation, which originally arose more or less out of necessity. From 1945 that consensus rested on two pillars: one was the protection of the class interests and power ambitions of the workers, the other was the Soviet Union's contribution to the victory over Hitlerism. However, whenever the second factor was spoken of, the emphasis was placed on the Soviet Union's assistance in transferring the Hungarian population out of Czechoslovakia. It was this aspect that was stressed by the Communist Party of Slovakia during the pre-election campaign of 1946. In the 1950s and 1960s, this factor was pushed into the background. After 1968, and particularly after the start of so-called 'consolidation', the consensus between the regime and the society of the majority nation was renewed in the same terms as in 1945. In other words, it was necessary to ensure a standard of living in line with the consumer requirements of the majority of the population, while at the same time convincing the Czech and Slovak populations that the protection of national (i.e. Czechoslovak) sovereignty was the Communist Party's prime concern. The main way they try to win over the Czech nation is by having the mass media portray the evacuation of the Germans after 1945 as having been an act of supreme national interest carried out in the most humane manner. Anyone who doubts this, or maintains the contrary, is an enemy of the nation and state. At the same time, it is stressed that the only guarantor of national and state sovereignty is the Soviet Union.

The programme of *Lebensraum* proclaimed at the above-mentioned Communist Congress of 28 February 1945 is once more being implemented in Slovakia. One plank of this programme is the loudly trumpeted construction of Slovakia as part of the Federation which Husák's policy successfully achieved. The second was the quiet liquidation of the Hungarian minority. The achievement of the second goal was greatly assisted by the existence of a centralized administration, because apart from anything else, the Communist Party has created both a discriminatory economic policy for the territory inhabited by the Hungarian minority and an anti-minority educational and cultural policy. In addition it has taken decisions, mostly in secret, aimed at the minimum implementation of minority rights. There was one minor factor which serves to document clearly that the regime is fully aware in whose favour and to whose detriment it is pursuing its nationalities policy, or rather who it needs to win over to its anti-minority policy. The fact is that the official materials so far published in Hungarian carefully exclude the above section of Husák's speech of 28 February 1945. This passage was also omitted from the Hungarian edition of his book *Testimony about the Slovak National Uprising*, along with others. On the other hand, when that event is commented on in Slovak language texts, stress is always laid on his anti-Hungarian statement.

It must be realized that even during the First Republic there existed no effective weapon against the nationalism of the majority nation. The pre-war system was admittedly far more democratic, but it was a majority democracy, i.e. for the benefit of the majority population. Majority in this respect implies both a political and a national majority. Thus it was a political system organized for the benefit of the majority nation because not one of the major political parties (i.e. the coalition partners) upheld the interests of the national minority. The parties of the national minority obviously had no hope of entering the coalition and therefore no hope of influencing government policy.

It is likely that the politicians who assumed the leadership of the Czechoslovak state in 1918, particularly Masaryk and Beneš, regarded the total suppression of the national minorities as incompatible with the democratic idea, even if they regarded their presence as a necessary evil. Their idea of democracy derived from the idea of personal freedom. Unfortunately, in the process of transforming the right of personal freedom into a collective right – which is an essential process in the creation of a state – it can too easily happen that the democratic principle is defined too specifically in terms of the priorities on which the state is organized. Thus the democratic principle can be modified in terms of national priorities into 'national' democracy or according to class principles into 'socialist' or 'people's' democracy. This sort of limited democracy is not an invention of the West. In our part of Europe, modified democracy – the 'democracy of the Estates' – existed back in the Middle Ages. [...]

President Beneš's anti-German and anti-Hungarian stance – both during the period of exile government and during the subsequent 'national democratic revolution' – also goes to show what were the priorities of Czechoslovak democracy. The fact is that Beneš's attitude was virtually anti-democratic and totalitarian. The only basic difference between it and the position of the Communists was that it was anti-Communist to boot. However it requires just as much cynicism to distort democracy in line with national priorities as it does to distort the idea of socialism and transform it into national socialism.

The idea of a limited democracy serving the interests of the majority nation evolved well before the ethical crisis which occurred during the Second World War. Its features could already be discerned in the months following the proclamation of an independent Czechoslovakia. Justified doubts started to emerge within the national minorities regarding the declared programme of an 'Eastern Switzerland'. By now we know how even Masaryk himself played a moderating role over the Hungarian issue. As he told Vavro Šrobár, minister plenipotentiary for Slovakia: 'We have to Slovakize slowly lest we antagonize international public opinion'.

Quickly or slowly? That is solely a question of tactics, not of principle. The main thing was to liquidate the Hungarian minority in Czechoslovakia. Where is the Slovak or Czech these days who would dare propose a positive alternative to such moderate tactics, that is, a policy for the protection of the minority nations? Not even the non-conformist intellectuals opposed to the system have made any public attempt at it. Not even the most tolerant Slovaks or Czechs have suggested replacing the unorganized policy of assimilation pursued by the state and society of the ethnic majority by a legal solution ending the minority status, in other words emancipating the national minority by recognizing it as a constituent nation with the same rights as the majority population. The idea for a solution along these lines has yet to take root in the tradition of our geo-political region. [...]

At the time of the break-up of the Austro-Hungarian monarchy, relations between the different nationalities were in such a state of confusion that the outcome could only be the extinction of Austria-Hungary as a state. However, the 70 years since then have not seen any serious attempt to eliminate those original underlying contradictions, including those between the Hungarians and the majority populations of the emergent states. Nor was the German problem settled for that matter. Instead it was got rid of by deporting the Germans. [...]

One can only conceivably talk about the development of cosmopolitan relations between the Hungarians, Slovaks and Czechs (i.e. relations based on a mutual affinity of views, intellectual outlook and concepts of democracy in Eastern Central Europe) in the conditional tense, in terms of something eminently to be desired. This is not solely because the creation of such links between these nations – including the involvement of the national minorities – has always been contrary to official Czechoslovak policy to date. The present authorities, even more than their predecessors, reject the traditional idea of 'bridge building' between nations, which was already being mooted within the Hungarian minorities of the emergent states after the First World War and was incorporated in spirit in the Final Act of the Helsinki Conference in 1975. The Czechoslovak authorities do not reject the idea solely because their plan is to write off the Hungarian minority, but also because they are opposed to the current more liberal policies of Kádár's Hungary. Of course their rejection is not based on national convictions alone, but is conditioned by the very nature of totalitarian power, that is, the *a priori* rejection of any private and unregulated initiative. [...] The fostering of relations between the two peoples is now considered undesirable. Of course it is remarkable that the views of a section of the Czechoslovak public both at home and in exile in the West closely resemble this nationalist state-oriented attitude. It should be added that the chief motivation for the official attitude is that the regime would find it hard to keep tabs on such relations if the ethnic minorities themselves took an active part in fostering them. Certain unofficial circles (both Czech and Slovak) share the offical position on this issue, their fear being that state borders in Central Europe, including its eastern reaches, do not correspond to ethnic frontiers. Either the territory of the state or of the nationality is greater and this clashes with the idea of a national state held by the countries which emerged from the Austro-Hungarian empire, and hence it conflicts with the very idea of a Czechoslovak national state. We should also bear in mind in this respect that the regime has a similar attitude to the development of relations between Slovaks and Czechs (as well as between Slovakia and the Czech lands). After all, it is well known that the forces of repression do all they can to prevent any links being forged between Czech and Slovak members of the unofficial public and between them and the Hungarian minority. [...]

There would seem to have been no great improvement in conditions for a settlement between neighbouring countries in Eastern Central Europe, despite the fact that the countries of the area share such a similar past. For centuries there have been parallels and links between Polish and Hungarian history. Czech – these days Czechoslovak – and Hungarian history, which evolved for a long time in quite separate political regions, have come to display increasing similarities over the recent past. The Soviet military invasion of Czechoslovakia in August 1968 marked a culmination of the experiences acquired within the Soviet system up to then by the Polish, Hungarian, Czech and Slovak nations. It was still possible in 1956 for many Czechoslovaks to view the events in Hungary of that year as a consequence of the Hungarians' defeat at the end of the Second World War, or as the last uprising of those traditional Hungarian political forces and social classes which had been conquered. They therefore regarded the Soviet Union's military intervention of November, against the already victorious revolution, as a logical outcome. However in August 1968, the point was very cruelly made that not even Czechoslovakia – regarded at the end of the war as a victorious power and extensively supported by the Soviet Union – could be considered an exception and it was just as subordinate to Soviet power interests as Hungary which lost the war. I believe that was the cruellest but also the most telling lesson of the period since 1945 or 1948. There could be hardly any more eloquent demonstration of how similar the destinies of the Eastern Central European nations are.

We have a fairly clear notion of what gave rise to the contradictions between the nations living here. We have quite a good knowledge of the tragic history of Eastern Central Europe over the past century or more. It is clear enough to us that whereas blame for the conditions in the Monarchy must be shared by the Austrians, Germans and the Hungarians, responsibility for the situation after the disintegration of the Monarchy must be borne by the policies of the emergent States, because the international decisions that most influenced the situation in the area were taken on the basis of the demands which they tabled. If we manage to appreciate the real significance of this latter fact, then there may be a faint hope of reducing the defencelessness of the nations of this part of the world. And that is the only way we will hasten, at least spiritually, our return to Europe. For so long as suspicion rules on one side and unwillingness on the other, the hopes of creating a common European future are truly slim.

In his anti-Fascist writings, which could well be unique even in international terms, the Hungarian journalist and critic Zoltán Fábry who lived in Czechoslovakia, singled out Fascism as the enemy of European culture and European traditions. He did not regard Fascism as an isolated phenomenon limited to a particular time and place, however. In his view, Fascism is a sort of anomalous distortion within the human value system, a view that contrasts with the doctrine that it was defeated and annihilated with the armistice of 1945. The latter doctrine does not hold water even when the cardinal enemy was the genocidal and militant Fascism which held sway during the Second World War. In Fábry's eyes, the idea of Fascism and Europe were antithetical. Fascism was the antithesis of the European idea, of

European cultural traditions, and of all the trappings of modern Europe: democracy, pluralism, anti-barbarism, freedom, the protection of the individual, anti-violence, anti-totalitarianism, etc. According to him: 'The law of Europe is freedom. It is a law which rules out terror, dictatorship, and the one-party systems on which Fascism thrives'. These words were written in 1946 in his political plea 'A vádlott megszólal' (The accused speaks out) against the collective indictment of all the Hungarians living in Czechoslovakia on the charge of war crimes.

But let me focus on the last words of this quotation, which are even more topical now than they were 40 years ago. One may deny the existence of terror or dictatorship and call the first 'decisiveness' and the second 'law and order', for instance. What one calls them depends on one's traditions and political culture. But there is no denying that what we have here is a one-party system. Our experience bears Fábry out. The one-party system (the political monopoly) means in general terms anti-pluralism. In this respect, however, the lack of democracy is more crucial than the lack of political pluralism, or a system of multiple political parties. Respect for pluralism is the most European of our modern traditions and is the guarantee of democracy. Whenever lack of respect for pluralism infects a society, the European spirit is at mortal risk. However, the meaning of pluralism is much wider, richer and more profound than is traditionally understood by politicians. Political pluralism (the multi-party system) is admittedly an important and indispensable tool of democratic practice, but it is unable on its own to ensure that the democratic idea takes root in society. By its nature it can, of course, permit the expression of different opinions and interests, but it classifies them according to the hegemonistic system of the majority. Political pluralism emerged in Western Europe particularly as a means of resolving social, political and ideological conflicts or competing power interests. Politics evolved rather differently in the eastern parts of Central Europe. Apart from the classic conflicts of interests referred to, of equal importance were conflicts of national interests or the political ambitions of the different nations. This meant *a priori* that political pluralism – that is, democracy based on the majority principle – was not an adequate principle for the organization of society, so long as it did not ensure that the different nations could enjoy equal rights. In other words, the system lacked the principle of national pluralism. This was why from the 1860s, the system of parliamentary democracy was incapable of balancing the interests of the different ethnic groups of the Austro-Hungarian Monarchy. This meant that despite the demonstrative withdrawal of the representatives of the minority nations, the Hungarian Diet was able to adopt a nationalities law in 1862. The national principle was accorded the lowest priority among those governing the way society was organized, and it was a majority principle anyway, that is, not only did it do nothing to protect national rights, but it actually disadvantaged those peoples with minority status. I do not intend here to go into the rights or wrongs of the policies of those days, merely to point out that lessons of those times have yet to be learnt and put to good use. The idea of structuring society according to this principle so as to respect national pluralism is alien to the political forces that run the successor states. The most they have done is to recognize the right to national self-determination, although this has been used solely to advance their own power ambitions. In my opinion, only the simultaneous operation of political and national pluralism in Eastern Central Europe is capable of providing the requisite political framework without which the idea of democracy cannot be implemented as it is in the Western democracies.

The very fact that the establishment of new political structures in the central and eastern parts of Central Europe in 1918 resulted in the creation of relatively large minority populations which could have been avoided on the basis of ethnic ratios, only goes to show that it was not the aim to do away with national antagonisms. There was only a regrouping in favour of other nations according to the majority principle. So in fact it was not a democratic settlement at all, because a system of majority democracy into which the national principle has been injected is essentially hegemony of a kind and is a step in the direction of totalitarianism. We should realize this before we go any further. In Eastern Central Europe (but this also applies to the Balkans) the principle of democracy can only be applied in practice if, in the interests of respect for the equal collective rights of national minorities and majority nations, respect for national plurality (the plurality of nationalities) is guaranteed by constitutional provisions. If in our region an eventual prospective democracy will continue to be based on the majority principle – preserving the advantages of the majority nations – the danger of totalitarianism will remain. To quote Fábry once more: 'Minority rights are the touchstone of democracy. When the capacity for autonomy fails in a democracy, it has taken the first irrevocable steps towards barbarism'.

Such a concept of pluralism is absent from the traditional political culture of the Eastern Central European countries. It can even be said to run counter to our traditions. The point is that for national pluralism to be implemented as a principle governing the social order, it would have to entail a democratic curtailment of the political rights of the majority nation. It would imply power-sharing, or, in other words, respect for the social and political rights of national minorities as well as their recognition as an equal partner in the state. In reality it implies autonomy.

But let us now return to the question we posed at the beginning, namely, whether the idea of Europe is a reality or no more than wishful thinking on the part of the Eastern Central Europeans.

The answer is not an encouraging one because apart from the monolithic political system imposed on our region's countries and peoples and the supremacy of Soviet power – to which European traditions are alien – there are other factors tending to move these nations away from Europe. I refer to traditions rooted in their recent past, such as those of limited democracy and pluralism based on national power interests. These latter traditions, which also fuel the aspirations of the majority nations aimed against the Hungarian minority living in Czechoslovakia, are as great a threat to the implantation of the European idea as the monolithic power system that holds sway in Eastern Central Europe.

In conclusion, I would merely point out that the traditional tension in the relations between the nations of this part of Europe combine with surviving national antagonisms to render the region automatically defenceless. The Soviet Union can go on strengthening its influence undisturbed so long as the Rumanians continue to oppress the Hungarian minority in Transylvania; so long as tension governs official relations between Hungary and Rumania; so long as the unofficial opposition in Hungary is obliged to criticize the government for dragging its feet over the matter of Hungarian minorities living in neighbouring states and so long as that same government – albeit under pressure from neighbouring states – takes measures to suppress this opposition; so long as private travel from Czechoslovakia to Hungary is restricted; so long as Hungarians in Czechoslovakia are involved exclusively in the minority rights campaign; so long as Czechs and Slovaks fear that the Hungarian minority is not loyal to the republic, and so on. However this situation is not identical to the classic 'divide and rule' policy for which the Habsburgs may be justly criticized. For although they protected the dynasty's interests in that way, they also defended the eastern and western frontiers of the empire, in other words of our region: *Eastern Central Europe*. And in the final analysis, the nations of this area were able, albeit with varying degrees of difficulty, to follow their own line of development and live according to European traditions. However, when the Central European nations turned their backs in this way on their common interests and aims they soon found themselves borne along on conflicting currents – in those cases where they did not actually fall immediate prey to dictatorial power. There is no need these days for Soviet policy makers to stir up fresh dissension among their satellites; it is sufficient to make sure that the old 'home-made' national controversies are not settled. However this principle for governing our nations no longer serves, as it once did, the general interest of defending the natural political region we inhabit. On the contrary, each of our nations is increasingly aware of its defencelessness and its constantly dwindling defensive capability. In such circumstances, the leaders of the individual states have no choice but to jostle for position. By repeatedly swearing oaths of allegiance to the supreme Soviet leadership or to their delegated representatives in the different countries, the vassal states can managed to pre-empt each other in their efforts to shore up their positions and widen the bounds of their power. By stubbornly exploiting traditional quarrels they can win advantage for themselves and their subjects, but at the expense of others. These are all reasons why we are already a long way away from Europe and moving further away all the time.

(Translated by A. G. Brain)

8
Central European Attitudes
Czesław Miłosz

While most mappings of Central Europe have recourse to political, socio-economic and cultural criteria, the following two writers attempt to construct the image of Central Europe that resides in the literary imagination. Czesław Miłosz sketches the literary profile of a Central European consciousness and sensibility, and Csaba G. Kiss looks at how Central European literature simultaneously affirms and expresses the dilemmas of self-identity.

I assume there is such a thing as Central Europe, even though many people deny its existence, beginning with statesmen and journalists who persist in calling it 'Eastern Europe' and ending with my friend Joseph Brodsky who prefers to reserve for it the name of 'Western Asia'. In these decades of the twentieth century Central Europe seems to exist only in the minds of some of its intellectuals. Yet, the past of that area – a common past in spite of the multitude of languages and nationalities – is always present there and is made very real by the architecture of its cities, the traditions of its universities and the works of its poets. Neither is the present deprived of signs indicating a basic unity underlying diversity. When reflecting on literary works written now in Czech or Polish, Hungarian or Estonian, Lithuanian or Serbo-Croatian, I perceive a tone and a sensibility not to be found elsewhere, in West European, American, or Russian writings.

In this chapter I have assigned myself an ungrateful task: the attempt to define specific Central European attitudes. The task is ungrateful since, in an attempt of this kind, I do not have at my disposal precise instruments of analysis and must, therefore, accept in advance a certain unsolicited vagueness.

Central Europe is hardly a geographical notion. It is not easy to trace its boundaries on the map even if, while walking the streets of its cities, I do not doubt its survival, whether that be in my baroque Wilno, or the differently baroque Prague or the medieval-Renaissance Dubrovnik. The ways of feeling and thinking of its inhabitants must thus suffice for drawing mental lines which seem to be more durable than the borders of the states.

The most striking feature in Central European literature is its awareness of history, both as the past and the present. It seems to underlie the treatment of various subjects, not necessarily themselves historical, and can be detected in love poems or novels dealing with love imbroglios. Personae and characters who appear in these works live in a kind of time which is modulated in a different way than is the time of their Western counterparts. Events of the political decade in which the characters live, of decades which formed and marked them, but also those of their parents' lifetime, constantly lurk in the background and add a dimension rarely met with in Western works. In the latter, time is neutral, colourless, weightless, it flows without zigzags, sudden curves, and waterfalls. In the former, time is intense, spasmodic, full of surprises, indeed practically an active participant in the story. This is because time is associated with a danger threatening the existence of a national community to which a writer belongs. I suspect that the historical imagination always comes from the collective memory and from a sense of menace. In this respect there is an affinity between Central European and Jewish literature. Nations in that part of Europe, despite some of them having once lived through periods of prosperity and glory, have spent long times under foreign domination, threatened with the loss of their national identity, oppressed by the enemy, whether by the Turks, the Austrians, the Germans or the Russians. The defeat of Germany in the First World War and the disintegration of the Habsburg and the Tsarist Empires were followed by the appearance of two names symbolic of any potential federalist tendencies in the future: Czechoslovakia, composed by the Czechs and the Slovaks, and Yugoslavia composed by the Southern Slavs. After a short breathing spell, the Russo-German pact of 1939 put an end to the hopes of national independence in that area, while the Second World War resulted in the return to the oppressive situation of the preceding century – the Soviet empire taking over from the defunct big monarchic powers.

A sad history. Yet it is far from certain that the size and might of states are accompanied by fertility in science, arts, and letters. Examples to the contrary abound and it is possible that incredible tangles and mazes of political circumstances are necessary to incite the human spirit, if only to liberate itself from them and to manifest its sovereignty. Anybody who speaks of Central Europe may be reproached with bringing back the phantom of *Mitteleuropa*, as that whole region must anyway belong either to the Russian or the German sphere of influence. My answer is that, should this remain true for ever, the Molotov-Ribbentrop Pact of 1939 which divided territories has to be regarded as epoch-making, indeed. I recognize, though, that my Europe, the domain of acute nationalism, both resisting external control and turning against one another, may be dismissed for that reason as a potential troublemaker to be kept in check by a guardian – the Soviet empire. If not for Moscow's rule, goes the argument, the nationalities of the area would be at one another's throats. One need look only at the Hungarian-Rumanian, Slovak-Hungarian, Polish-Ukrainian, Polish-Lithuanian quarrels. Here I touch upon a problem too complex to be dealt with in a short chapter. In any case, I see sufficient reasons to believe that the most energetic minds in those countries successfully resist the temptations of national chauvinism and represent a considerable force working for the unification of Central Europe. At least, they share a perception of its common destinies and of peculiar traits that make it different from its big neighbours, West and East.

Humiliated national pride usually gives rise to delusions, to self-pity, and mythologies. Observing that, a Central European writer receives training in irony. The very condition of being a Pole or a Czech or a Hungarian becomes an object of his irony, which colours his approach to life. Thus, the brave soldier Švejk, who repeats the pattern of the slave Aesopus and his master, acquires a durable significance. Irony finds nourishment in the present international set-up which is an offence to reason. In an era of anti-colonialism, at the very moment the British Empire and the French Empire were crumbling, independent states of half of Europe were converted into colonial satrapies controlled from outside. Those satrapies send their delegates to the United Nations – more correctly, not united nations but disunited governments. The basic fact is the border of the empire and the garrisons of its army, while the mentality of the masters is felt by the subdued populations as alien, nearly incomprehensible and barbaric. Russian self-admiration (more than that, self-worship) goes beyond the habitually expected range of national vanity and bears the mark of a nineteenth century messianism which in that part of the world left no good memories. Similarly, Russian contemporary art and literature, obstinately clinging to clichés, frozen by censorship, seems sterile and unattractive. Yet innumerable soldier Švejks in their dealing with Russians must pretend their reverence and gratitude for Big Brother.

There is, of course, Marxism. The decades of Communist rule have radically transformed the whole area by lifting social barriers, urbanizing the populations, and creating a mass society. The process paralleled transformations that occurred in Western Europe owing to technological progress. There they exemplified the general egalitarian tendency of our epoch. However, what happened in the process of the Communist take-over in my part of Europe may be compared to the fairy-tale of liberating a genie from a bottle. No longer peasants, who were rather indifferent to national heritage, the industrial workers appear as harbingers of both national and libertarian aspirations. For example, the Solidarity movement in Poland typically combines social unrest and national resentment of foreign rule. A forceful and enforced leap carried those countries in a few decades far from what they were before the Second World War, with resulting new conflicts and new pains.

Now, let us imagine a Central European intellectual in his confrontation with the world at large, with his colleagues from Western Europe, America or Latin America. As long as he keeps silence or, if he talks, spares the sensibilities of his interlocutors, everything is fine. As soon as he begins to talk frankly, he has the impression that he is regarded as a monster of irony and cynicism. That rift is certainly one of the strangest phenomena to be observed today and its thorough elucidation would probably lead us to the core of the modern man's predicament. The clue is undoubtedly our intellectual's position on Marxism. He perceives a certain aura around that term, a kind of awe and veneration even among people who are far from having any political commitment. He himself does not claim to be a Marxist or an anti-Marxist; he just shrugs and smiles, for he knows too much. There are, in his opinion, certain demonic subjects which must be approached warily, as many hidden traps and temptations wait there for the imprudent. Marxism appeals to the noble impulses in man, and thence its force of seduction. It is impossible to communicate the truth about it to anybody who has not seen it at work. However, its product, the totalitarian-bureaucratic state, monopolizing all political and economic power, has been prophetically described by a Central European writer, Franz Kafka. Direct experience is responsible for the fact that the most thorough survey of Marxist philosophy ever written comes from the pen of another Central European, Leszek Kołakowski. The adjective 'demonic' applied to Marxism is not an exaggeration. First of all, the number of people killed and tortured to death in its name surpasses many times the total number of victims of Hitler's National Socialism. Second, a doctrine promising 'the withering of the state' has led to the emergence of an all-powerful state and its omnipotent police. Third, instead of ending the oppression of man by man and getting rid of alienation, a realm of nearly absolute alienation came into being, where the individual does not belong to himself, both literally and figuratively.

And yet, a confrontation of my intellectual with his Western counterparts is made even more intricate by the durable influence of this system on his way of thinking. Lifeless and petrified, the Marxist doctrine receives in his countries no more than lip-service as a tribute, but some of its practical results are tangible. In the first place, great numbers of people have been liberated from the curse of Adam, namely, work. If, as the Polish saying goes, 'The State pretends that it pays us, we pretend that we work', we can speak of a reversal of the capitalist conditions, namely, the economic fear, fear of unemployment, to a large extent disappears, while work time is used for parallel activities, for securing goods and money through private deals, standing in lines, etc. This does not apply perhaps to heavy industry, but masses of white-collar workers, often half literate, confirm the pattern, no less than peasants, whether they are collectivized or not, with their private sector of the economy. A habit has been formed regarding the role of the only employer, the State. It is supposed to provide a minimum of subsistence for everybody and is held responsible for empty shelves in its stores. Fear is thus shifted from the sphere of the economy to the sphere of political surveillance. Immigrants to Western countries from the Soviet bloc have great difficulty in comprehending the principles of the self-reliance of the individual which implies misery, homelessness or starvation as penalty for failure. All this cannot remain without impact upon the mind of the Central European intellectual. When looking for Western interlocutors open to his views, he notices that only the conservatives take his horror of political oppression and his defence of freedom seriously. The liberals seem to close their ears, for their true passion is a breast-beating and hatred of the capitalist system. Yet the character I discuss cannot be an ally of the conservatives except, perhaps, in foreign policy, as he takes for granted that the welfare state fulfils the human need of decency and minimal security. He understands the dilemmas involved by relying upon the State and its plethoric bureaucracy, but feels they can be resolved without renouncing the free decisions of the individual.

If his thinking appears bizarre to Westerners, it is, I suspect, due to a shade of Hegelianism which has become nearly instinctive with him. He reasons in terms of the movement of history and the life of ideas whose ascendance or decay indicates the direction that will be taken by human societies. The fascination exerted for several decades by Marx upon most creative artists and thinkers, testified, in his opinion, to the vigour of the revolutionary trend. But now Marxism has already been abandoned at the top, by the elite, both in the East and West, while at the same time it attracts lower-level minds and spreads among people just emerging from illiteracy. A similar descent from the top down to the layer of everyday myths characterizes the thought of Freud. What, then, is the prognosis? Probably this: the nineteenth-century notion of what is 'scientific' has to run its course. Marx wanted to dedicate *Das Kapital* to Darwin and though Darwin declined the offer, a link between various scientific or pseudo-scientific theories of evolution is obvious. Since modern man is brought up in the spirit of the nineteenth century science, Marxism still has large appeal, though withering gradually from the top where its coherence as a philosophy has been found wanting. Exaggerating a little, I would say that my intellectual from Central Europe is inclined to divide people, wherever he meets them, into three categories: proto-Marxists, Marxists, and post-Marxists, to such an extent he is serious about ideas – forces incarnated as the main philosophical currents of his time.

Is his world apocalyptic? Not in the sense that the minds of many writers in the West are. It looks as if he has rejected mediation on the possible effects of nuclear war as futile and has moved the very possibility of war into the realm of the absurd joke, to write a story about a peasant wedding where drunken guests start to fight, using not knives but atomic weapons, or about an intercontinental missile placed by the authorities on somebody's private balcony. But dark visions of the future in a different, and perhaps deeper sense, seem to be a specialty of Central European writers. Let us not forget that the word 'robot' now internationally accepted, was introduced by Karel Čapek, and that Stanisław Witkiewicz's novels and play of anticipation proved to be prophetic. He had already described, before Orwell, totalitarian rule by the Party of Levellers and the predicament of artists controlled by what he called the Ministry of Mechanization of Culture. The future in such works is envisaged in the function of internal disintegration of the bourgeois society which is too weak to present an effective resistance to the Levellers who would seize power and liquidate their opponents. Here we have the main component of criticism addressed by my Central European to the West, parallel but not identical with anti-Western propaganda conducted day and night by the Levellers, i.e. by the Communist parties. That propaganda speaks of the decadence of capitalism as opposed to the health of the so-called socialist societies. However, one has no need to be a very perspicacious observer to notice that the word 'decadence' may be applied to both sides, if, and this I assume to be correct, it means the loss to the notion of good and evil. Complete relativization of good and evil, by making them dependent upon social criteria of a given historical moment, is a major event in the history of the European mind and in this respect Nietzsche, who foretold 'European nihilism', was no less apocalyptic than Dostoevsky who, in *The Possessed*, outlined the essential features of the Russian revolution. And the refusal to see the loss of the metaphysical foundation as a great tragedy characterizes people today, just as it was foreseen by Nietzsche. Man loses, however, his subterfuges, which allow him to escape the issue, when he is confronted by the totalitarian state. Scorned by the rulers and no longer protected by the Ten Commandments, a victim, one of expendable millions, discovers, so to say empirically, the unmistakable line separating good from evil. In the geographical longitude I deal with, the experience of Nazism sufficed to prove that one could not relativize the basic values and compromise on them without becoming guilty of connivance with criminals. Yet – and here I return to my question as to the apocalyptic frame of mind in Central Europe – things ceased to be so simple with the advent of Communist rule. A long-range programme aimed at gradual absorption of society by the State means that all clear-cut differences are obliterated and it is difficult to distinguish between baseness and integrity, lie and truth. Everybody is tainted and everybody is a victim. Orwell's *1984* astonishes by its accuracy, even if he pushes his negative appraisal of the proles' ability to think too far and does not take into account private economic endeavours, that margin without which the system could not survive. All in all, however, an observer of the system is no more optimistic than was Orwell. According to him, it is not impossible that a totalitarian State is a logical outcome of the spiritual deprivation of modern man, a kind of punishment, as in the biblical story of Babel. If such is the case, the future of the planet is gloomy indeed.

But, another peculiarity of the human type I describe battles against those depressing predictions. Anybody familiar with the history of the Czechs, the Hungarians or the Poles knows that certain codes of behaviour mandatory for the intelligentsia go back several centuries. A civic commitment, a pursuit of a dream as to what the political and social life of a country should be, animated socio-religious movements of the Czech Hussites, of the Polish Socinians, produced voluminous utopian works on the ideal Christian state such as Andrzej Frycz Modrzewski's *On the Improvement of the Republic* of 1543 and is visible in the pedagogical, scholarly, and theatrical activity of Commenius. Undoubtedly libertarian and directed against the supremacy both of the church and the state, those trends were predecessors of a great romantic and democratic elan at the end of the eighteenth century and the first decades of the nineteenth century, a specific confluence of sober Enlightenment ideas and of a Schillerian enthusiasm. All this is far from being forgotten and gives to Central European writings a tinge of nostalgia, of utopianism, and of hope.

There is no reasonable basis for hoping that the present international set-up will be changed in the foreseeable future. After the Napoleonic wars the big powers divided the spoils among themselves at the Congress of Vienna and the established order lasted, with some modifications, for a hundred years, till 1914. The long struggle of revolutionaries against villainy of the allied monarchs did not prevent the repetition of this pattern at Yalta. From Moscow's perspective, the newly acquired area is a property to be gradually assimilated and sovietized, though, until now, their programme has to a large extent failed, as the events of 1956 in Hungary, of 1968 in Czechoslovakia and of the 1980s in Poland indicate. Yet the Russian tanks are there to stay and to teach a lesson. In such circumstances let me state boldly that the humanistic imagination should be separated from and even opposed to the political imagination, for dealing with probabilities, including that of the survival of the planet, with strategy, with evolutionary trends, etc. is a quite debilitating occupation for a person engaged in the humanities. As to myself (now it is clear that in this chapter I am also drawing a portrait of myself), I think that that Central Europe is an act of faith, a project, let us say, even a utopia, but my reasons for adopting it are quite realistic. As the name of numerous Centres for Russian and Eastern European Studies demonstrates, a division of Europe into West and East is accepted by American universities. That acceptance can be objected to on the grounds that it confuses a political borderline with cultural borderlines of the past. Those who object advance the argument that a cultural division of Europe into two halves has been for centuries identical with the division into the realms of Rome and Byzantium and, thus, the Latin language of the church and Roman law determined the Eastern borders of the West. Behind that argument we can detect the complaint of nations proud of their belonging to Western culture and now easternized by force. There is a validity in that complaint. And yet, let us confront the facts and say that neither had the old religious frontier between Catholicism and Orthodoxy been a very precise indicator, nor were these countries, situated between Germany and Russia, pure-bred Western. Ideas from abroad penetrating these lands, diluted and transformed, acquired a specific quality, local habits were persistent, institutions took forms unheard of in the Western part of Europe which could only wonder at Hussitism in the late Middle Ages, at a bizarre parliamentary system in Renaissance Poland or at the 'paradise of heretic', (*paradisum hereticorum*) in Poland and Transylvania, to give just a few examples. And even today the average person in France or America is unable to say what the Uniate or Greco-Catholic church is. Moreover, snobbery and love of things Western notwithstanding, we, from those mostly agricultural marshes, had many axes to grind in our encounters with Western mercantile and manufacturing societies. The present ambiguous attitude towards the capitalist West is nothing new. A hygienic reason behind our choosing the term Central Europe is that it authorizes us to look for the specificity of its culture and protects us from the temptation of misleading analogies. A curious phenomenon could be observed in European literature and the art of the last decades: the iron curtain and the differences of two political systems only in part stopped the circulation of ideas and fashions in spite of all the efforts to close the borders hermetically and to impose Russian models. In poetry, in painting and in the theatre, Warsaw, Prague and Budapest have been more similar to Paris, Amsterdam or London than to Moscow. And yet it would be rather unproductive to search in Central Europe for echoes of Western surrealism, existentialism, structuralism, or the theatre of the absurd. If there are influences, they are transposed, often changed into their opposites under the impact of a unique collective experience. I am inclined to agree with Milan Kundera when he says that at present there is more energy and vigour in the literature of our Europe than in its Western variety.

Another aspect of cultural interchange can be brought into relief by the idea of Central Europe and that is the place of Russian art and literature in a cosmopolitan epoch before the revolution, at the time Russian writers and artists had their share in the European movement of modernism and symbolism. A study of symbolism may provide interesting examples, for Russian symbolism did not resemble French symbolism, but, on the other hand, Polish symbolism (forgive me my referring so often to my own yard) was not like the Russian, as the odd theatrical works or plays of Stanisław Wyśpianski or the paintings of Jacek Malczewski so clearly demonstrate. A study of diverging paths within the common trend would be useful for the future, when Russian art and literature again recover their spontaneity.

Summing up, I do not regard my talking of Central Europe as just an expression of regret that things are as they are. Much can be done, in literary and art scholarship, in criticism and in intellectual history. By delineating how we all, who speak the languages within our pale, are akin, by practising a long overdue comparative investigation of our patrimony, we can make national conflicts less likely, even if the day of one or another kind of Central European federation is distant.

9
Central European Writers about Central Europe: Introduction to a Non-Existent Book of Readings
Csaba G. Kiss

A book of readings on Central Europe? Does such a thing exist? Sadly, no. Yet there is a need for it. There are anthologies, of course, collections of texts from the various national histories and even handsome volumes in one or other of the major world languages may be found. These are unlike the national histories and histories of literature compiled for foreign consumption, for the wider world to be precise, which generally contain the great figures of the past fitted rather uncomfortably into a 'European' uniform or else looking ridiculous in local costume.

My non-existent book of readings would help to bring out the individual colours of Central European literature, difficult though these may be to define, to make its original features apparent so that its strengths and weaknesses – measured against itself – will be visible in the appropriate historical and cultural context, the one that ensured that it came to look as it does. Since the Enlightenment and romanticism, a particular variant of European literature has appeared in the region between the Russian and German language areas. The causes of its particularity should be sought in the complex network of historical, social, ethnic and literary development. I would refer to only one of its consequences, the best known, that over the last 200 years literature has been accorded a far greater role in the formulation of the nation and society in our region than in Europe's more fortunate parts. I want to lay down at the outset that I have no doubt that there exists a particular cultural-historical region at the centre of Europe, even if its frontiers have changed and some of its features define greater or lesser transitional zones.

And with this, we are in the thick of things. Where, actually, is Central

Europe? Or to be more modest, if we are looking only at literature and at the nineteenth and twentieth centuries, is there a Central European literature, is it at all justified to classify writers on this basis? After all, these writers generally knew nothing of each other, seeing that they cast their glances towards Paris, from Warsaw and Prague, Belgrade and Bucharest just as much as from Hungary. The question is all the more justified because over the last three years one has begun to encounter the idea of Central Europe ever more often, sometimes nostalgically, sometimes critically or with curiosity and scepticism or with the pleasure of rediscovery and disturbing errors. This Central Europe is often nothing more than *Mitteleuropa* – the word used occasionally in this way even in French and Italian and mostly meaning the blossoming in Vienna at the turn of the century of Art Nouveau, Freudian psychoanalysis, Rilke, Kafka, Musil. The 1985 exhibition in Vienna extended this period both forward and backward in time. It showed in an illuminating panorama through various aspects of culture the disintegration of a unified and hierarchical world picture, the birth of the twentieth century in the imperial city and the emergence of ideas and artistic expressions which have acquired a decisive significance for the whole of Europe.

Also included in this is the variety of languages, the meeting of national cultures and assimilation. But the Czech, Polish and Hungarian facets of Central Europe are often faint, as if they were shrouded in a mysterious fog, with only the occasional feature visible. Yet the Polish Wyśpianski, the Hungarian Ady and the Croatian Krleža – to name only a few – were an organic part of the world of the turn of century as expressed in decadence, the literary expression of *Lebensphilosophie* and the radical reformulation of national mythologies.

The Pole Czesław Miłosz was absolutely right when he expounded his views at Harvard,

> The literary map of Europe, as it presented itself to the West, contained until recently numerous blank spots. England, France, Germany, and Italy had a definite place, but the Iberian peninsula was no more than a vague outline. Holland, Belgium, and Scandinavia were blurred; while to the east of Germany the white space could have easily borne the inscription *Ubi leones* (Where the lions are), and that domain of wild beasts included such cities as Prague (mentioned sometimes because of Kafka), Warsaw, Budapest, and Belgrade. Only farther to the east does Moscow appear on the map.[1]

We may have an inclination towards extreme reactions in Central Europe, our self-esteem is uncertain and we pay great attention to the judgements of the so-called great literatures. We respond as emotionally to a sentence of praise as to criticism. All the same, perhaps it is no misunderstanding if we conclude that over the last five to six years attention to our area has intensified. In literature, however contingent the yardstick may be, two Nobel prizes (Miłosz, Seifert) hint at something along these lines. But the bibliographies of journals would also seem to support this assertion, and the number of Czech, Polish and Hungarian names published appear to be greater than before. It is as if the blank spots mentioned by Miłosz were beginning to acquire colour here and there. Anthologies are published, for example one in the United States by Emery George (*Contemporary East European Poetry, 1983*), there are special issues of journals, and the burgeoning Central Europe debate in a growing number of languages.

The Central Europe of the Monarchy may now exist only in its relics – in the furnishings of coffee-houses in Prague, Trieste and Cracow, the railway stations typical of the region from Transylvania to Silesia, from Western Ukraine to the Tirol. But literary tradition has conserved the memory of this shared world, with its own contradictions naturally, an odd mixture of pain and nostalgia, negative sentiments, affection and hate, gibes and national injuries. The Habsburg myth in Austrian literature may be complemented by the serried ranks of heroes from plays and novels, representative of so many different nuances, like the figures drawn by the Czech Hašek, the Pole Bruno Schulz, the Hungarian Krúdy and the Croat Krleža. This line can be continued forward to the literature of our day. A few years ago, the Czech writer Bohumil Hrabal declared in a self-interview in the Hungarian monthly *Kortárs* that, apart from Prague, he could conceive of living only in Lemberg, Cracow, Vienna or Budapest. So it may be that Central Europe is no more than a phantom, as François Bondy wrote in the *Frankfurter Allgemeine Zeitung* (21 December 1985), but the trail of the phantom can be found in the cultures and intellectual life of the peoples living here. Central Europe is present in the consciousness of the writers of this region.

This is what I would like to illustrate in my argument, to present a sketch-in-the-round of how writers in this century have seen and now see this intermediate Europe. Obviously my survey will have gaps and will be somewhat out of proportion, seeing that my interests in and commitments to Polish, Czech and Slovak are considerably denser than elsewhere. Even so, many important traits of the Central European consciousness will become evident. It is another question, of course, whether the literary angle distorts. I do not regard answering this as a part of my task. I take the view that literary reality is already a reality. It does not become real by being palpably open to proof. We have had quite enough opportunity to experience the truth of this assertion. National ideologies and social aspirations have been formulated more than once in literature. It was not by chance that Milan Kundera made mention of the role of literature in safeguarding Europe's cultural heritage:

> For if European culture seems to me under threat today, if the threat from within and without hangs over what is most precious about it – its respect for the individual, for his original thought, and for his inviolable private life – then, it seems to me, that precious essence of European individualism is held safe as in a treasure chest in the history of the novel, in the wisdom of the

novel. ('"Man thinks, God Laughs"', *New York Review of Books*, 13 June 1985)

I am going to attempt to sketch the Central European state of affairs by looking at three literary problem areas of this century. The first is the circle of reactions linked to the intermediate and frontier character of the region and interpretations of being in between West and East. The second is the literary formulation of the fate of small nations; and the third is the linguistic and cultural variety of the region, as well as their coexistence.

Central Europe, as is known, is far from being an unambiguous concept. It means something different in German to what it does to a Pole or a Hungarian; it meant something different at the turn of the century; it is differently interpreted by historians or by politicians and differently again by writers. It would be hopeless to try and explore this wilderness of interpretations, although it is necessary to order it and look at it scientifically, though not on this occasion. The sense that this region is a frontier area regularly emerges from the literature of the twentieth century. Here many of the cultural innovations of European culture and literature appeared as a challenge, from symbolism to the avant-garde. Complete models, conventions and forms arrived from the centres of European culture and were often not appropriate to the systems of tradition and the structures of reality that had taken shape in national cultures. A typical example is the story of the modern novel. The classical realist novel was received in an ambiguous fashion, with a time-lag and with discontinuity. Being on the frontier means something transitory, some uncertainty about belonging. One of the characteristics of Central Europe is that its frontiers are not defined precisely. All that is certain in linguistic, cultural and consequently literary terms is that it has a German half and another half which is represented by a series of small peoples – starting with the Poles, through the Czechs, Slovaks, Hungarians to Slovenes, Croats, Serbs, Rumanians, and Bulgarians; but there are intermediate zones to the north, east and south, starting with the Finns and the Baltic peoples, through the Belorussians and Ukrainians and ending with the Greeks. In this entire region, literature was subordinated to the realization of national goals and this made it decisively different from Russian literature. The principal concern of writers was national liberation and the formulation of the national ideology. Let us not forget how vast the difference was between the Russian Pushkin and the Pole Mickiewicz. The Russian poet had to struggle for literary and social goals as the subject of an existing empire. The Polish poet did not have a country in the political sense and could not expect the Tsar to undertake the censoring of his poems.

The consciousness of being in a borderland reaches back furthermore to one of the more significant frontiers of European civilization – the one between Western and Eastern Christianity. Miłosz began his lecture series at Harvard, by stating that he was from the frontier between Rome and Byzantium, the marchlands of Catholicism, where the eradication of an Orthodox culture was immediately tangible through its differentness, its otherness and imperceptible assimilation. From the opposite side of the divide, Serbian and Rumanian writers of this century would probably have had a similar experience of the impact of West European 'Latin' values, stimuli and forms of expression. It was not by chance that Ady wrote of Hungary that it was a 'ferry-land' and, extending his phrase to the region as a whole, it might be called 'Europe's ferry'. A decade and a half ago in Bratislava, the Hungarian Árpád Tőzsér wrote that we lived 'in the waist of a sand-timer'. It has not been easy to remain upright in Europe's waist and to hold on tight, while innovations, armies, cultural goods, infections and messianic ideals rushed through from one bulb of the timer to the other.

Intermediacy means, therefore, consciousness of the marchland and it is not hard to discern the widespread tradition among the peoples of the region that Europe's defensive bastion, the antemurale, stretched precisely through their lands. The correctness of this cannot be denied and it is quite useless to discuss to what extent a people was entitled to lay claim to this distinction. The essence is that the sense of mission has been integrated into the national traditions articulated through literature. It can be found equally in the historical novels of the Pole Sienkiewicz, the Hungarian Gárdonyi or the Rumanian Sadoveanu. The sentence used by the Croats about their past is familiar elsewhere – in the Turkish period, 'Croatia was an open wound on Europe's body'. The situation between Western and Eastern Europe can be given a positive or negative interpretation. It can be assumed, for one, that the influences arriving from different directions are mutually cross-fertilizing and have brought a unique cultural entity into being.

This is the modernized version of the sense of mission, transcending the limits of the traditional and the national. Dezső Szabó, the Hungarian writer of the inter-war period, wrote as early as the late 1920s in this sense, namely, that there exists a community of fate of the peoples of Eastern Europe and, a little later, László Németh used the term 'foster brothers' in the Journal *Tanú*. In their terminology, especially where Dezső Szabó was concerned, they sought to differentiate their ideas from the German aspirations put forward before and during the First World War, which emphasized the 'disorderliness' of the region and attempted to construct a unified Central Europe under German overlordship.

But the need for this particular kind of rapprochement, based on mutual understanding, in the region between the Baltic and the Adriatic was recognized by writers from many other national cultures. I would like to quote Stanisław Vincenz (1888–1971) here. A son of the Carpathians, he knew at first hand the coexistence of peoples and nationalities in one-time Eastern Galicia – through a complex conglomerate of Poles, Ukrainians, Jews and Rumanians. He spent the Second World War in Hungary, in Budapest and Nógrádverőce, and among other things, he taught his friend Lajos Áprily, who lived on the far side of the Danube, Polish and Russian. In 1942, he wrote:

> If the Central European region does not unite its forces into some kind of intellectual and cultural alliance – each one of its parts will of necessity become the dependency of a greater unit. Through rapprochement, however, each separate component can safeguard its individuality and can gather significant strength, moving in a direction different from the existing one. It looks as if efforts made by the Jagiellos were moving instinctively in that direction. Except that at the time, the Czech lands were decapitated and silenced and then a significant part of Hungary's territory was torn from Europe by the Turk, and finally Poland fell, not capitulating in spirit, but without a visible body. Tradition remained. Whatever happens, one feels despite the great turning points and dreadful aspects of the world nowadays, the nation that accepts this tradition and seeks to achieve it, knowing the risks and paying the price, as well as trying to remain true to the tasks which result, cannot suffer degradation.

The only possibility, when a kind of intellectual no-man's-land emerges in the intermediate zone, is the loss of character. This was the danger of which Witold Gombrowicz, another of the great Polish writers of the century, warned mostly in his *Diary*. These were his arguments:

> I was a Pole. From Poland. What is Poland? A country between East and West, where Europe somehow all but comes to an end, a transitional country where East and West mutually weaken each other. But let me mention a characteristic Polish danger, one that derives from the intermediacy of the Polish situation, namely that our country is a little bit of a parody of the East and of the West. The Polish East is a moribund East in consequence of its encounter with the West [and vice versa], after which something here 'is losing its strength'. Imagine Miłosz's pain, when, say, he is writing of a tiger from here. The stumbling-block is, is this tiger a tiger at all or a stray cat mewing on the tiles?

In many respects, certainties were and are lacking in Central Europe, even as the borders of the region are ambiguous. Often its inhabitants may have come to feel that there are no irrevocable truths, no certain criteria to establish what truth is and what it is not. The experience of the first half of the twentieth century only deepened these perceptions and intensified suspicion towards History with a capital H. They felt perhaps that events were open to numerous interpretations. Hence their suspicion of phrase-making and illusions. It is understandable that the history of Central Europe should have appeared as a labyrinth in the eyes of those who suffered it and survived it. The world of Kafka did not seem to be a fiction at all; far from having been an absurdity, it had the force of a living documentation. In the loss of certainties, in all probability this area preceded the rest of Europe.

Appearance and reality were not sharply divided, it was rather as if they spilled over into each other, so that what was unreal was real and what was real was unreal. In other words, one of the most important questions of European culture received a much clearer definition – the nature of the relationship between subjective and objective, the basic recognition that there can be no consciousness without object, that consciousness is always a consciousness of something. Thus it is hard to conceive of the so-called 'objective' reality, since we, its viewers and judges, are in it.

This is a key question of modern prose and it is not chance that the contemporary pioneers of the genre are from this region. Kafka or Musil or Gombrowicz are far from certain that everything can be told as it is; the narrators of their works have lost the confidence of their predecessors, for the authors know full well that the competence of the speaker is not without limits, that the reader addressed by them must also be taken into calculation and that language or the system of cultural prejudice can erect many traps in the process of communication. The changed order of the communication between author and reader is connected with one of the leading values of our shared European culture – tolerance. Dialogue and reciprocity have a better chance. Paradoxically, it is as if in backward Europe, beyond the Elbe and Leithe, in the complicated interpenetration of feudal and bourgeois elements and the constraints and cataclysms of the twentieth century, that there are fewer doubts about the fundamental values of European culture. The essays of István Bibó and the poetry of Zbigniew Herbert both testify to this, to name only two instances from among the greatest.

Beyond any doubt, one of the most striking features of the region is the schizophrenia of national consciousness and one can find countless examples to illustrate it in the literature of the most recent decades. The frontiers of the nation were in themselves ambiguous. Some homelands were parts of the great empires and often the limits of a nation were not marked even by the internal boundaries of provinces. State frontiers have changed often in the last seventy years (especially in the first half of the century) and it was at all times an agonizing dilemma for those affected to know on what basis one should identify with a national community – did it depend on what language one spoke or where one was born? And professing a country in these parts could easily 'lead to a hastily dug ditch', to use the words of Zbigniew Herbert. When looked at from more tranquil regions, the hysteria and old-fashioned gestures of Central European national consciousness undoubtedly seemed anachronistic and comical. And we too can be sceptical of this ideal, which had its halcyon days in the nineteenth century, seeing that its intolerant variants can lead us astray even nowadays. Nevertheless, we are under an obligation to look into the mirror of literature to come to know our prejudices.

The schizophrenia of national consciousness can also be defined as the unhappy and mostly unsuccessful experiment to integrate the concepts of nation-state and national culture. But one can equally mention the tragic excesses of Central Europe on national consciousness, that is, that national identities failed to evolve proportionate forms, that the nation regularly appeared either as an all-encompassing value or as a total negative to be sacrificed at the altar of any and every alternative ideal.

> At last I'd like to know
> where indoctrination ends
> and true links begin

as Zbigniew Herbert·expressed all these uncertainties in his poem 'Reflections of the National Question'.[2]

Peoples, languages, religions and state frontiers represented difficult opportunities for identification. Often it was possible to choose between nations, to assimilate voluntarily or in obedience to economic or political constraints. I regard Miroslav Krleža's passage, from one of the pieces of the Glembay Family cycle of plays and short stories as emblematic. Here he offers this insight into the dilemmas of the identification of his hero in turn of the century Zagreb:

> it was a mystery from his earliest days of understanding why his mother knew no Croatian, why the Glembays spoke German, seeing that they did not claim to be Viennese or why the Fabricys professed to be Hungarian ... Why did they not teach him to speak Croatian properly at home, when all his school books were in Croatian and at school, everyone spoke Croatian, whereas at home nobody spoke it ...?

In such circumstance, the aspirations of nation-states and state-nations necessarily resulted in exclusivity in the nineteenth and twentieth centuries, and a significant part of these aspirations was automatically injurious to the interests of neighbouring peoples. The maps of the new homelands intersected each other and it looked as if each nation could attain its goal only at the cost of its neighbours. It is enough to place the maps of the different national movements on top of each other – those of the exclusively monoglot Hungarian kingdom in the historic Crownlands, or of the Czech homeland made up of the historic provinces (Bohemia, Moravia, Silesia) which ignored the German minority, or of the projected territory of Slovakia that stretched from the Tatra mountains to the Danube where all non-Slovak speakers were regarded as degenerates, or the Greater Rumanian homeland lying between the rivers Dniestr and Tisza.

The relatively limited ethnic resources of small peoples, political dependence, unfavourable geographical situation, ethnic intermingling, and the absence of territorial autonomy taken together had the consequence of a powerful sense of being threatened by the prospect of the destruction of the nation.

A wealth of illustration can be mustered from every national literature to demonstrate that small nations have been conscious of being under threat. The particular compound of hopes and desires, of illusions and scepticism characterizes these declarations – the sudden flaring of the flame side by side with darkly brooding pessimism, the simultaneous over- and underestimation of strength. I shall quote only a few examples, Karel Čapek in his work *A Place for Jonathan* (1932–1936) wrote:

> A neurotic Czech writer asked himself whether it was worth being a member of a small nation and would it not be better for them if they merged with larger ones. I could never understand this. I felt as if a melancholy beaver was pondering on whether it was worth being a beaver, when there are far fewer beavers than mice or horses. The real beaver does not ask whether it is worth being one, but asks how he can secure his existence if he is what he is. Securing his existence is an undertaking with moral significance. The instruments at the disposal of a small nation are modest. Its possibilities are limited. Its choice of persons and resources is restricted. Everything it has attained borders on the miraculous and the heroic. Every one of its successes was born in spite of its limited possibilities and in great tension. If someone crosses the ocean in a large, well-equipped ship, that can be a record or just a part of the time-table. If, on the other hand, someone crosses the ocean in a small boat, that is an adventure and is more of a moral than a technical success.

In 1970, Vladimír Mináč, one of the most decisive personalities of contemporary Slovak literature and an investigator of our painful past, wrote:

> Our self-consciousness and pride, if they exist at all, are without content, nothing more than a tap-room gesture. In their subconscious, particularly in the subconscious of the younger generation of intellectuals, there is a fear that we have no meaning, that it will be hard for us to acquire meaning. Yet we do want to be something, to mean something, even if the price is that we lose our identity as we are.

The uncertainties of identity, national self-flagellation and strutting arrogance can appear in surprisingly similar guises. Interesting lessons may be drawn from a comparative analysis of the poetic 'curses' pronounced on one's own nation. Another characteristic definition of the consciousness of small-nationhood in Central Europe is taken from the *Paris Notebooks* of the Slovene writer Edvard Kocbek:

> Our history shows no kind of undistinguished passion at all. By reason of its poverty it cannot sustain any serious mission, it rests on no original declaration of faith or shared moderation. Our community is convex rather than concave, has no centre of gravity which would constitute a centre geographically or

morally. This is why we have no thinkers of centripetal value, intellects convinced of our independence, of our having a predetermined destiny. As against this, during our long history we have come across many bearers of apostolic ideals which, rather than unify the people, scatter them. ... We never regarded our national boundaries as a yardstick, as a safe passage, a standard and an inspiration, but rather as a temptation, shame and covert opportunities.

The next complex of questions is the interpretation of the coexistence of peoples and cultures. As is known, there are many lands and settlements in Central Europe which are the homelands of peoples of different mother tongues.

If multilingualism is frequently encountered anywhere, it is in this region, so that after the national programmes placed monolingualism on their agendas, their implementation – whether in Hunagry after 1867 or elsewhere after 1918 – meant that members of minorities suffered as a result. The coexistence of cultures and multilingualism could be given positive or negative attributes. They can be perceived as the ideal arena for mutual respect and tolerance, of cultural exchange where the coexistence of national groups enrich each other and learn from one another's cultural differences to enhance national particularities. The century of nationalism tended to favour the negative perception of cultural variety. Linguistic homogeneity received the seal of approval and assimilation (from the standpoint of the state-constituent nation) was meritorious. To differ was to err. Exclusivity received too great an emphasis in the concept of nationhood, as did the politically determined and much desired cultural-linguistic homogeneity. What a triumph it was when the national and linguistic composition of a town changed! Magyarized Pest and Buda, Prague acquiring a Czech majority or Zagreb a Croatian one exemplify this. Just as the awakening of nationhood was a necessity for Central Europe, so it was accompanied by an equal amount of impatience and exclusivity, which continued into the twentieth century. Yet in this region, the positive traditions of multi-culturalism lived for centuries in some places, in cities like the Lithuanian-Polish-Jewish-Belorussian Wilno, the Czech-German-Jewish Prague, the German-Hungarian-Slovak Bratislava to name only a few. It is as if thinking in state-national categories had forced these traditions out of our consciousness. How striking it is that our very reflexes seem to protest against a place having several names, different in different mother tongues. One illustration of the cultural variety of Central Europe should suffice. The example is from one of Ivo Andrić's short stories, about Sarajevo:

> Anyone spending a sleepless night in Sarajevo will hear the nocturnal sounds of the city. The bell of the Catholic cathedral strikes the hour precisely and weightily. It is two hours after midnight. More than a minute passes ... and only then is the bell of the Pravoslav church heard, a softer though penetrating

sound, to toll 2 o'clock. Shortly thereafter, in its hoarse and remote voice, the clock on the Beg-Jami sounds, but it strikes 11, a haunting Turkish time, by the calculation of far-away, wondrous, alien worlds. The Jews have no bell tower and only the Good Lord can say what hour is struck by Sephardic and Ashkenazi reckoning.

Many motives may be hidden behind the discovery or rediscovery of Central Europe. During the construction of modern national culture, roughly over two centuries, writers and thinkers have been confronted by the dilemma – sometimes sooner, sometimes later – that they must expound the backwardness of their own national cultures and the differences from that European culture from which they sprang. This was how two possible solutions were formulated and these have, in effect, recurred repeatedly since the Enlightenment and romanticism. One of these is the imitation of Europe and the other is total differentiation from it, the exclusive quest for local particularities. The two were conceived of as mutually exclusive. I take the view that it is not difficult to locate literary movements and currents in this complex. An enormous quantity of raw material could be brought up in the debate – from any of the literatures of the region. That one is dealing here with a characteristically Central European dilemma – an interpretation of certain facts of the particularities of cultural development, which enjoys laying down definitions in decisive questions – is clear from the relections of Gombrowicz, who essentially disagreed with the proposition that the choice was between two possibilities:

> My generation of Polish writers generally chose between two roads. They could restrict themselves to a Polish cosmos and condemn themselves to being second-rate. Alternatively, they could strive to be European, but this equally condemned them to be second-rate, seeing that theirs was a secondary kind of Europeanness which only wanted to reach Europe and to imitate it.

So Gombrowicz, who sought to extricate himself from the cul-de-sac of false alternatives by synthesizing sameness and differentness. The Polish writer was discussing his dilemmas, but the moral of what he pondered is valid for all of Central Europe and, with only slight exaggeration, one can say that we must use it as a guide. There was nothing of the schoolmaster in him, but all the same it is hard to avoid the temptation of using his words for guidance in defining a Central European identity.

> One of the most important questions of our culture is our relationship to Europe. We cannot become a truly European nation until we separate ourselves from Europe, since our Europeanness does not mean submergence, but that we become a part of it, indeed a very particular part not interchangeable with any other. Consequently, only by opposing the Europe that created us can we ultimately ... create a life of our own. ... Our 'superficiality', our 'carefreeness' are essentially aspects of an irresponsible infantile relationship to

culture and life, our lack of faith in reality as a whole. The origin of this may be that we are neither properly Europe or Asia. This is expressed all the more strongly the more we are ashamed of it. If modern thinking does not commit itself to the necessary clarity and, alarmed by the discovery, tries at all cost to imitate the West (or the East), to eliminate these 'shortcomings' and transform our character, then we shall only create yet another distortion of ourselves. If, on the other hand, we have the sense simply to accept ourselves as we are, we are certain to discover hitherto unknown and unexplored possibilities in ourselves – we shall certainly be capable of assuming a beauty fundamentally different from what we have had until now.

NOTES

1 Czesław Miłosz, *The Witness of Poetry* (Harvard University Press, 1983) p. 7.
2 Retranslated from the Hungarian.

PART 2

10
Milan Kundera's Lament
George Schöpflin and Nancy Wood

As the previous part indicates, the idea of Central Europe has been a longstanding topic of reflection for modern historians, political theorists and the like. However, the question of a distinct, Central European *identity* was given a more insistent and critical impetus in very recent years following the publication of the seminal essay by Czech writer-in-exile Milan Kundera, 'The Tragedy of Central Europe' (*New York Review of Books*, 26 April 1984). The essay, whose title hints at Kundera's pessimistic appraisal of the fate of the Central European legacy, sparked a lively discussion and a debate, heated at times, that continues to this day. (The publication of this essay in the British journal *Granta* (No. 11, 1984) bore Kundera's own more forthright title, 'A Kidnapped West or a Culture Bows Out'.) For what Kundera injected into the Central European medley was the proposition that the erosion of the *idea* of 'Central Europe' in our times has sealed the political and cultural fate of some of the countries included within its embrace.

The chapters in the following part represent a range of responses – by no means exhaustive – to Kundera's essay. It will be immediately apparent that the discussion which has evolved is by no means an academic one, but one with important political and cultural implications. While it is true that the authors of the essays draw upon an astonishing range of historical, sociological and literary sources, the final stakes of their respective arguments concern the political present and future of so-called 'Central European' societies currently under Soviet domination.

The argument that there is an inseparable link between the declining fortunes of the notion of 'Central Europe' in our times, and prospects for social change in the region increasingly referred to as 'East-Central Europe' may not be Kundera's invention, but his essay undoubtedly crystallized a set of inchoate ideas and lent them a timely, direct and poignant voice with far-reaching reverberations for Europe as a whole. Naturally, the editors asked Kundera for permission to include his essay in this volume. Kundera, for reasons of his own, refused. What follows, therefore, is a summary of the main contours of his argument.

Kundera's opening challenge is the assertion that nations like Poland, Hungary, and Czechoslovakia, whose current geo-political reality would seem to fix them now and forever within the boundaries of 'Eastern Europe', in fact have legitimate claim on a European identity more broadly understood. For Kundera, any backward glance at the common historical and, above all, *cultural* traditions of these countries will attest to their essentially European orientation and character. Hence Kundera recasts the turbulent upheavals which have marked this region in the post-war period — Hungary in 1956, Czechoslovakia in 1968 and Poland in 1956, 1968, 1970 and 1981 — not as 'a drama of Eastern Europe, of the Soviet bloc, of communism', but as quintessentially 'a drama of the West — a West that, kidnapped, displaced and brainwashed, nevertheless insists on defending its identity'.

In a very short space, then, Kundera throws down several gauntlets: against the grain of current *realpolitik*, he refuses to endorse the primacy accorded to political definitions of European reality, and he discerns within these eruptions of popular resistance in the post-war period continued strivings to preserve an identity — European, Western — obscured and usurped by such definitions.

In Kundera's schema, it is not politics but *culture* which must be seen as the decisive force by which nations constitute their identity, express that identity and give it its own distinctive mould. Armed with this criterion, Kundera sets out to support his assertion that Central Europe was just such a 'cultural configuration' by virtue of the shared traditions, sensibilities and forms of expression of the 'family of small nations' which composed it. Indeed in the course of unravelling some of the common threads from this tangled historical skein we find Kundera making the case for a distinctively Central European cultural heritage which stands in direct counterpoint to a Western model. In the seventeenth century, for example, Kundera identifies the explosion of baroque art, the predominance of the irrational, and the primacy of visual arts and music as specifically Central European in contrast to France's preoccupation with the classical and rationalistic modes and the primacy of literature and philosophy. Nonetheless, in Kundera's cultural profile of Central Europe, it is Western traditions which served (and continue to serve) as the main points of cultural reference, with which Central European culture remained in productive tension.

In Russia's traditions, on the other hand, Kundera identifies features which are the direct antithesis of those constitutive of the Central European experience. Before drawing this conclusion, however, Kundera tests it by anticipating the argument that it is communism which has deprived Russia of its essential identity and therefore the current imperatives of Soviet bureaucracy – above all, centralization and standardization of cultural, linguistic and ethnic diversity – should not be subsumed within a timeless notion of the Russian nation.

Kundera is sympathetic to an extent to this defence and acknowledges that a case for the discontinuity or rupture of certain Russian traditions (especially religious ones), with the advent of communism can be made. He also concedes that in the nineteenth century, far from a stand-off between East and West, a virtual 'cultural betrothal' of Europe and Russia was enacted, evidenced in the impact the great Russian novels exerted on the European literary imagination and the reciprocal fascination of many Russian authors with European cultural trends. But if communism denied this liaison a future, Kundera believes it did so by reviving the part of the Russian heritage that was *always* hostile to such courtships with Europe, and bent on fulfilling long-standing imperial ambitions.

In other words, Central European nations which have had the unhappy fate of being subjected to communist Russia's centralizing and expansionist policies feel part of a drama which has been staged before. Poland's direct experience of Russian occupation for two centuries, and the fear that Russian imperial might aroused in other countries (Kundera cites František Palacký's 1848 warning of Russia's expansionist designs), suggest to Central Europeans that their fate today is the fulfilment of ambitions embedded within the Russian legacy itself. This is why Kundera maintains that, finally, it is an image of continuity between the Russian past and present which remains deeply etched in the historical memory of Central European nations. A memory, moreover, that is reinforced by the awareness that as an 'uncertain zone of small nations between Russian and Germany', their 'very existence may be put in question at any moment; a small nation can disappear and it knows it'.

Kundera asserts, then, both the continuity of Russian traditions and their profound *difference* from European ones. This explains why in his view Central Europe's adherence to the West is a natural disposition, arising as it does from a constant and intimate intermingling of cultural traditions, whereas Russia represents an 'other' civilization, a fundamentally different culture, despite its periods of cultural reapprochement with Europe.

The 'tragedy' of which Kundera speaks is precisely that, with the exception of Austria, the small nations of Central Europe have been forcibly yoked to this 'other' civilization and have lost the distinct identity that Central Europe once carved for itself out of the larger European panorama. The rest of Europe, meanwhile, has let the demise of Central Europe go both 'unnoticed and unnamed'. Kundera's explanation for this cool disregard returns him again to the decisive role which he attributes to *culture* as the key bearer of traditions, memories and experiences. In the absence of this appreciation of culture's vocation, notions of common destinies and identities inevitably lose out. Precisely because in his words, 'Europe no longer perceives its unity as a cultural unity' culture has 'bowed out', been deprived of its vital function, and Central Europe has been the victim. Prospects for a renewed assertion of Central European identity are bleak in Kundera's estimation precisely because the rest of Europe has sacrificed the only dimension which might serve as the basis for such a revival. Kundera concedes that perhaps other values will step in to perform this task of unification, but he confesses that he doesn't know which these might be, and in any case, their appearance would not assist the case of Central Europe, whose essential identity is synonymous with its cultural life.

But Kundera's pessimism is not reserved for Central Europeans alone. On the contrary, the warning which emerges from his essay is primarily aimed at a Europe which, having long ago abandoned its other half to 'the East', may now look into this space and see reflected back an image of what its own future may hold: 'In our modern world', notes Kundera, 'where power has a tendency to become more and more concentrated in the hands of a few big countries, *all* European nations run the risk of becoming small nations and of sharing their fate. In this sense the destiny of Central Europe anticipates the destiny of Europe in general, and its culture assumes an enormous relevance'.

But speculation about Europe's future cannot be separated from a final question posed by Kundera which bears immediately on our political present: does Central Europe still exist? The continuing, creative output of Central Europe, and the revolts which frequently remind us of its citizens' enduring aspirations, suggest to Kundera that Central Europe has 'not yet perished'. But if a condition of any sense of that identity is recognition by a significant 'other', then Europe, which 'sees in Central Europe only Eastern Europe', has by this very gesture condemned Central Europe to non-existence. It is this conclusion which gives so much poignancy to the underlying meaning Kundera discerns in the history of Central European revolts against Soviet domination: these societies are fighting for an identity their counterparts abandoned long ago, for an image in which Europe no longer even recognizes itself.

11
Central Europe – What It Is and What It Is Not
Egon Schwarz

> Central Europe is not a state:
> it is a culture or a fate. Its
> borders are imaginary ...
> Milan Kundera[1]

Ladies and Gentlemen, permit me to keep my contribution totally subjective.[2] You have chosen a sceptic and outsider for today's speaker. I came upon the idea of a Central Europe late, having spent most of my life, nearly half a century, in South and North America. Nevertheless, I am of course aware that it is a widely-known term, imbued with much meaning and history, and I have noticed that recently it has found its way even into the Italian language in the form of *Mitteleuropa* and *mitteleuropeo*. Still, the frequent use of a term does not prove anything. On the contrary, the repeated appearance of a catchword reminds one of Arthur Schnitzler's remark that 'the things which are most often mentioned do not actually exist'. Schnitzler was referring to love. The quotation is taken from the *Reigen*, and what, if I may ask, is the topic of this misunderstood work if not the lack of love, or rather the consequences of its absence?

My scepticism probably stems from the fact that although I was born in one of the great cultural centres of Central Europe, Vienna, the strong centrifugal forces of that time drove me to the other end of the earth, to the so-called underdeveloped world before my intellectual development was completed. I have no intention of describing to you the crazed countenance which the Central Europe of my youth presented to me. But you must understand that no mild breezes waft over the highlands of the Andes, where I grew up, and that in the Bolivian tin mines, where my conscience of the world was created, the perception of European civilization is totally different from that in the Café Griensteidl or the Café Central where a large part of the mythological web was woven with which we are occupied today. In that thin air – but perhaps not only there – it might be easier to say what Central Europe is *not* than to define it convincingly. If one wanted to approach the subject with humour one could come up with facetious examples of things which are under no circumstances part of a Central European culture. For instance, anyone who has eaten a meal in, let us say, a Scottish village knows that that is not Central European. Jokes about Frisians and drugstores in Asiatic Turkey are not Central European, nor is crossing the border in an Eastern European country. But we have more serious intentions, and so I would like to add only that I would not have accepted the request to talk to you as a confessed sceptic if I were not convinced of the salutary power of scepticism which after all does not only uncover the weaknesses of a belief, but can also strengthen it by freeing it from untenable ballast, and if I did not know furthermore that much connects me with the Central European idea because of my origin and my profession as a historian of literature.

That a multitude of possibilities is contained in the so simple-sounding words 'Central Europe' has been capably pointed out by the historian Henry Cord Meyer. 'Few slogans', he says in his book *'Mitteleuropa' in German Thought and Action*,

> have had greater international implication or provoked such strong reactions. Writers and speakers of varying occupations in many countries endowed the term with a host of vague and different meanings. Geographers sought to give it definition; economists, politicians, and journalists manipulated it; and idealists caressed it with romantic devotion. The more current the expression became in Germany and abroad, the more vague, ambiguous, and emotional was its use. Later captured by the pseudo-science of German geopolitics, and fortified with a strong injection of race theory, it became one of the slogans of a political dynamics which sought control of the European continent from its German centre.[3]

To this summary Henry Cord Meyer attaches the noteworthy warning, 'the analyst who would unravel the threads of the 'Mitteleuropa' story must initially recognize the existence of this state of semantic confusion.[4] But exactly the opposite occurs. The term is generally used without definition, as if there existed total agreement of opinion so that every reader or listener can provide his or her own highly personal interpretation. The situation becomes totally hopeless when connections are made which at best could be considered as 'retrospective': The Holy Roman Empire, the arising Habsburg Monarchy, the up-and-coming Prussia, the fight for the unity of Germany: they were all 'Central Europe'. Frederick the Great, Prince Eugene of Savoy, Leibniz,

Metternich, Friedrich List, Bismarck are all said to have had the 'Central European' vision.

Henry Cord Meyer outlines the more recent history of the term. During the First World War, Friedrich Naumann's concisely titled *Mitteleuropa*[5] gave it impetus. Because of the blockade and their defeat, the Germans became painfully aware of their central position, and the terms Central Europe and Central European were therefore used *ad nauseam*. The influence of the geo-politician Karl Haushofer and his school made sure that these expressions stayed alive in the 1930s. Opponents of the German desire for expansion, especially the Slavs and Western Europeans, thus associated 'Central Europe' with the drive toward the East, the idea of a Berlin-Baghdad axis, the pan-German movement, and they equated it with aggression, Prussianism, conquest, an imperial ideology, suppression and annexation. That is to say, this term which evoked enthusiasm from many Germans created fear and revulsion in others. Only now can one understand Friedrich Naumann's remark, 'Central Europe is war harvest'.

Before we turn to Naumann, to whom 'Central Europe' owes its popularity or notoriety in the twentieth century to a large extent, and who probably shares the responsibility for the fact that a British geographer, Alice Mutton, could talk of a 'German obsession with "Mitteleuropa" during the last half century',[6] we should state that those quantitative scientists, the geographers, for whose help the term seems to cry out, are of no assistance at all. Alice Mutton herself, in her *Central Europe. A Regional and Human Geography*, calls Central Europe a '"problem" region', and, even more strangely, includes 'the Alpine lands, the Czechoslovak lands, Western and Eastern Germany, and finally the Benelux countries', but not Poland and Hungary, Italy or Yugoslavia, although she does admit that her selection is 'arbitrary'.[7] She excuses her procedure with the remark that all attempts to define Central Europe as an independent geographic area 'defied objectivity' and that 'attempts to find a common element' had been 'singularly unrewarding'. In the modern world the human scene has changed so often, so kaleidoscopically, that one should not be surprised that the term Central Europe 'appears as the assessment of a particular writer, be he geographer, historian or politician'.[8] As early as 1876 a French geographer, A. Himly, had written similarly, 'Central Europe is far from permitting itself to be defined with accuracy. ... Aside from its very vague name it has no noteworthy common elements'.[9]

Those geographers propounding German unity, among them Josef Partsch and Albrecht Haushofer, were no more successful. In his book *Mitteleuropa* (1904), Partsch felt obligated to complement his unconvincing geographic definition with a cultural one. Accordingly, Central Europe would be that 'territory where German culture provides the common denominator. ... All of Central Europe belongs, knowingly or unknowingly, to the sphere of

German civilization.'[10] A quarter of a century later he is joined in his opinion by Haushofer who has also found a place in German post-war literature through his *Moabiter Sonette*, published posthumously. In one of these poems he attempts to justify the ideas and intentions of his father, the infamous geo-politician. In an essay entitled 'Mitteleuropa und der Anschluss' (Central Europe and the 'Anschluss', 1930) he writes as follows: 'Central Europe is a term arisen from political forces. ... It owes its creation to the Germans. It would not exist without them.'[11]

Since the division of the continent by the Iron Curtain, the number of geographers is increasing who would do away with the term Central Europe altogether. One realist summarizes his conclusion aptly with the metaphor '"Mitteleuropa" has contracted to a line.'[12] At the same time Jacques Droz, also basing his statement on the political situation, comments that 'the idea of a Central Europe no longer makes any sense.'[13]

Let us return then to a time when the term still roused passion and take a look at the well-known book by Friedrich Naumann which exploded in the middle of the First World War like a bomb. The reasons for its far-reaching impact can be found as much in its passionate rhetoric as in its potent mixture of economic fantasy and strong political aim. Let us first consider the innocent side. Who, for instance, could object to the following dithyramb, which reads better than many of today's travel ads: 'I am thinking of the first years after the war', Naumann begins and then asks himself, 'Where should the journey go?'. The answer to this question is presented in a language which the sober Anglo-Saxons have termed 'purple prose'; a language which explains why this particular work with its often dry political-economic content has found so many enthusiastic readers:

> Journey, you travellers, to the Carpathian Mountains, take along the mandolin, let gypsies play songs to you in mountain villages! Climb, you mountaineers, no longer in Tyrol and the Dolomites, but turn farther east to Styria and the Karst and bathe in wide and sunny Lake Balaton! You students of art, travel to the beautiful, secret corners, to the castles and churches, to the quaint buildings in the cities, visit Prague with its oddities, Cracow with its ancient relics, the city of Graz, so beautiful and proud! There are the Gothic and the Baroque and many worthwhile modern buildings. In Passau take a boatride on the Danube to the imperial city and then on to Gran [Esztergom] and the fabulous castle and city of Ofen and Pest.'[14]

But upon closer reading of Naumann's book one discovers that the main concern is less with travelling, nature worship and art appreciation than with economic matters, cars and machines, and a huge area in which the Germans would undoubtedly have the upper hand after the war. The mixed reception of Naumann's work within and outside the German realm can be foreseen in the careful arrangement of such sentences in which the idea of human companionship and the desire for German predominance are strangely intertwined. 'Central Europe', it says there, for instance, the elements of the sentence carefully balanced as if on an apothecary's scale, 'will be German in its core, will use German, world language and language of mediation, as a matter of course, but from the first day on it must also show indulgence and flexibility towards the other languages involved for only then can harmony prevail.'[15]

For the warring countries, but also for many inhabitants of the Habsburg Monarchy, Naumann's vision was simply the cleverly disguised preparation of a giant territory under German control, from the North Sea to the Middle East, and the calls for tolerance and flexibility contained in the book were only a sugar coating to make the swallowing of the bitter pill more palatable. Nevertheless even some of Naumann's political opponents were fascinated with his idea, for example, the Austrian social democrat Karl Renner, who was firmly convinced that Naumann was a man of peace and his Central Europe a haven of historic validity which would acknowledge social democrats and in which even proletarians could profit.[16] On the other hand, Rudolf Hilferding opposed the idea in an essay whose very title reveals his message: 'Europeans, not Central Europeans!'.[17]

The most damning response was delivered by Karl Kautsky who was not fooled by Naumann's pseudo-poetic rhetoric.[18] Derisively he quotes Naumann's 'enraptured'[19] exclamation: 'In poetry and prose, arise, rise to the heights, Central Europe',[20] and then continues with unfailing logic to strip Naumann's lofty structure of its poetry and to expose its basis: the German drive for hegemony not only over the small countries of Scandinavia and the Balkans, but also over the Danube Monarchy. In the course of this discussion he explains plausibly that Naumann's aversion to pacts with Russia and England is based on half-admitted fears that Germany might be absorbed by these powers or at least be relegated to a subservient position.

Kautsky's most effective weapon against his opponent is the quotation. Thus he lets Naumann proclaim with his own voice that 'Central Europe came about through *Prussian* victories'[21] and that 'as long as the sun is still shining we must maintain the thought of joining the ranks of the top economic powers'.[22] Kautsky condemns most strongly Naumann's idea of a 'Central European trench community' and juxtaposes instead that of a socialist, supranational alliance of equal states. Indeed, not only does Naumann proclaim that the German element will be predominant in a Central Europe, but he promises Europe after the war, whose end, as he says, will by no means bring 'the blissful state of eternal peace', 'two long trenches from north to south, one of which will run somehow from the lower Rhine to the Alps, the other from the Courland to the left or right of Rumania. ... First the long trenches must be dug, paid for, manned' – obviously Naumann is concerned with practical matters, seeing in 'the trench the basis for the defence of the homeland'. Indeed there will be 'trench politics', and 'the military state [will] go beyond the borders of the national state'. It will 'comprise a trench community'.[23]

Echoes of such militaristic insanity can be heard even in the present, and the nonsense is still concerned with Central Europe, as for instance in a news item which I found in an American paper in December 1984 after a group of terrorists had damaged an oil pipeline in Belgium. It said there, 'the oil pipelines which go through Belgium are part of a network of NATO fuel lines belonging to five nations. They comprise 3,680 miles and cross Central Europe so that in times of war the NATO's oil supply is guaranteed'. One can imagine what that would look like in times of war. Hidden and totally subconsciously, the notice contains the image of the future in its lines: the words 'Central Europe' and 'fuel' draw the picture in horrifying laconism.

Little else has remained of Naumann's dream to change a constellation created by war into a permanent political and economic entity. Nevertheless, his demand for co-operation is by no means completely outdated. 'He urged industrialists, labour unions, artisans, farmers, landowners, historians, lawyers, physicians, and men of other occupations of all the nationalities to talk about their mutual interests and problems.'[24] The conferences of the 'Istituto per gli incontri culturali mitteleuropei' in Gorizia have indeed been continuing these efforts on an intellectual level for nearly twenty years, and today it is due to this unique institution, as far as I can judge, that the idea of 'Central Europe' is not completely forgotten. I need not tell you about these conferences, which you yourselves have initiated and which you have kept viable through your organizational talents and your intellectual contributions. I have not participated in any of these meetings and can only speak of my reaction to the volumes in which the essays and lectures have been collected since 1966. I have read several of them and have noticed that, as one would expect, the personalities of the authors and their intellectual orientations are too different from each other for me to be able to express a general opinion of everything printed there. It is impossible to agree with every view held in these volumes; but the spirit emanating from most of these speeches, replies, and discussions is informed by a universalism, with which I can sympathize. Repeatedly the important intellectual contributions to the Central European culture by the Slovenes and Slovaks, the Croatians, Austrians, Italians, Serbs and Jews are pointed out. In 1982 a whole conference was dedicated to the latter, as was the impressive volume of 1984. All groups, be they ever so small, have been considered. Everywhere a cosmopolitan spirit is detectable, supranationalism and its presupposition, the renunciation of nationalistic relics, are stressed. And these are not merely vague statements of a general nature. Instead, concrete details which after all tend to contain the truth are offered. One simple remark such as that by Franz Tumler surely contributes greatly to alleviating old fears of a German-

Austrian drive for hegemony: 'I do not hold with those expectations which envisage a sort of rebirth of Austrian ideas and which see in them hope for *our* Central Europe. To take that path would be wrong, it would mean disregarding the great changes which all European nations have experienced.'[25] And I would like to include another remark which approximates my own feelings. One should, says Aurelio Ciacchi, overcome the fear of euphemisms and have the courage to exchange the term Central Europe with much more precise and fitting expressions such as: Jewish, Slavic, Habsburg, internationalist, socialist. And the so-called Central European meetings at Gorizia should be defined with more frankness as concrete attempts to overcome the politics of ideological superpowers through culture and to recreate a civilized exchange of ideas in the heart of Europe.[26] I must also agree with the same author when he would obliterate any trace of nationalist sentiment and fight any suspect and outdated taboo in the literature of Central Europe.[27]

It must be pointed out, however, that these remarks and many other worthwhile and intelligent contributions to the symposia of Gorizia stand out in three ways: first, they make liberal use of subjunctives, auxiliary verbs, and the conditional tenses, such as *potrebbe, sarebbe, potrebbero*, 'if – then', 'we must', 'we should', all of which indicate how hypothetical are the foundations on which these convictions and postulates are built. Second, in all these volumes – which are frequently dedicated to dual themes such as myth *and* Central Europe, the Jews *and* Central Europe and other similar ones – there can be felt a definite preponderance of the first component over the second. One gets the distinct feeling that a fear of commitment keeps the contributors from taking a close look at the *relationship* between the two terms and that they would prefer to deal with the unproblematic part. This creates the impression that they had less to say about Central Europe than about the item with which they paired it, or that they simply assumed a consensus on Central Europe. And finally, one notices that when geographic – cultural notions are introduced, Central Europe soon becomes Europe, or that Europe provided the frame of reference to begin with. Such cautioning interjections as the following are characteristic: 'I feel that the actions and relationships can be expanded beyond the narrow Central European confines', or 'it would now be even less wise to draw up borders and to exclude countries as well as cultures which do not directly gravitate to Central Europe.'[28] These remarks are characteristic of the feeling of uneasiness which Central Europe seems to cause as a term of scientific usefulness. One is reminded of Goethe's words with which Henry Cord Meyer, not coincidentally, prefaced his book on Central Europe: 'For when terms are lacking/the fitting word will come at the right time' ('Denn eben, wo Begriffe fehlen,/Da stellt ein Wort zur rechten Zeit sich ein.').

Recently, however, the idea of a Central Europe had a rebirth when the influential Czech novelist Milan Kundera (who now lives in Paris) published a passionate article entitled 'The Tragedy of Central Europe' in the American journal *The New York Review of Books*.[29] His idea of Central Europe is so unique and so different from any previous conceptions that a short explanation of his thought processes seems necessary.

At the beginning of his essay Kundera recalls the fact that in 1956 the editor-in-chief of the Hungarian news agency MTI met his death with the words 'We are going to die for Hungary and for Europe' on his lips. Such a sentence, Kundera says, could be found neither in Moscow nor in Leningrad but only in Budapest or Warsaw. From this premise he develops his definition of Central Europe with logical consequence. In his opinion Central Europe is comprised of those nations which until recently 'had always considered themselves to be Western', but which in 1945, after the Russian border had been moved several hundred kilometers to the West, awoke 'to discover that they were now in the East'. Consequently Central Europe is 'the Eastern border of the West', it consists of those nations which became independent after 1918 and must now live under the yoke of the Soviet Union, the polar opposite of Europe, in danger of losing their very being and which therefore cater to their culture – as the only power really capable of providing an identity – with an intensity unknown in the West.

In his passionate indictment, which is not only directed at the actual oppressors but also against a Europe which has forgotten these nations because it has stopped believing in itself, Kundera commits many small sins which must be less attributed to false judgement than to the omission of relevant facts. He states, for instance, that for two centuries Poland was oppressed by the Russians. For the sake of completeness one should add that the Prussians, Saxons, and the Habsburg Empire[30] were also party to this oppression, and that Poland itself ruled Russia for a while, acting every bit the oppressor, as any other nation would if given that chance. An insignificant but symptomatic event is noteworthy in this context: When Czechoslovakia was dismembered in 1938, Poland and Hungary joined the scavengers sharing the carrion. It should also be mentioned – but Kundera ignores this as well – that the Czechs themselves had treated their minorities with anything but kindness.

Equally, Kundera forgets to report that anti-Semitism occurred in these countries in a particularly virulent form and led to special laws and excesses against Jews long before the National Socialist regime. This fact deserves mention because in his scheme of a Central Europe Kundera bestows a central role on the Jews. He finds kind words for them and establishes a strong connection between them and Central Europe; indeed, he very nearly postulates the identity of the Jewish spirit with the Central European spirit. According to Kundera the Jews became the most significant cosmopolitan and integrating element in Central Europe in the twentieth century – the intellectual glue which held it together, the creators of its intellectual unity. Imitating Biblical diction, he confesses to love the Jewish origin and to espouse it with as much passion and nostalgia as if it were his own. 'Indeed', he proclaims, 'no other part of the world has been so deeply marked by the influence of Jewish genius. ... Another thing makes the Jewish people so precious to me: in their destiny the fate of Central Europe seems to be concentrated, reflected, and to have found its symbolic image.' And elsewhere he states that Central Europe has lost its soul through Auschwitz. Yet he neglects to mention that Auschwitz was a product of National Socialism and that National Socialism was a quintessentially Central European affair. In fact, one can pointedly state that the movement of the Soviet border to the West, the cause of all of these phenomena so fervently bemoaned by Kundera, was started by Hitler, the personification of Central European Fascism, because it was he who lured the Russians so far into Central Europe with his pact with Stalin. In hardly any of the many books which I have read that dealt with the essence of Central Europe is Fascism even mentioned, nor is it recognized as a consequence of certain socio-historical factors in the Central European countries.[31]

For Kundera the Jews are the 'small nation par excellence', and to the question, 'What is Central Europe?' he provides his own answer: 'An uncertain zone of small nations between Russia and Germany.' A small nation, on the other hand, is for him 'one whose very existence may be put in question at any moment.' Kundera forgets, however, that these small nations which for him make up Central Europe have not practised in the past, nor do they now practise, true solidarity among themselves. Jacques Droz feels, as do many others, that as early as between the two world wars 'it would have been impossible to return to the nations spawned by the dissolution of "Danubian Europe" any kind of unity, not even economically, due to their wildly exaggerated nationalism.' 'Even long before that, during the nineteenth and twentieth centuries, Central Europe had fallen victim to a nationalistic principle which continuously undermined the nations' desire for a shared fate and instead roused in everyone the passionate urge to lead a separate existence within one and the same state.'[32] I am emphasizing all this because it is important to me to show that the seeds of its destruction lay in Central Europe itself and that one must be very selective if one wishes to identify with the powers which are active in Central Europe.

Although Kundera speaks of culture in general, he also thinks specifically of the art which he exercises himself. He enumerates the works which he considers 'the greatest Central European novels': *The Sleepwalkers, The Man without Qualities, The Good Soldier Švejk*, the Kafka stories. They are Central European not in the sense that they document a common possession, but on the contrary in their irretrievable losses: Broch's work shows history as a process of gradually declining values; Musil draws the picture of a euphoric society which does not recognize that it will perish the next day; Hašek uses the pretence of ignorance as the very last means to preserve one's personal freedom; Kafka's novelistic visions speak of a world of memory which will exist after history has passed. The picture in which Kundera combines his view of literature past and present is negative to the point of condemnation: all the great Central European works of art of this century must be seen – and this is still valid today – as long meditations about the possible end of European mankind. Of course, the list could be expanded by the names of hundreds of works which guarantee a high artistic ethos and which for this reason alone would fit in well. Some – like *Die letzten Tage der Menschheit* (*The Last Days of Mankind*) or *Die Welt von gestern* (*The World of Yesterday*) – already reveal in their titles the uselessness of their quest. As for Stefan Zweig, the most believable of all Central Europeans: the exuberance with which he greets at the end of the First World War 'the long-promised realm of justice and brotherly love' and of which he has dreamed, is meant for 'the shared *Europe*'[33] and not Central Europe, and the subtitle of his memoirs is 'Reminiscenses of a European'. Books printed nowadays show no indebtedness to Central Europe – whatever the individual might imagine that to be – not even sadness at its demise. They are either full of dark aggressions against those tough, ever-surviving powers of stupidity and malevolence, or they drip with absurd joviality as if they wished to tell the reader: if annihilation has become unavoidable, there is no longer any need for pessimism.

What about Milan Kundera himself? He has not only written essays about the world situation but also well-known novels. It seems characteristic to me that this Czech prophet of the Central European theory does not articulate his concern in his narrative work. In all his works the entanglements of the private lives of his characters with the political life are shown most credibly, and the far-reaching influence of Czech history down to the erotic behaviour of the individual is made most visible. But nowhere is there any mention of Central Europe, not even in the strange sense which the author has given this term. I have found only one place which points to a Central European direction: in the novel *Life is Elsewhere*. With blind political enthusiasm the young hero, Jaromil, composes a poem for Lenin's birthday, and in it he lets the branch of an apple tree slide into the waves of a river so that it might float 'all the way to Lenin's homeland'. The ironic narrator, who never hides completely behind his fictional story and in whom we may suspect the later Kundera, disappointed by the Communist takeover of Czechoslovakia, comments sarcastically on this line: 'No Czech river flows to Russia, but a poem is a magical land where rivers change their course.'[34] That is all. Perhaps historiography is a similar wonderland. At any rate, the expert feels the historic passion in such remarks of the author. But do such sparse signs as these constitute a 'Central European' literature? Hardly. And so the latest defender of the Central European idea, the writer Milan Kundera, becomes a deserter as soon as one turns from his critical to his fictional texts. My explanation for this strange lack is that his concept has too little substance to take on poetic form.

It is obvious why I have included Kundera so extensively in my argument: today he propagates his passionate belief in a Central Europe before an indifferent audience, but at the same time he presents an idea of Central Europe which is so alien and deeply pessimistic that we become painfully aware of its chimeric nature; and because this exiled writer, fighting for his Central European identity, appeals to a greater spiritual power – Europe – but a Europe in which he has lost faith and which is in the process of giving up on itself.

Let me summarize. When I look at what I have read and experienced, when I compare these controversial and largely incompatible concepts, I come to the inevitable conclusion that all efforts which might have led to the creation of a Central European community have either long stopped or are being phased out. Long before the Holy Roman Empire was dissolved officially in 1806, it had ceased to exist in reality. The last witnesses to the Habsburg Monarchy in which, in spite of all its faults, a coexistence of several nations and ethnic groups might have been possible, are dying. The emancipated Jewry, with its tolerance, its cosmopolitanism, and its cultural openness, has disappeared. Even basically negative influences such as German imperialism, which saw Central Europe as a territory in which to execute its power, no longer exist. And even the advancing Soviet Union has not been able to effect a coming together of European nations, let alone of European splinter groups.

In these circumstances Central Europe can be seen today only as a cultural concept. But usually, manifestations of culture are even more elusive than those of economics or politics. At the time of Italo Svevo, Stefan Zweig and other contemporary advocates of the idea, it might still have had an aura of historic feasibility and durability. Most of those who use the term today know that these possibilities have disappeared and that they must restrict the meaning to the sphere of cultural, artistic effort and emotional content. This is accompanied by at most a few historical memories and a strong uneasiness in view of the increasingly hysterical confrontations between the ideological powers, which threaten to crush everything in their path and under whose rule we find ourselves searching for spiritual freedom, an identity of our own, and a more peaceful and less deceptive self-conscience. But even here one must tread carefully. I hope to have shown that even a cultural concept contains ideological components and can be misused.

For all these reasons I feel that we should make the best of the situation. Since there is no definable Central Europe, we are free to postulate a utopian one. It is permissible to call the quest for such a vague entity as Central Europe – an entity which contradicts the historical 'givens' – a utopian project, because the search for Central Europe stems from the same suffering under the historical conditions as a utopia. Like any utopia, it also attempts to free the people from their inevitable political encumbrances by transporting them to another dimension. Let us admit, then, that this Central Europe, weak in the past, elusive in the present, and more than uncertain in the future, is a symbol for what is not but should be, a spiritual attitude, an ethos. Let us assign it to the realm of Heine's Bimini, the island of eternal youth and *joie de vivre*, or to Mörike's Orplid, the land which beckons in the luminous distance.

We should not make the mistake of considering such a utopian concept esoteric or altogether ineffective. Whenever a group of people is formed in the name and spirit of utopia, it gains *ipso facto* the power of existence. True, its effect on the world cannot be fathomed, but luckily the spiritual efforts of mankind have always eluded definition and, I hope, will continue to do so.

Universalism, anti-racism, sympathy for all ethnic, linguistic, and religious differences, the right to criticize, the renunciation of aggression, the abandonment of ready-made ideologies, respect for the human being, the control of harmful illusions in oneself, the spiritual resistance against lies and hypocrisy, with which we are faced today from birth until death, protection of the environment, so that enough is left for the coming generations, social justice, equality between men and women, raising the living standard of the Third World, support and propagation of cultural activities: if we apply to this programme the term Central Europe – and I do not see why we should not do so in view of the many already existing interpretations of the term, most of which are no less arbitrary and therefore all the more dictated by special interests – if such a Central Europe is the land which beckons in the distance, then I am willing to give up my initial scepticism and to declare enthusiastically: I, too, am a Central European.

NOTES

1 Milan Kundera, 'The Tragedy of Central Europe', *New York Review of Books*, 26 April 1984, p. 35.
2 This essay was originally delivered as a lecture in the spring of 1985 in Linz at the invitation of the PEN Club of Upper Austria.
3 Henry Cord Meyer, *Mitteleuropa in German Thought and Action* (The Hague: Martinus Nijhoff, 1955), pp. 2–3.
4 Ibid., p. 3.
5 Berlin: Georg Reimer, 1915.
6 Alice F. A. Mutton, *Central Europe. A Regional and Human Geography* (London: Longmans, 1961), pp. VII–VIII.
7 Ibid., p. VII.
8 Ibid., p. 3.
9 From A. Himly, *Histoire de la formation territoriale des États de l'Europe centrale*

What Central Europe Is and What It Is Not 155

(1876), quoted in Jacques Droz, *L'Europe Centrale. Evolution historique de l'idée de 'Mitteleuropa'* (Paris: Payot, 1960) p. 17 (my translation from the French).
10   Quoted in Jacques Droz, pp. 17–18.
11   Quoted from Haushofer's essay 'Mitteleuropa and the Anschluss' in the essay volume *Die Anschlussfrage* (Wien, 1930), in Jacques Droz, p. 21.
12   E. Fischer, 'The Passing of Mitteleuropa' in *The Changing World. Studies in Political Geography*, W. G. West and A. E. Moodie (eds) (1956), chapter 2, p. 62, quoted in Alice Mutton, p. 6.
13   Jacques Droz, p. 15.
14   Friedrich Naumann (see note 5), pp. 101–2.
15   Ibid., p. 101.
16   In 'Wirklichkeit oder Wahnidee?' *Der Kampf*, IX (1916), pp. 15–25.
17   In *Der Kampf*, VIII (1915), pp. 357–65.
18   'Mitteleuropa' in *Die neue Zeit*, 34. Jahrgang, Bd. 2 (1915/16), pp. 423, 453ff, and 494ff.
19   p. 424.
20   Naumann, p. 231.
21   Naumann, pp. 57–8.
22   Naumann, pp. 177–8.
23   Naumann, pp. 7, 8, 254.
24   H. Cord Meyer, p. 199.
25   'Einspruch von Franz Tumler' in *Mito e realtá della Mitteleuropa. Atti e documentazione sul convegno* (Gorizia, 1971), p. 107.
26   Aurelio Ciacchi, 'Internazionalismo e letteratura nell'ambito della Mitteleuropa', *Mito e realtá*, p. 59 (my paraphrase of the Italian original).
27   Ibid.
28   Eros Sequi, 'Mitica poeticitá di realtá profondamente radicate', *Mito e realtá*, p. 139.
29   26 April 1984.
30   To strengthen this argument I have selected from many testimonials only that by Jacques Droz (see n. 9), a friend and supporter of the Danubian Monarchy, who nevertheless spoke of the 'suppressed nations' (*peuples opprimés*) in the Habsburg Empire. p. 16.
31   A few authors who published responses to Kundera's essay in the Czech exile journal *Svedĕctví* are the exception. Milan Hauner writes: 'Hitler himself, who does not appear at all in Kundera's long article, was a product of the Central European culture par excellence ... that same Central European culture spawned also Auschwitz and the mass deportation of millions'. And in the magazine *Le Débat* François Bondy responds to Kundera's essay: 'the catastrophe of Central Europe came from within. The carelessness of the Habsburg Monarchy, which was neither a protector nor a defender for its Slavic people but a "nation prison", did not make the slightest concession towards participation in government. The German movement, which was after all in no way Asiatic, started the Second World War. And in the long run it was also the small nations' inability to show solidarity in the time between the wars, which contributed to the tragedy of Central Europe'. Quoted from a report by Thomas Rothschild in the feuilleton section of the *Neue Zürcher Zeitung*, Sunday/Monday, 7/8 April 1985, mailing edition No. 80, p. 39.

32 Droz, p. 15 and 16 (my translation).
33 *Die Welt von gestern* (Frankfurt A. M.: Fischer Taschenb., 1974), p. 205.
34 *Life is Elsewhere*, tr. Peter Kussi (Faber, London, 1986), p. 194.

12
Another Civilization? An Other Civilization?
Milan Šimečka

I read Milan Kundera's article 'The Tragedy of Central Europe' in the *New York Review of Books* of 26 April 1984 at the beginning of summer. I remember noting how intelligently it was written and was pleased that our national 'story' was still capable of arousing interest. I also disagreed with him profoundly on a number of points. It is unlikely, though, that I would have returned to the article and discovered just how seriously I disagreed with it were it not for Lev Kopelev, a person I esteem highly for his thoughtfulness and unassuming wisdom. [...] It was in a lengthy report by Pavel Kohout on the election campaign of our old – new European parliamentarian [Šimečka seems to be referring to Jiří Pelikán, Member of the European Parliament for the Italian Socialist Party – Ed.] that I came across a reference to some meeting where Lev Kopelev had appealed to Milan Kundera not to exclude Russia from Europe. I realized that I would second such an appeal, even though, in view of the trials endured by Slavdom, my motives can only be intellectual.

The actual Central European tragedy is quite poignantly depicted by Kundera. He presents his American readers with a grandiose historical tableau of the Central European spiritual tradition, supported by all the names now familiar to us from his writing: Freud and Mahler, Bartók and Janáček, Musil and Broch, Kafka and Hašek, Gombrowicz, Miłosz, Palacky, Derý, etc. He demonstrates just how prolific was the cultural tradition of Central Europe – an entity so difficult to define – and how great a loss it is. In all events, he does a nice job of explaining to the Americans that there is no comparing the spiritual contribution made by the Central European nations ('the victims and outsiders of history') with the politically engendered sterility that occupies that area nowadays. He enlivens his article with an account of how the secret police confiscated a philosopher friend's 1,000 page-manuscript and adds a few choice and highly quotable phrases. He also frames hypothetical questions just as provocatively as he used to in the days when he would have us worrying our heads about whether it really had been worthwhile resuscitating the Czech language and literature in the nineteenth century. But what had he done to Russia to hurt even Kopelev's feelings?

I follow the trend and employ the term 'Russia' just like Kundera. That doesn't mean I like it, however, and I have avoided it for years, even though it is nice and short and much easier to type than Soviet Union. These days 'Russia' as an expression has clear ideological overtones. We're all of us aware how much of a distortion it is. Most seriously it involuntarily ignores the existence of all the other nations of the Soviet Union and tempts one to perceive Estonians and Armenians in terms of Pushkin and Dostoevsky. It's probably not altogether fair to isolate the Russian aspect of Kundera's article. I have in front of me the sentence in which Kundera excuses himself at the outset: 'but Russia isn't my subject and I don't want to wander into its immense complexities about which I am not especially knowledgeable'. The trouble is, how can one talk about Central Europe and not talk about Russia? Doesn't the tragedy of Central Europe derive precisely from being next-door neighbours of the Soviet Union in whose brotherly embrace we gasp for breath? On this score, Kundera leaves no one in any doubt that in his view Central Europe's membership of the West did not end until the post-war upheavals: 'the countries of Central Europe feel that the change in destiny that occurred after 1945, is not merely a political catastrophe: it is also an attack on their civilization.' As part of an explanation of the demise of the Central European spiritual tradition, this statement is not entirely correct. Kundera would have his American readers believe that the beginning of the end for Central Europe was when Russia came on to the scene.

I share Kundera's admiration for the Central European cultural tradition. I never fail to be moved when I discover that someone I have always taken to be a typical Westerner turns out to have been born somewhere in Galicia or Moravia, and that their grandparents migrated from place to place with my own grandparents within that bizarre 'prison of nations' which Austria-Hungary indeed was. I agree that the way nations here intermingled, and their influences, languages and traditions have intertwined, gave rise to some of Europe's supreme spiritual achievements. I agree that this old tradition was broken and that the political regimes which currently occupy this area deliberately suppress it. However, we should not disguise the fact that it was not Russia which ushered in the beginning of the end of the Central European tradition. It was Hitler who tore up by the roots that certain decency of political and cultural standards which the Central European nations managed to preserve more or less intact up to 1937. It was chiefly due to the insane acts of the Nazis that the nations of Central Europe became the victims and outsiders of history. It was Nazism, after all, which so effectively silenced the 'Jewish genius' which had been part and parcel of Central Europe's spiritual evolution. At the moment the tragedy of Central Europe began to unfold, Eastern influences were negligible or, at any rate, the Russian factor played scarcely no role at all. The cancer which finally put paid to what had gone before was nurtured on Western European history and fed on the decaying legacy of Western European intellectual innovations. That was the real succession of events: it was only the remnants of the old Central Europe that breathed their last in Russian arms. Let us not forget though that they consigned themselves there voluntarily – spiritual inclinations having been tempered by historical disappointment with the West and by utopian hopes. However, these hopes were to founder on Soviet power ambitions and everything else followed on from that.

We who live here in Central Europe have an historical alibi. We live in the awareness that our unhappy situation on the borders of two civilizations absolves us from the outset from any responsibility for the nation's fate. Try as we might, there is nothing we can do to help ourselves within the Russian sphere of influence. It's good to see how Kundera lets everyone know that we are not to blame for any of it: 'when the Russians occupied Czechoslovakia, they did everything possible to destroy Czech culture. This destruction had three meanings: first, it destroyed the centre of the opposition; second, it undermined the identity of the nation, enabling it to be more easily swallowed up by Russian civilization; third, it put a violent end to the modern era, the era in which culture still represented the realization of supreme values.'

I wouldn't like to say that this sentence is typical of Kundera's article, but it testifies nonetheless to a tendency to assign a demonic power to the Russians. We are not too distant from the events, however, to forget that it was not the Russians who put paid to Czech culture which seemed to be evolving so promisingly to us in the 1960s. It was our lot: Central Europeans born and bred. I'm under no illusions about the importance of the instructions and 'advice' received from the imperial centre (to borrow a phrase from György Konrád), but I saw with my own eyes how avidly our colleagues in culture, education and science set about the task of 'cleaning up' culture. Our spiritual Biafra bore an indelible local trademark. It had a very special local pungency too: envy, hopes for promotion, anticipation of rich pickings, fear, cowardice, short-lived solidarity, etc. And the people who have done so much in the past 15 years to spoil the lives of my friends and myself and hamper our efforts to salvage something of 'the authority of the thinking, doubting individual', all spoke Czech or Slovak; in fact, many of them I once knew, when they pretended to be friends of mine. We all share with Kundera the same memory, so he shouldn't be blaming *everything* on Russian civilization. It would be far better to tell the Americans that if ever (perish the thought), the Russians invade, it's not the Russians they should fear so much as their own compatriots. What is noteworthy about Central Europe is not that it has a Russian civilization but rather the variety of ways in which its nations have coped with Russian influence. Just a stone's throw away from us we have the Hungarians who have to put up with the same welter of instruction and 'advice', but still manage to live in a decent manner in a state of cultural tolerance and spiritual heterogeneity which continues almost strikingly the Central European tradition. And one scarcely need mention that after all the upheavals in Poland, things there would hardly seem to conform to Kundera's model of Russian civilization.

Kundera resurrects Solzhenitsyn's question about the relationship between Russia and Communism, but answers it differently. To the question, 'is Communism the negation of Russian history or its fulfilment?', he replies, 'it is both its negation (the negation for example of its religiosity) *and* its fulfilment (the fulfilment of its centralising tendencies and its imperial dreams).' At the same time, he adds that the Central European nations feel more powerfully the second aspect. Of course, one could go on discussing indefinitely the second point. But the discussion would have to go back to Peter the Great and the controversy between the Slavophiles and Westerners and deal with the cultural duality present in almost all Central European traditions. In Solzhenitsyn's view, communism is an evil Western import, whereas Kundera sees it as a system so totally russified and transformed by the Russian environment as by now to be utterly alien to Western traditions and Western thinking. In short, it has become virtually a Russian civilization. Kundera has confirmed the idea prevalent in the West that Communism is an incomprehensible Russian disease. Just to what degree Communism is Russified is a matter for academic debate: plenty of books have been written on the subject. All the same, I can't help feeling that the concept of Communism as 'Russian civilization' is no more than the primitive ideology of my daily newspaper stood on its head. I'd even go so far as to say that I find this particular 'book of forgetting' a trifle immoral. As a doctrine, Communism was cultivated in the West, researched in Germany, tested in combat in the French revolutions, and assigned to the shelves of the British Museum. As a former reader of Lenin's writings, I recall how Lenin used to strike me as particularly un-Russian. His ideological accent was that of Paris, London and Zurich. To forget all that seems to me as immoral as sending a new-born child to be brought up in foreign parts and then rejecting it when it doesn't behave as it should, when it speaks a foreign language and is hard to understand.

Likewise, we should not forget how a large proportion of European intellectuals looked on enthusiastically as Russia transformed the Western European legacy. It's no good pretending that it was obvious from the outset that the Russian experiment was doomed. If someone were to put together an anthology of the expressions of devotions which burgeoned among Western intellectuals, particularly in the 1930s, the younger generation would be amazed. No doubt the Soviets have to answer for the change in perception of their role in Europe, but the fact remains that, in terms of the regime's internal rigidity and the closed nature of Soviet society, Russia is no worse now than it was in the 1930s. Russia isn't worse, it's just more powerful and that's the whole problem. All the more reason, therefore, to heed the voice of common sense and not exclude Russia from Europe and European civilization. However, try as I might, I am unable to put any other construction on the following sentences from Kundera's article: 'on the Eastern border of the West – more than anywhere else – Russia is seen not just as one more European power but as a singular civilization, an *other* civilization ... totalitarian Russian civilization is the radical negation of the modern West, the West created four centuries ago at the dawn of the modern era: the era founded on the authority of the thinking, doubting individual, and on an artistic creation which expressed his uniqueness.' Were I a Russian, even an emigré Russian like Kopelev, not only would that sadden me, but I expect I'd also take offence. If Russian is an *other* civilization, then I suppose it means that all is hopeless: all one can do is sigh, like they used to in the days long before communism – 'East is East and West is West'.... Disparate civilizations inevitably are forced on to the defensive, and we here on the eastern border of the West will just have to go on dutifully playing our roles as the victims and outsiders of history.

Europe is undoutedly in a very bad state at the moment, and anyway, the Central European tragedy is not the only European tragedy ever. Europe has been a mass-producer of tragedies, and if things go on the way they are, we will be faced with the last and final one. The separation of Russia from Europe, even in a purely spiritual or cultural sense, doesn't improve Europe's chances one bit. The reconciliation of Russia and the West by whatever means of détente would be an act of self-preservation on Europe's part, and, in that sense, superior to the intellectual pastime of scoring points in a debate about whether Russia is a part of Europe or whether it represents a different civilization. I know the arguments of either side off by heart, but precisely because I live on the frontier of East and West, I choose of my own free will to employ those arguments which do not exclude Russia from Europe and do not widen the gulf. The decision freely to opt for the thesis that Russia does not represent another civilization has the added virtue of allowing one to examine dispassionately the processes involved in the Russian transformation of the Western European legacy and make out glimmers of hope. Of course it's no easy job keeping to this decision when state television undermines it day by day and unconsciously confirms Kundera's case. But when this happens, I pick up any Russian novel published here and have a read. Where else is one to find solace but in books?

Kundera's thesis about the area known as Central Europe makes good reading but I find it depressing because of the sense of hopelessness it fosters. The last thing I'd do would be to persuade the Americans that the East is the total negation of the West: some of them believe it anyway, just like some of the Russians, no doubt. It is more hopeful to stress Russia's European traditions, rather than its isolationist tendencies, which Kundera and I have both experienced. Without distorting the facts, there is no reason why the West should not accept the idea that the transformation of communism did more than anything else to bring Russia closer to Europe; Russia has endured one historical option which the West was preparing for itself and which, by chance, it has been spared. As a thinking, doubting individual living on the western border of the East, I would merely add that everything that the Europeans have brought upon themselves so far has been of their own contriving, and likewise, there can be no white-washing our responsibility for any future misfortunes either.

(Translated by A. G. Brain)

13
Is the Russian Intelligentsia European? (A Reply to Šimečka)
Jane Mellor

Šimečka has little respect for the academic debate about whether Russia is part of the West, or part of an other, Eastern tradition. Yet it is curious that although he makes this clear, he none the less employs academic argument to bolster his own cause as and when it serves his purpose. Indeed, the academic 'is' and the hypothetical 'ought' are totally confused in his article, so that by the end, the reader is left with no more than a plea for reconciliation between Russia and Europe, as 'an act of self-preservation on Europe's part' to ward off some final cataclysm.

Šimečka's motives may well be well-intentioned. To search for the common ground between Russian and the West, to reconcile (and obscure) such differences as exist between them, 'by whatever means of detente', may lessen the tensions within Europe and create a climate favourable to the re-emergence of cultural traditions independent of either superpower.

The facts of history and the meaning of a historical tradition, however, cannot be white-washed or wished away. If Šimečka wishes 'to choose of my own free will to employ those arguments which do not exclude Russia from Europe and do not widen the gulf' he is free to do so. But he is not helping anyone a jot to understand the problems, the possibilities and the limits of change in Central Europe, nor the depth and nature of the rich cultural traditions of this part of Europe. In the hope that 'what is not expressed does not exist', he is merely creating more 'memory holes', as the only way to make the uncomfortable facts fit the more pleasant mould of detente.

Detente is in fact a key word here. What this term meant in the 1970s to the USSR and what it implied to the West were very different, and it was precisely because the West could not understand the Soviet meaning given to it that the USSR was able to capitalize on this, and turn detente into a monopoly of foreign policy initiatives and benefits. This misperception by the

West goes beyond semantics, and underlies a huge difference in norms and values which it is foolhardy to obscure.

Indeed, it borders on irresponsibility to deny the deep gulf which exists between the dominant Russian tradition, which is characterized above all by a monism and an exclusivism towards other competing ideas, and the markedly more pluralistic tradition of the West. The Western tradition, for all its seeming anarchy and waste, its perpetual conflict and argument, draws its strength from these elements. It is very different indeed from the stress on unity, coherence and intolerance of alternatives which are central to the Russian tradition, whether one is talking of Lenin or of Solzhenitsyn.

The academic debate as to whether Russia is part of the West remains as relevant as ever. Šimečka finds it both 'cheap and immoral' to see Communism as something totally Russified. He argues that Communism derived from Western ideas and that Lenin was himself 'particularly un-Russian'. Moreover, from the fact that many in Central Europe and in the West welcomed Communism in the early days after the Second World War, he infers that Communism and Russia were not perceived as alien phenomena. Yet this is a spurious argument. Lenin, un-Russian?! The idea is so absurd that Šimečka cannot expect it to be regarded as anything other than an intellectual joke.

The genesis and development of the Russian intelligentsia in the nineteenth century, which spawned Lenin and the ideas to which he subscribed are, in my view, the clearest expression of the differences between East and West. Marx was indeed a Westerner, a German, who derived his models from very Western sources. Yet the character of the social formations (the bourgeoisie in the West, the intelligentsia in Russia) which carried these and earlier 'utopian socialist' ideas had a profound impact on the way they were understood and implemented. In the West, the bourgeoisie and later the working class which took up 'radical' thought had a *practical* inclusive role in society, be it an undesirable and inhumane one, which nevertheless added a realism about the nature and depth of change possible.

In Russia, the intelligentsia was, by definition, a group of men and women without a role in the given order, 'wandering Hamlets', to use Herzen's graphic phrase, with a profound dislike of Western economic systems. It is a curious feature of nineteenth century Russian intelligentsia thought that although Western ideas and literature were avidly sought after, the economic and political niceties of change were obscured in favour of an emphasis on chiliastic elements and ontological philosophical discussions. In this way Chernyshevsky could read the whole of *L'Organisation du travail* and comment more on the evils of capitalism than on the viability of Proudhon's economic blueprint. Because the Russian intelligentsia became more alienated as the century went on, the debate about change and revolution necessarily became more abstract and philosophical, further from the constraints of reality and the more convictions took root about the possibilities afforded by the 'proper' socialization and creation of universal Man.

As already argued, the Russian intelligentsia, which worked out and elaborated both new and Western ideas about the future of Russia, was, *a priori*, a group of men and women without a role in the given order. When Catherine the Great broke historical tradition by relieving the nobility of mandatory state service, she inadvertently created the conditions for the slow but sure growth of an independent, critical line of thought, which before long would be directed toward the overthrow of the centralized state over which she and her heirs presided. The group which emerged, the intelligentsia, was therefore aristocratic by origin, and although 'intelligents' made it a *sine qua non* of their new position as critics of the regime to break family ties, and deride their own traditional class value, inevitably they carried with them the strong sense of class, family, culture and loyalty to the Russian state with which they had been imbued for centuries.

Once cut adrift from the all-embracing body of the Russian state and from service in the bureaucracy, the self-styled 'intelligents' found themselves alienated and powerless. The radical ideas flooding in from Western Europe were read with alacrity, particularly after Russia's Crimean defeat, yet the intelligentsia felt powerless to act in the face of the Russian Leviathan. The timing of the intelligentsia's formative years, the 1940s and 1950s, is important too; the main body of thought emanating from the West consisted of a harsh critique of capitalism, its immorality and cruelty. This was compounded in the Russian intelligentsia's view by the 1848 'betrayal' of the working class by the Western Liberals in France and Germany, and the seeming hypocrisy of parliamentary and other institutional forms in their claims to safeguard the people's interests. The intelligentsia then represented from the outset a *moral* revolt against the evils of capitalism and this included those who saw it as an inevitable stage for Russia. At the same time, it pushed them towards looking to recreate in a consensual vision of Russian society the strong sense of fraternity, loyalty, duty and equality that they had experienced as a class, but without the dichotomy of us/them that had made the aristocracy possible.

This notion of 'alienation', which accompanied the formation of the intelligentsia, is pivotal in understanding both Russian thought and how Western ideas were transmuted as they passed onto Russian soil. The intelligentsia's initial sense of psychological alienation led to an all-pervasive 'quest for self', which was mirrored endlessly in its assessment of Russia's problems and how to overcome them, in the strength of its obsession with Russia's historical past and culture, and in an overwhelming sense of guilt towards 'the people', the *narod*, whose labours had made possible the knowledge and high culture of the 'intelligents'.

In turn, the ideas generated by this group reflected the single, underlying idea, that lost, alienated powers (rather than mere economic ills or some formal malfunctioning of the political mechanism), were the key evil in Russia and in the West, and the sense that to discharge its *guilt* towards the *narod*, to do its *duty*, the intelligentsia must struggle to find the way forward towards an equitable future for Russia. (The self-inflicted asceticism of the men of the 1860s, the idea of total revolutionary dedication, are both in some way part of this attempt to share the *narod's* suffering and to identify better with them.)

The quest for identification with 'the *narod*' in Russian Populism, the anarchism and messianic calls for change attest to the psychological malaise and alienation; even the sense in which 'democracy' was understood was particularly Russian, eschewing formal mechanisms and legal safeguards and counting instead on the spiritual symbiosis of all Russians. The Russian Liberals, with their stress on poverty, law, parliament and individualism were in this sense the oddballs in the Conservative, Liberal Radical/Socialist troika. The majority were in government service rather than rootless 'intelligents', and Liberal thought within the intelligentsia was branded, by association with the hypocritical meliorism of the bourgeoisie in the West, and the betrayal of the workers in 1848. It is clear that there was a very high level of abstraction and detachment from reality in Russian thought and a corresponding disbelief in half measures; power arrogated by the state to itself, could and would be totally reabsorbed by the people. The 'how' remained unanswered.

The only acceptable professions for these sons of nobles were either in teaching or publishing, both of which added an academic, literary quality to the Great Russian Debate which, in retrospect, seems so far from the immediate and practical demands for economic betterment by bourgeois or working-class spokesmen in the West. Such conditions meant that Russian thought included a very high level of abstraction and philosophy with little need to test them (when they did, as in the *To the People* movements of the 1870s, the dislocation between thought and reality was all too obvious), and as the prospects of organic, incremental change grew less likely as the nineteenth century wore on, the need to adapt ideas to present conditions lessened, the philosophical 'ideal type' was confused further with everyday 'reality' and the expectation of what change could achieve grew increasingly.

These particular circumstances of the Russian intelligentsia and its many impracticable ideals were reinforced by the problems facing Russia as a 'backward' country. Due to pressures on late developing societies, the role of the native intelligentsia is often both enhanced and diminished. Enhanced, because as old values become inappropriate for new needs of society, increased communications and literacy allow new groups to rally around values which did not previously exist; diminished, because the state tends to respond to the new centrifugal pressures it has to face by increasing central control over society in an attempt to maintain order, and thereby fuel radical grievances. Such a pattern of events was certainly evident in Russia.

Lenin's achievement was to blend the modern, i.e. impersonal, change oriented, universal norms, with the abstract messianic *Weltanschauung* of the intelligentsia, and to do so in a language comprehensible to the Russian people. Firstly, Lenin offered the radical intelligentsia a role. Through his commitment to a Vanguard Party, his stress on strict discipline and organization, and the promise of 'inevitable' success, Lenin showed a way to overcome the paralysis of alienation, as well as the guilt and moral dilemmas of the 'intelligents', by means of offering this foolproof and ultimately *moral* means of *engagement*.

Secondly, he retained the abstract, philosophical views of futurity and change (*malgré lui?*), and spoke to the intelligentsia in their own language. In his clearest delineation of the future form of society, in *State and Revolution*, the 'state' is clearly far from any Western concept of 'state' with its anarchical view of democracy and illusory notions about the economics of society. Yet this blend of Western elements into a Russian situation, in such a way as to appeal to the harbingers of change, the 'intelligents', was Lenin's genius; his success derived from his being at the end of the day, a Russian.

So in the light of the foregoing, the Communism of Lenin and his Bolshevik followers must be seen as a specifically Russian answer to specifically Russian problems. This is not an argument about the rights or wrongs of different variants of Communism or of the Russian tradition, but is set forth to illustrate the vast difference between Russia and the West, large enough in fact to denote Russia as *another* civilization. By agreeing with Kundera, I would be arguing that it was the imposition of this one variant – a Russian variant, of Communism upon Central Europe that constituted and constitutes the rape of the long, rich, spiritual and cultural traditions of this diverse area of Europe.

14
Who Excluded Russia from Europe?
(A Reply to Šimečka)
Mihály Vajda

'Lev Kopelev had appealed to Milan Kundera not to exclude Russia from Europe' (Milan Šimečka). My question is whether it was Milan Kindera, or Russia itself which did so. I think I esteem Lev Kopelev just as highly for his thoughtfulness and unassuming wisdom as Milan Šimečka does. I cannot, however, accept the civilization or culture of that country as a European one, as long as it fails to respect those who think in another way, as long as it also tries to expel from itself all 'Europeans', among others Lev Kopelev himself. I do not deny that there are and were many 'European' Russians. But as long as their fate is the holocaust, imprisonment, banishment, exile, or, at best humiliation and neglect, not even one of the finest of them can convince me that the culture or civilization of that country as a whole is a European one. Admittedly, even a non-Russian European can be fond of Russia – an argument of Milan Šimečka's to which we shall later return. Moreover, he or she may do everything in order to make of his or her beloved Russia a European country (this was, I think, even a possible alternative in earlier decades); nonetheless, this does not alter the fact that in Russia one cannot find the main features of the civilization we call European. Russia, in Kundera's words, 'reveals its terrifying foreignness' to us. And, citing him again (and it is a pity that Šimečka neglects to quote this most important sentence, without which the whole meaning of Kundera's essay would be something else): 'I don't know if it is worse than ours, but I do know it is different.'

European civilization is a notion which is not so difficult to define, even if the different national cultures within it are very different from each other in many respects. The leading value of Europe is *freedom*, conceived – more and more – in a very simple and understandable way: namely, as the freedom of the individual limited only by that of others. This does not mean, of course, that the notion 'freedom of community' has no meaning for this civilization. A community is free if it renders possible the freedom of its members. The individual should thus submit to the common goals of the community if – but only if – these enhance the free initiative of individuals, the condition of which is that such goals are democratically accepted by the community. Behind this notion of freedom lies, of course, the interpretation of the human being as a rational being, who is fully capable of deciding on his or her own affairs, as well as on those of the community. This means from the outset that this form of civilization is dynamic, that it dissolves its own traditions again and again (that is, the possibility is not excluded that at some time or another it will abolish its key traditions, and thus itself). This is not the place to explain how the development of this civilization of free individuals has led *necessarily* to the separation of state and civil society – a more and more characteristic feature of this civilization as a whole.

I am aware of the fact that my very sketchy notion of 'Europe' is not absolutely identical with that of Kundera. He has, in my view, the inclination to idealize this civilization. The above definition, examined closely, does not exclude some possibilities which are anything but ideal from a European point of view (and who would or could deny that even modern European history – the above definition sees Europe as realized only in modern times – has produced in abundance abhorrent events and states of affairs). This fact itself, namely, that the main value of this civilization has almost always been realized in a partly self-contradictory form (and I am almost convinced that it *cannot* be otherwise), explains why European intellectuals could anticipate the 'redemption' of their own world by Russia, by a civilization which (unlike Europe) had not been 'spoiled' by individualism. Milan Šimečka is surely right when he states: 'We should not forget how a large proportion of European intellectuals looked on enthusiastically as Russia transformed the Western European legacy.' Only the meaning of the sentence is something other than the one Šimečka wishes to give it. This transformation was *not a development, but an annihilation* of this legacy, and this large number of European intellectuals looked on enthusiastically *precisely because of this fact.*

Before examining each of Šimečka's arguments in turn, I would like to raise a question which I am not sure I can answer. Why are most Europeans terrified at the very moment someone wants to state or prove that another nation also has another culture, another form of civilization? Even before reading Šimečka's article, I had had arguments with Hungarian friends who wanted to convince me that Kundera was, unfortunately, anti-Russian, a position which one could of course understand, but not condone. Is Kundera, indeed, anti-Russian? Reading, and re-reading his very elegant essay I could not find a trace of this alleged anti-Russian attitude. He evidently cannot accept not only the occupation of East-Central Europe by Russian troops; the main tragedy of this part of Europe is, in his view, that as a result of this occupation, East-Central Europe is forced to accept a political system which does not correspond to the European character of its civilization. My friends and seemingly, Milan Šimečka, are as little pleased with the military occupation of this part of Europe and the system forced on it by the Soviet Union, as Milan Kundera. They want to believe, however, that the system forced on Poles, Czechs, Slovaks and Hungarians (and other nations of the East-Central European socialist countries) is just as unacceptable to the Russians as to them, just as alien to Russian civilization as it is to these nations. I do not want to demonstrate here that this is not true (though I am convinced, with Milan Kundera, that it is not). I would only like to know why it is almost impossible to discuss the problem even with those (or, above all with those) for whom it is a life and death question whether we can or cannot preserve our Europeanness.

The answer lies, in my view, in the false univeralistic claims of European rationalism which cannot accept that the free individual (and, as a consequence, a free society) is not an inalienable feature of human beings, but *a chosen value*. The enlightened European has always been afraid to acknowledge that there have been cultures where freedom has not been a value (or, at least, not a leading value), because he/she thinks that to admit this is to deny the dignity of others. As I see it, just the opposite is true. If freedom is an inalienable feature of human beings, then in all those cultures where freedom seems not to be among the main values, people have let themselves be deprived of their human dignity. Just because freedom is a universal value *for us*, we contradict this main value if we judge and condemn all those who have chosen other values. Every civilization has the right to be an *other* without being conceived by us as less human, or inferior.

On the other hand, we Europeans are surely justified in defending ourselves against civilizations which do not want to acknowledge our right to choose our own values. Up to this point everything is clear. Now we have arrived, however, at a point where things begin to become obscure, and the universalistic claims of European rationalism seem to justify themselves. Lev Kopelev, having appealed to Milan Kundera not to exclude Russia from Europe, surely had good reasons for doing so. For if, on the one hand, he accepts the thesis that Russia is an *other* civilization, and, as a European-minded Russian, accepts the right of his own country to preserve this other culture and not to accept European values, then, on the other hand, he effectively justifies those who banned him from his own country! Is there really, then, no justification of those who want to defend from the outside the rights of a minority inside a civilization which does not accept the existence of minority rights at all? Or, more precisely, is the only justification to declare our own values to be universally valid, thus identifying

Europeanness with humanity as a whole?

The encounter between different civilizations has always been difficult. However it is a tragic situation only for those cultures which acknowledge the right of other cultures to be 'other', but are then compelled to struggle against the threat which the latter may pose. The tight independence of all human beings of our planet (a phenomenon of our age created certainly by the technological means of European civilization!) has deepened this tragedy to a degree which is almost intolerable. There is no theoretical – even less a practical – solution to the problem which would be acceptable to the European conscience. In my opinion, it is nonetheless more honest (intellectually as well as morally) to confess that we want to defend all those who have chosen our civilization as against their own, than to universalize our own values by appealing to a God in whom we no longer believe. The theory of natural rights does not function without the support of a Christian faith. God is dead, traditions are alterable, values are valid only where they have been chosen.

The case of Russian civilization is, of course, not identical with that of other, even geographically non-European cultures. Russia had and has much in common with Europe (a fact Kundera does not deny and even emphasizes). That is why for centuries and until recent times it remained an open question which path Russia would take: a European one, or another. I am almost convinced that after the death of Stalin, an alternative was still open (or was once more re-opened), and that the choice to become non-European was finally made only in the last decades. If one takes this fact into consideration, then it should come as no surprise that in Russia there are many more 'Europeans' than in other non-European civilizations, even if these 'Europeans' are in a minority. European values, a European spirit, is not an import article there. This is not a minority which has chosen something absolutely alien to its own culture. It is a minority which could have become a majority, a minority which did not revolt against its own civilization, but which wanted to transform it – and was defeated in centuries of struggle. The European spirit in Russia is not a product of European intervention (as it is in the case of most other civilizations). And if there is an oppressed European Russia, and we Europeans consider it not only our right but our duty to defend it, then we should have the courage to admit that we are defending its members because they are European, and not because they are in the right. A conflict of cultures – who could deny it?

In the case of those Central European nations which, before being occupied by the Russians, were already European or at least were in the process of becoming European, (their revolts against the imposed system is the clearest proof of this fact), there is no place for any kind of moral doubt. One can say that the sovereignty of Western nations is limited by their belonging to the

American-led Western alliance. This is a problem in itself, to be sure. But none of these nations has been obliged to give up its genuine civilization in the manner of the Poles, Czechs and Hungarians. Kundera is perhaps more bitter than anyone else, though I can understand why. The process of annihilation of genuine culture went further in Bohemia than anywhere else – perhaps precisely because it was among the most European of Central European cultures.

At least this is my conviction, and one I share with Kundera. I do not want to dwell on this further here, but I do want to scrutinize whether Šimečka's arguments support the opposite view. His arguments are as follows:

1. To use the term 'Russia' instead of the 'Soviet Union', though the former is 'nice and short and much easier to type', has clear ideological overtones: 'it involuntarily ignores the existence of all the other nations of the Soviet Union and tempts one to perceive Estonians and Armenians in terms of Pushkin and Dostoevsky.'

Was it Šimečka or Kundera who wanted to call attention to the fact that 'one of the great European nations (there are nearly 40 million Ukrainians) is slowly disappearing'? (Milan Kundera, 'The Tragedy of Central Europe', *New York Review of Books*, 26 April 1984, p. 33). The term 'Russia' has, indeed, clear ideological overtones. It means that the country officially called the Soviet Union is not a free Union of free nations, but a centralized imperium led (and oppressed) by Russians who want to 'Russianize' the whole. Such a statement may be called into question, and if Šimečka does not agree with it, he should refute it. But instead of doing so, he laments Kundera's ignorance about Russia.

2. Šimečka agrees that the old tradition of Central Europe 'was broken and that the political regimes which currently occupy this area deliberately suppress it. However ... it was not Russia', he says, 'which ushered in the beginning of the end of the Central European tradition. It was chiefly due to the insane acts of the Nazis that the nations of Central Europe became the victims and outsiders of history ... it was only the remnants of the old Central Europe that breathed their last in Russian arms.'

As far as I know the Nazi movement was born in Germany. The first European country which the Nazis 'incorporated' into the Third Reich was Austria, and German troops occupied Paris before Budapest. Why is it, then, that the outcome of their terrible deeds had protracted influence only in that part of Central Europe which now belongs to the Russian Imperium? Let me take only the Hungarian example. Hungary has never been a democratic country. If there was a real opportunity for this finally to happen, then it was after the Second World War when the traditional ruling strata were totally compromised by their alliance with the Nazis. This left Hungary as a corporate entity without a ruling stratum and ruling institutions – a curious historical event. The only obstacle preventing Hungary from becoming a democracy following the collapse of the Nazi regime was the Russian occupation.

3. Continuing this line of argument, Milan Šimečka also stresses: 'it was Nazism, after all, which so effectively silenced the "Jewish genius" which had been part and parcel of Central Europe's spiritual evolution.'

This is surely true, but Kundera does not claim otherwise. And it is also true that, with some exceptions, the communist regimes did everything to silence the remaining Jews (witness Poland 1968!).

4. Kundera's article, according to Šimečka, 'testifies to a tendency to assign a demonic power to the Russians ... it was not the Russians that put paid to Czech culture.... It was our lot: Central Europeans born and bred.' Milan Šimečka witnessed with his own eyes how avidly his colleagues in the spheres of culture, education and science set about the task of 'cleaning up' culture. The Russians gave only instructions and 'advice'.

These innocent instructions and advice were, of course, supported by some tanks but, without Czechs and Slovaks, they could not have been executed. However Šimečka neglects to explain why it was necessary – in a situation where instructions were backed by tanks – to expel half a million people from Czech culture before the regime could find those who would assume the task of cleaning up culture. I want to stress that I also view collaborators as no better – they are even worse – than invaders. But without invaders there cannot be collaborators.

5. Šimečka has one further argument to support his case, especially concerning point 4. This concerns Hungarians 'who still manage to live in a decent manner in a state of cultural tolerance and spiritual heterogenity which continues almost strikingly the Central European tradition.'

It must surely reflect primarily on the Czechoslovak state if Hungarian life appears so idyllic from the vantage point of Bratislava. This is not the place to argue about Kádár's Hungary. That my country is more tolerable than Šimečka's could only be denied by someone with no sense of reality whatsoever. Šimečka's next sentence, however, explaining why this is so, proves just the opposite of what he seemingly intended: 'and one scarcely need mention that after all the upheavals in Poland, things there would hardly seem to conform to Kundera's model of Russian civilization.' I hope Šimečka is right. But if upheavals are necessary in order to be able to live under Russian occupation in a form which is not absolutely identical with the life-form of Russia (though in its main features very similar to it), this fact proves only that Russians are incapable of tolerating another civilization, an other form of life in that part of the world which 'belongs' to them. And this is one of the main features of Russian culture: it is, as Kundera writes, 'uniform, standardizing, centralizing.' If today Hungary is in some *important* respects different from the Russian model, then it is the consequence of the 1956 revolution, of the biggest upheaval Russians have ever experienced inside their post-Second World War imperium.

6. Šimečka states that 'cultural duality' is 'present in almost all Central European traditions.'

This is an undeniable fact (though less true of the Czechs). But the periodically recurring upheavals in Central Europe, the (at least implicit) aim of which is the creation of a Western type of democracy, have proven that Poles, Czechs and Hungarians have opted for the Western tradition. The total petrification characterizing the rigid, centralized, hierarchical system in the Soviet Union indicates that the Russian choice was the opposite.

7. Šimečka believes that in Kundera's view, communism has become virtually identical with Russian civilization. I can't help feeling, he says, that the concept of communism as 'Russian civilization' is a trifle immoral. One should not forget, he continues, that as a doctrine 'communismn was cultivated in the West, researched in Germany, tested in combat in the French revolutions, and assigned to the shelves of the British Museum.'

No one could deny that this communism cited by Šimečka, and the contemporary version are interrelated. But is it simply a historical accident that in *geographical* Europe, it was only in Russia that communism was *realized* without the use of external force?

8. As I have mentioned already, Šimečka writes of the erstwhile enthusiasm of many European intellectuals as Russia transformed the legacy of Western Europe.

Once again, this admission is not a refutation, but a proof of Kundera's thesis. The majority of these intellectuals saw in Russia a redeeming force against a spoiled, rotten Western civilization. Yes, one could put together an anthology of expressions of devotion which burgeoned among Western intellectuals, particularly in the 1930s. While I certainly cannot share their faith in redemption, I am shocked, indeed, that anyone would want to use the naive faith of those men and women (how many of them died in the Gulag having fled to the Soviet Union from Nazism?) in order to prove ... finally, I don't know what. Šimečka writes: 'Russia is no worse now that it was in the 1930s.' Alright. And then? What follows? If there were thousands upon thousands of European intellectuals who looked enthusiastically on the Russia of the Gulag (mostly because they did not know what was happening there, or because they wanted to share Lukács' horrible faith formulated by him with the words of Hebbel: 'and if God has put sin between me and the deed imposed on me – who am I that I could back out of it?'), are we obliged in turn to be enthusiastic in the knowledge that Russia is better today than it was in those times?

9. 'If Russia is an *other* civilization, then I suppose it means that all is hopeless: all one can do is sigh, like they used to in the days long before communism – "East is East and West is West."'

The statement that all is hopeless may be true, or it may be false. But the hopelessness or hopefulness of our situation has nothing to do with its theoretical description. Is Russia an other civilization, or is it European (only suppressed, together with other nations of East-Central Europe, by the communist regime)? Regardless of how this question is answered, we East-Central Europeans must do something to safeguard the possibility of remaining Europeans – if Europeans we wish to remain. Kundera is surely right: the task is almost hopeless if even the West is inclined to forget what the meaning of Europe is.

10. 'The separation of Russia from Europe, even in a purely spiritual or cultural sense, doesn't improve Europe's chances one bit. The reconciliation of Russia and the West *by whatever means* of detente [my emphasis] would be an act of self-preservation on Europe's part and, in that sense, superior to the intellectual pastime of scoring points in a debate about whether Russia is a part of Europe or whether it represents a different civilization ... It is more hopeful to stress Russia's European traditions, rather than its isolationist tendencies, which Kundera and I have both experienced.'

The point at last becomes clear: please, do not annoy the beast on our borders with this intellectual hair-splitting. If you increase its feelings of inferiority it will be more aggressive than it has been. It will return to the politics of the cold war years. I suppose this is the central meaning of Šimečka's article. At this point, however, I do not wish to argue further. I have been trained neither as an animal tamer, nor as a politician. But I am convinced that we will suffer the worst intellectual and moral catastrophe if we let ourselves be guided by so-called tactical considerations. If we think the truth is harmful, we would do better to remain silent.

15
Which Way Back to Europe? (A Reply to Mihály Vajda)
Milan Šimečka

Budapest is three and a half hours away from Bratislava by train. It's a journey I myself once made – back in the mid-1960s. Many people continue to go that way to Budapest with no problems, mostly on shopping trips. For those of us who don't go on shopping excursions but instead worry our heads about the future of Central Europe, communication is not quite so simple, as can be judged from the fact that it was many moons before I got to know that my comments about Kundera's piece had been published in the *East European Reporter*, and many more before I was able to read Mihály Vajda's critical reactions to my views. Moreover, further long months will certainly pass before Vajda gets to know my response. A rather intermittent dialogue, but thank God the opportunity exists at all.

The pauses in the dialogue have at least served some useful purpose, though. Over the past year, the subject of our debate – that 'other civilization' – has, like some enormous beast, been rolling from side to side, trying to find a more comfortable position, and I hope against hope that it will end up facing in Europe's direction. I don't believe, of course, that the civilization in question is doing it for my sake, so that in my debate with Kundera and Vajda I should have further arguments to back up my plea for Russia not to be excluded from Europe.

In reading Vajda's objections to my arguments I am startled to find myself suddenly cast as a champion of 'Russian civilization.' It doesn't pay me to be one – quite the opposite, rather. I feel that there is part of me that is capable of accepting all the arguments that Vajda wields against my assertions. The fact is that I'm capable of taking an even more gloomy view than he: after all, I vividly recall the mind-shattering effect of watching that 'other civilization' in action in August 1968. In trying to trace the origins of my present state of mind, I have quite honestly failed to find any hidden motive for my apparent Russophile tendencies. Unless, that is, you count the fact that I was once a student of Russian and can still recall my enchantment with Russian literature. What is more, these days I am a bit of an eccentric in that I continue to read the better portion of Soviet literature. Not long ago, I even started watching Soviet TV. The list of my favourite authors only half tallies with the one Kundera included in his article. Dare I admit that I only read *The Man without Qualities*[1] so as not to have a gap in my education? On the other hand, I'll never forget the thrill I got from reading Bulgakov.

I doubt that this has any substantial bearing on my attitude to the 'other civilization', though. My concern lies elsewhere, and Vajda reveals it at the end of his article. It is in the fact that in discussions of this type I am incapable of ignoring the practical-political aspects. It is my belief that it is part of our 'dissi-pline' here in Eastern Europe to think in terms of practical politics, whether we like it or not. And it was above all my awareness of this obligation that straightaway made me wary of Kundera and raised my suspicions about an argument conducted exclusively on the intellectual plane. It also put me on my guard against his persuasive, though biased, choice of evidence and his elegant construction of an intelligent micro-ideology. After all, we are all aware how people read things. They are not going to appreciate Kundera's judicious choice of phrase nor the moderation of his language. What they will fall for essentially is the uncomplicated idea of a 'different' civilization. It is something that automatically saves people the trouble of going more deeply into the origins of that civilization and the historical influences on it. It is for this self-same reason that even now I would take issue – albeit mildly – with Mihály Vajda.

EUROPE: OUR VISION AND THE REALITY

Kundera is from here, Vajda is from here and I am from here – i.e. the East. We are all marked by the experience of occupied nations. We all realize that that is the main cause of our thirst for freedom which people in the West sometimes find hard to understand. Unhappily, since it is largely an intellectual phenomenon, it makes little sense to many of our 'normal' fellow-citizens either. If it did, they would hardly stay so mutely submissive or retain their healthy appetites. That's why our dreams about Europe are almost entirely one-dimensional: that dimension being freedom and tolerance towards people with different ideas. There is only one of Europe's values that fascinates us, and it is one we regard as somehow the core of the European idea: 'the leading value of Europe is freedom, conceived – more and more – in a very simple and understandable way: namely, as the freedom of the individual limited only by that of others.' I am 100 per cent in favour of

Europe's leading value thus formulated, but I think it is unfair for it to be used ahistorically as a stick to beat a society that developed in quite different historical conditions.

Vajda knows as well as I do that such a formulation of Europe's highest value tends to be used in the West mostly as a refrain in official speeches. However, if you take the intellectual expression of 'Europeanness', it is ferociously critical – almost incredibly so, in fact. When I was reading the speeches of several writers at a meeting of the US PEN Club, there were moments when I felt uneasy at just how incommensurate our experiences are. I don't intend to argue with their experience; the best we can do is say to them: 'if you don't like things over there, try living here and see what you think.'

Vajda is naturally aware that Europe has not always been guided by respect for its 'leading value', and he himself writes that 'even modern European history.... has produced in abundance abhorrent events and states of affairs.' Europe truly has not always been an oasis of freedom. Rather it has always been a Faustian kitchen in which all the good and evil essences of the human spirit have happily hubbled and bubbled away side by side. Does one have to point out that the Russian Revolution was the direct consequence of one of Europe's most terrifying catastrophes? Naturally it no longer forms part of our own personal experience, but were our forebears lying to us when they were overcome with horror and disgust at the memory of how Europeans slaughtered each other in the trenches of the First World War? And at that time it was not a matter of freedom to think differently, but quite simply freedom to speak a different language. If we are to juxtapose Europe and that 'different civilization', then we should use a true picture of Europe, particularly if we intend to refer to Russia's past, as Milan Kundera does in his essay. I quite simply don't like the fact that Kundera's representation of Europe contains hardly a whiff of that malodorous excretion of the European spirit that was Nazism.

When placed side to side with Russia, Europe can in no way be passed off as a vestal virgin. It will detract not a jot from the value or importance of Europe's contribution to the experience of freedom if we present all the contradictory features of European development, of which 'Russian civilization' is one component. There is no way that Europe will stay for ever divided; sooner or later, the Soviet Union is going to join the debate about Europe. But discussion with the newcomer will be no easy matter if all we do is to demonstrate, wrongly, that he was always someone different, someone evil, while Europe was ever spotless.

GUILTLESS NATIONS?

Though it is never expressed in so many words in our discussion, all of us – Kundera, Vajda and I – make the assumption that were it not for Soviet influence, the Central European nations would be integrated into Europe just like their Western neighbours. We assume that in the absence of Soviet occupation we would have proceeded directly, in friendship and peace, to fulfil the European ideal. The trouble is, that after the war we were not the people we are now, and we have come to European ideals only as a result of our actual historical experience.

No doubt most people in Czechoslovakia imagined that we would resume the exemplary path of Masarykian democracy and merely endow it with greater social justice. All the political parties, the Communists included, vowed to take such a course. If it hadn't have been for the Russians! Vajda presumes the same about Hungary: 'The only obstacle preventing Hungary from becoming a democracy following the collapse of the Nazi regime was the Russian occupation.' If it hadn't have been for the Russians! I'm sure that the Poles also believe they would have created a model democracy. If it hadn't have been for the Russians! The same goes for the Rumanians and the Bulgarians, not to mention the Yugoslavs who managed to achieve the dictatorship of the proletariat in the absence of Russian occupation.

It is just possible – but only just – that things might not have taken that course, but it would most likely have required the Western powers to have kept an eye on developments here. The awful thing is that there is no way we can prove it. What can be proved is that, after the war, the Central European nations were neither particularly mature, nor quite as innocent as Kundera would have us think. There was nothing dove-like about them, as the Czech historian Milan Hauner has pointed out in an article (in the Paris-based journal *Svědectví*) which also reacts to Kundera's position. After all, none of us is unaware how things were in our part of the world, with everyone trying to grab as much as they could for themselves and take advantage of their good relations with the major allies. The 'leading value' in those days was the 'national interest', so-called – not internal freedom. A plan for a Czechoslovak-Polish federation was mooted while the war was still raging, but neither side took it seriously, and the Czechoslovak government subsequently bent over backwards to out-rival the Poles for Stalin's favours. In the end it was Stalin who mediated in the dispute over the Těšín[2] region. His greatness grew and grew when he consented to the expulsion of the Germans.[3] I don't have to remind Vajda that Czechoslovak democrats tried very hard to make the Hungarians[4] share that same fate. Many disputes remained unsolved until settled by 'internationalist' decree. This charming Central Europe of ours provided the setting for executions galore. And while some people suffered confiscation to universal acclaim, others fought tooth and nail to get themselves off to the best possible start in the new era. What evidence do we really have for us to judge how we might have been, if it hadn't been for the Russians?

It gives me no particular pleasure to evoke the memory of all this. It's far more pleasant to pass oneself off as a guiltless nation which would show the world if it only got the chance. I just think that it serves a purpose – if only a therapeutic one – to be reminded that a lot of the evil was of our own creation, and one of the reasons why the influence of the 'other civilization' was so effective was because, to a certain extent, we provided it with fertile soil. I have read quite a bit about the interesting period when the Hungarian communists came to power. Did their bloodthirsty deeds derive from the logic of the power struggle or was it done on Stalin's advice? What made Rakosi egg Gottwald on to murder his comrades? What did 'Russian civilization' have to do with the brutal way in which the Czechoslovak Communists, in the wake of their victory, treated their opponents of other political parties with whom they had socialized in the pre-war parliaments? What made them resort to executions? The Poles didn't, even though they were under the same influence.

There are plenty of mysteries in the Central European closet and they can't all be explained in terms of the Russian occupation. That was what I had in mind when I criticized Kundera's 'demonization' of Russian influence. Moreover, I believe that, should we return to Europe, we would be received with greater trust were we to show a readiness to share the blame for our own past. I believe that Germany's integration into the European community has been so successful precisely because the Germans – whether voluntarily or because they were obliged to – have analysed their own guilt more thoroughly than any nation before them in history. There is nothing for it but for us to accept our history in the form we helped make it. There is no way we will ever manage to calculate precisely the degree of foreign influence within it. (Incidentally, there has been the odd occasion in the course of our history where one can even point to a certain degree of success.)

In this connection, I have a feeling that Vajda tends to make light of the Hungarian contribution to the Europeanization of our part of the world over the past 30 years.

In saying this, I do admit that Bratislava is not the best vantage point from which to assess the specifics of the Hungarian case, but unfortunately I have no other. Vajda should be capable of imagining, though, just how attractive the Hungarian cultural scene has looked to us for years now. Were the sort of meeting that our Hungarian colleagues organized on the fringes of the Budapest conference to be held here all of a sudden, without notice, the unexpected joy would cause us severe shock.[5] I believe that the Hungarians have made the best possible use of the era of limited opportunities and are, out of the Central European nations, the most well prepared for European rapprochement. The process of national reconciliation has attained such a level that future development will not be determined by the sort of tense and deeply ingrained fear of political reprisals which is at the root of Czechoslovakia's present stagnation. The power elite here may well trust in the deep-seated non-violence and moderation of the Charter's representatives and of their intellectual groups, but they suspect the mysterious threat that people's mute indifference conceals.

However important Soviet influence has been over the past 40 years, the differences that now exist between the individual Central European nations are of their own making.

I am writing these lines just a few days after learning that Sakharov and his wife were returning to Moscow [in 1986 - Ed.]. I try not to overestimate the circumstances surrounding this event. Even so, had someone asked me to believe such a scenario just two years ago, I would have laughed at them in spite of my natural optimism. It's only in the East – in the other civilization – that things can happen in such a way, and this is a case where I accept Kundera's reasoning. Shortly before then, Marchenko had died in prison, and I have only just learned of Tarkovsky's death in Paris. In other words, the other civilization does display one truly European characteristic: i.e. that when it starts to move, it cuts both ways, and leaves in its wake both personal triumphs and personal tragedies.

In all events, the subject of our controversy no longer finds itself at the same point in history where it was at the commencement of our debate. The main issue now is what significance it will all have for us, the Central European nations in search of a European identity. Maybe Kundera and Vajda are now, like me, excited by matters other than those that gave rise to this polemic. In the new situation, I can happily accept all of Vajda's objections to my views, but I still stick by my original fundamental assertion based on the practical-political consideration (which I, for one, do not shun), that nothing would be worse in the present situation than to reject the currently emerging prospects of European rapproachement on the grounds that the internal laws of the other civilization are immutable. I don't want to introduce 'peace' considerations into the debate, but even so, I have them fixed in one half of my brain and they keep on asking the same question over and over again, viz., What's the alternative? Can Europe afford to go on keeping the 'other civilization' at arm's length indefinitely? Vajda concludes his article with the assertion that 'we will suffer the worst intellectual and moral catastrophe if we let ourselves be guided by so-called tactical considerations.' I find that an odd assertion and one that even has a familiar ideological ring to it. If the Europeans have an unswerving belief in their 'leading values' and a determination to be guided by them, then there is nothing to stop them engaging in the open-minded investigation of the other civilization's possibilities, and no dialogue based on respect for those values can ever lead to moral and intellectual catastrophe. However, the haughty rejection of the East's involvement in the future of Europe could well lead to a catastrophe of a different kind.

(Translated by A. G. Brain)

TRANSLATOR'S NOTES

1 Original title: *Der Mann ohne Eigenschaften*, a novel by the Austrian writer Robert Musil (1880–1942).
2 Czech: Těšínsko: Polish: Cieszyn: German: Teschen.
3 i.e. the Sudeten Germans.
4 i.e. the ethnic Hungarian minority in Slovakia.
5 The author is referring to an unofficial writers' symposium which was held in Budapest in October 1985 during the opening days of the CSCE European Culture Forum and gathered together a panel of writers of international repute. The meeting took place in private apartments when conference rooms previously rented for the occasion were withdrawn following a last-minute official intervention.

16
Central Europe Seen from the East of Europe
Predrag Matvejević

It is well known and frequently pointed out that the concept of Central Europe is, at the same time, historical, geographic and political in nature. Recently, especially in Western Europe, the specific features of Central European art and culture have been emphasized. This discussion itself stems from the conditions facing countries which, after the Second World War, found themselves incorporated into the Eastern bloc, that is to say, into the Soviet political sphere. Writers who fled to the West, as well as others who refuse to recognize the existence of a cultural frontier between Eastern and Western Europe, have together given the Central European theme its full dimensions. For some time now, the contributions of Milan Kundera have especially enlivened the debate:

> Today, all of Central Europe has been subjugated by Russia with the exception of little Austria, which, more by chance than necessity, has retained its independence. But ripped out of its Central European setting, it has lost most of its individual character and all of its importance.[1]

What should attract our attention here is his 'with the exception of little Austria'; he forgets that Slovenia, Croatia and other regions of Yugoslavia where Kundera is one of the most frequently translated authors, are also not under Russian domination. Hence, the issue which he raises is just as relevent for Yugoslavia.

Some twenty years ago, in *Conversations with Miroslav Krleža*[2], I asked our great writer what he thought of Central Europe and how he saw his place within it. His reply was very different from that of Kundera:

> The entity which is geographically and demographically considered as Central Europe doesn't represent for me, on the aesthetic level, a separate universe, in

much the same way that I don't believe that the concepts of Central America, Central Asia, or Central Africa make much sense from a literary point of view. Naumann's beloved theory of the unity of *Mitteleuropa* has been variously used either as a political pretext (pan-Germanism or Austro-imperialism at the beginning of this century), or as a nostalgic longing for the past, extending back, it seems to me, to the installation of the Austrian dynasty in Spain: *Die schönen Tage von Aranhuez sind vorbei* ... [The beautiful bygone days of Aranjuez] but the works of Kafka, Rilke, Musil remain ...

Here Krleža shows himself faithful to opinions formed in his youth: it's the perspective of a man who, as a Croat, endured the Austro-Hungarian empire as a member of a vassal nation.

In Yugoslavia, the Central European question has of late provoked responses different to those of Krleža: quite ambiguous in Croatia because of its particular situation, more open in Slovenia, where a certain distancing from 'Yugoslavness' has been evident. For example, in a 1985 colloquium in Ljubljana on the theme of 'Slovene People and Culture', novelist Marjan Rožanc stated:

> It is not just the end of the Slovenes, for with us is disappearing the entire baroqueish space extending from Trieste to the Baltic and which is designated by the vague name of Central Europe. All the nations and peoples shaped to such a large extent by Central European culture – the Croats, Czechs, Slovaks, Hungarians – I would almost include the Bavarians – are dying with us. We do not die alone; our fate is bound to the Jews of this region who, more Central European than anyone, and by virtue of this fact more exposed, disappeared in the smoke of the crematorium ovens.

I don't share this view and I dispute the fable – not a new one after all – of the death of these European nations. Moreover, we should understand the comparison of our lot and that of the exterminated Jews at the level of metaphor alone. I've heard the same theory voiced in Russia about the extermination of the Russian nation, which is allegedly faring worse than any of the client states of the USSR, and perhaps there's more truth in this. But the pathos which issues from certain declarations – Ljubljana, Zagreb in 1971, Belgrade in 1987-8 – can only provoke mistrust – pitting one Yugoslav nation against another – and leave a bitter after-taste. The past is too quickly forgotten.

Danilo Kiš, the Yugoslav writer who divides his time between Belgrade and Paris, examines identities and differences in an essay entitled 'Variations on the Theme of Central Europe', where one can find the following observation:

> It seems to me that to see today an all-embracing uniformity in this vaste heterogeneous space, among so many national cultures and languages, is above all the result of a certain simplification: it is to ignore differences in order to

highlight resemblances – a process exactly the opposite of that pursued by nationalists who disregard resemblances and emphasize the differences.[3]

Kiš's own views are forcefully illuminated through the fictional character of E.S. who appears in several of his novels, a victim of the holocaust, of the nationalist folly of Central Europe and its rampant hatred of the Jews.

The founding of the organization ALPEN-ADRIA, the collaboration of writers from Western regions of Yugoslavia with their Austrian and North Italian neighbours, and the emphasis on their belonging to Central Europe – all this has not transpired without provoking undertones of discontent in Eastern regions of the country, for example in certain Serbian circles, which in recent years (following events in Kosovo) have seen the resurgence of a nationalism which has long been the greatest scourge of southern Slavs. In a 1987 interview, the Serbian poet Miodrag Pavlović recalled that 'many important Serbian cultural figures – Dositej Obradović, Vuk Karadžić among them ... benefited from Central Europe. The notion of the Slav's positive mission was engendered in German philosophy of the Romantic period. We must take care not to judge the whole of Europe with reference to experiences with our closest Central European neighbours.'

The Austrian writer Peter Handke, a Slovene on his mother's side, recently expressed his views on *Mitteleuropa* in polemical terms:

> Central Europe is a notion which has only a meterorological meaning for me. This thought came to me often during my long walks in the Alps. While I was in the southern part and looked at the clouds adorning the summits, I thought of Central Europe as if from a country located on the other side, where it rained and where it was always shrouded in fog. I would say to myself, you see, you are from the north, and in the Karst gentle breezes blow, the sun shines and there are pines and fig trees. Central Europe – a term which I would never use with ideological connotations – is something linked to meteorological phenomena.

Here Handke is in his own way settling scores with everything that compelled him to become a temporary Austrian exile in Paris.

György Konrád, who, in his essay, 'My Dreams of Europe', sees in the notion of Central Europe an expedient utopia, has received a mixed response throughout Yugoslavia: 'one can think of Central Europe as a stubborn chimera.... Without the idea of Central Europe our great cities become like outposts, border towns, let's say front-line cities.' Konrád lives two identities: as a Jew who cannot forget the lot of Central Europe's Jewish inhabitants, and as a Hungarian who knows how his own 'dissident' views have been received in his country.

So we can see a settling of scores by various indirect paths. It is understandable that Kundera's perceptions of Central Europe differ from Krleža's: Kundera, a Czech, spent 1968 in Prague, now lives in exile and belongs to a different generation than the author of *Zastave* (Banners). Just think what Jaroslav Hašek, with his vision of 'louse-ridden history' and his good soldier Švejk might have to say today – undoubtedly something different again, neither quite like Kundera nor Krleža. In 1914, Gavrilo Princip fired, in the same instant, at both Austria and Central Europe in the name of the Southern Slavs and their unification, a fact remembered by some Yugoslav writers but forgotten by others – and this is what divides them still. But nor is it these differences which account for the contemporary division of East and West.

At this point it seems appropriate to turn to the topic of borders, an issue of long-standing importance in European history. The Jagiellonian Shield (the ancient frontier of Catholic Europe whose mapping from the Baltic to the Adriatic dates back to Carolingian times) is one prominent border which must be mentioned in any serious discussion and which is the Europe which must be borne in mind when one evokes the medieval concept of *christianitas*. This outline circumscribed Polish space and set Poland's eastern and western borders. The German episcopate, attracted by the prospect of a 'Carolingian' pope, assisted the conclave in electing as pope Cardinal Wojtyla. When the new pontiff cited the 'Ostra Brama' (the 'Sharp Gate' in Wilno) as the northernmost Catholic border, some believed that he was implying that he wanted to reinstate the Jagiellonian tradition (there is no space here to discuss the events which followed). In any case, prelates and cardinals of the Catholic church soon brushed with Communism on this point: the Greco-Catholic Archbishop of Galicia Josif Slipyj, Stefan Wyszyński, Primate of Poland and of Lithuania, the Archbishop of Prague, Jozef Beran, the Hungarian Cardinal József Mindszenty, Áron Márton, Bishop of Transylvania. Certain of these church dignitaries came close to collaboration (Stepinac, Slipyj) or manifested a nationalism with possible anti-Semitic overtones (Mindszenty); others joined the Resistance (Wyszyński, chaplain in the Armia Krajowa, Beran, and so on), but they all met similar ends. Regardless of our opinions of these men and their ideologies (unlike Churchill and de Gaulle, they all refused to accept Communism as an ally in the fight against Fascism), the issue of borders remains, and must to some extent constitute an integral feature of Central Europe.

To reflect on Central Europe is to raise the question of frontiers and centres. Perhaps, strictly speaking, Central Europe does not have a centre: we can of course point to Vienna, but Prague, Budapest, Munich and even Zürich are also centres in their own right. We can include Salzburg for its music, even Milan, the Venetian region and Dresden. Certain direct ties link Vienna to Zagreb, Lvov and Odessa. Bucharest in some respects is likewise connected to Central Europe and beyond Central Europe, to Paris. And, of course, Bratislava, Cracow, Wilno ('this Jerusalem of the North') must be included, Berlin, not in the context of state capital but rather as 'Berlin of the Cabarets' is sometimes even considered Central European, though today East and West Germany would probably dispute this point.

In contrast to certain contemporary German historians, Jürgen Habermas identifies in the idea of Central Europe the expression of right-wing tendencies. Stalinism suppressed the genuine right–left rapport in Eastern Europe, where now, many in the intelligentsia are harkening back to earlier, conservative traditions. Due allowance being made, this phenomenon is evident in Yugoslavia as well: the left-wing journal *Praxis*, critical of the nationalist orientation of the elite and the Stalinist remnants in the bureaucracy, was isolated by the intelligentsia and banned by the authorities. This is significant in more than one respect. To be for or against Central Europe in Yugoslavia is not something that can be defined in terms of right and left. This is true in other East European countries as well.

In some respects, Central Europe extends as far as the Adriatic (Trieste, Rijeka, summer resorts of the Habsburgs, Opatija, the Lido of Venice and some old hotels). It is difficult to pinpoint the border separating Central Europe from the Mediterranean: some Adriatic coastal regions are not Mediterranean while there are other borderline regions of Central Europe as far as the Dalmatian coast. In Northern Central Europe, marked by the confrontation of Catholicism and Protestantism and the dominance of the latter, well-defined borders give way to gradations and variations. Certain affinities exist between Hamburg, Amsterdam and Copenhagen on the one hand, and Vienna, or better yet Munich and Zurich on the other. In much the same fashion, the essayist Claudio Magris has presented convincing evidence in his study entitled *Danube*, which suggests that Central Europe, stretching into Pannonia, follows the course of the Danube perhaps even to its mouth.

Despite its 'centralism', Central Europe was pluricentrist. And despite its central position, Central Europe did not constitute a centre of Europe but incorporated many different regional, national and cultural identities. Yet despite all these, certain distinctive traits existed: *idem, nec unum*.

It is possible, moreover, to entertain the notion that a supra-national quality binds Central Europe as a community. The community is as centrifugal for those who live outside Vienna as it is for those who live in it: Vienna 'the experimental laboratory for the destruction of the world', according to the oft-quoted words of Karl Kraus, the experimental laboratory for destroying at least 'Kakania'. Nearly all the important writers of Slavic origin – Croats, Slovenes, Czechs, Slovaks – favoured dismantling the Austro-Hungarian Empire. Naturally, centripetal aspirations existed as well that were not only official and anti-nationalist; neither were they mere forays on behalf of centralization, nostalgia and myth. Social Democrats and Austro-Marxists greatly influenced the federalist thinking of Masaryk and Lenin, and that of the socialist Southern Slavs – Slovenes, Croats and Serbs in particular. The issue of federalism is nowhere so keenly felt as in Central Europe.

Perhaps a sort of 'koine' of ideas or views exists in Central Europe which has not yet been itemized. Behind all the disparities and differences, it is apparent that many are busy forging links between their cultures, or at least helping to mend differences. It is not an exaggeration to say that despite their differences, Central European Jews (Kafka, Freud, Mahler, Joseph Roth, Wittgenstein, Kraus, Svevo, Saba, Hofmannsthal, Kautsky, Otto Bauer and so many others whose names cannot be mentioned here) have played an important role in this process. In the *Confessions of Zeno* the narrator admits: 'the confession which I make in Italian can be neither complete nor sincere.... Who can provide me with the necessary vocabulary?' Differences of this kind are not negligible.

There were differences amongst the Jews themselves: some, wary of a nationalism whose consequences were easy to foresee, favoured assimilation; others were hostile and viewed assimilation as a betrayal. Both groups suffered less from the Eastern threat and a shared culture than from the particularisms specific to atomized states and fragmented national cultures. (Perhaps Marx himself can be seen as representative of these attitudes with his idea of the 'withering away of the state' and at the same time the necessary curbing of 'national cultures'.) Be that as it may, the Jewish contribution to the creation of a supra-national culture in Central Europe was not sufficient to unite and bind that which was disarticulated or contradictory in 'Kakania'.

The dominant ideas of national cultures in Central Europe are sustained only with difficulty and survive supra-nationalist initiatives badly. Today it almost seems paradoxical to defend national culture with reference to supra-nationalism, to defend one's allegiance to a particular state ('Državnost') via a kind of supra-statism. (In this respect, certain contemporary Central European nationalist aspirations – specifically those advocating the creation of a community of Central European or Danubian states – appear to contradict their very *raison d'être*). Yugoslavs are divided over the issue: are we just Slovenes, or Yugoslavian Slovenes; are we just Croats or Yugoslavian Croats? By the same token, is a Serb exclusively a Serb or is he also a Yugoslavian Serb and a European, etc.? The same holds true for the other Yugoslav national minorities, which I will not list here.

Moving beyond the narrow conceptions of national cultures, inherited from a past where particular characteristics were often accepted as values even before being confirmed as such, it is not surprising to find that each constituent culture projects itself into a space not bounded by the borders of a common State. The 'Slovene cultural space', for example, is said to extend as far as Italy and Austria where a Slovene minority resides. These projections (which constitute the subject of a good many polemics in Yugoslavia) must not be regarded *a priori* as a betrayal of Yugoslav cultural space: if authentic, they could considerably extend the existing cultural space with all its variable components.

But let us return to Central Europe and its distinctive traits. The oft-cited geographic, political and historical definitions must not be allowed to overshadow the equally important and sometimes decisive cultural and artistic definitions: the Central European gothic has acquired a certain distinctiveness; the Baroque is easily distinguished from its European counterparts; the *Biedermeier* derived from the average family's lifestyle; we can include the salon and facades of the Secession; and, loosely speaking, it can be said that expressionism occasionally supplanted surrealism in Central Europe.

Perhaps the frontiers of Central Europe are most easily distinguished with reference to style: Central Europe might even be said to extend as far as its styles – the Baroque, *Biedermeier* and Secession, or a certain distinctive music, painting and sensibility. Even though these designations may appear arbitrary, many of our current considerations are based on hypothesis and as such they can serve a useful purpose. We can recall here as well the many creators inspired by Central Europe: Kafka, Broch, Werfel, Musil; Hašek and Čapek; Schönberg and Bartók; Svevo and Saba in Trieste; the Polish trio Gombrowicz, Witkiewicz and Schulz; the Hungarian Tibor Déry; in Croatia Krleža and, at least in part, Andrić and Črnjanski in Bosnia and Serbia, Cankar or Vidmar in Slovenia, and others as well.[4]

But the important part is to highlight those characteristics which works share in common, especially in cases where a strong Central European influence can be detected: Broch's *The Sleepwalkers* and *The Death of Virgil*, Musil's *The Man without Qualities*, the theme of the absurd in Gombrowicz; Hašek's *Good Soldier Švejk*, Krleža's *Today's Europe*, and Miłosz's *Other Europe*, pamphlets by Kraus and parodies by Witkiewicz, diverse expressions of Jewish identity manifested in many works, Protestantism and the reform spirit, features of Catholicism and clericalism specific to this part of Central Europe, similarities and differences with the Catholic Mediterranean. Nowadays in Eastern parts of Central Europe, the forms which resistance to Stalinism has assumed and the subsequent 'thaw' are of particular interest: in Yugoslavia, for example, this resistance was wholly Yugoslav in character.

It is only recently that certain Western European countries have begun to pay attention to the Central European identity. This is, among other things, a case of bad conscience. The Entente powers (France, Great Britain, Tsarist Russia) did everything they could to deprive Austria-Hungary of its political – and as a consequence – cultural prestige. It is this fact which probably accounts for the considerable delay in recognizing Central Europe's existence.

A space of differences then, as well as affinities. Because they have escaped from the net of the East where Czech, Polish and Hungarian culture remains imprisoned, the cultures of Yugoslavia haven't experienced the type of polemic like that between Kundera and Joseph Brodsky in 1985: is the 'Russianness' of Dostoevsky such that it transforms everything into a feeling raised to the status of an absolute truth and value, as Kundera believes, and which is the key to understanding certain phenomena of power in the contemporary politics of the East? Or is it Brodsky who is on the right track when he recalls that 30 years before 1968, the invasion of Prague came from the West and that Eurocentrism of the continental variety, as represented by Kundera, is too tainted by its own partiality? And that when all's said and done, Marxism in Russia is itself an import of Western rationality. In this type of debate, each participant looks at history and universal culture through the visor of his own particularism, his own politics and so on.

It is really a matter of distinguishing what was the Central European culture of former times, what it might have been and the nature of its revived existence in the present. Amidst desires and nostlagic memories, reality has not yet triumphed over certain myths – myths which don't have the same importance in Austria or parts of Germany as they do for the Czech, Polish and Hungarian emigration, for those living in Prague, Budapest, Warsaw, Ljubljana or Zagreb. It is in this sense that one can speak in Western Europe about the 'resurrection of Central Europe', even though Central Europe, or what actually remains of it, is engaged in the laborious process of recovering from the losses it has suffered (the absence of cultural syntheses, of an intense cultural life, the aftermath of fascism, the disappearance of the Jewish component, and so on). Central Europe is adandoning itself to sweet memories, struggling with difficulty against its own provincialisms, and often proving itself ill-equipped to rejuvenate its old traditions.

NOTES

1 'The Tragedy of Central Europe' (1984). This famous essay was also published in Yugoslavia.
2 *Razgovori s Krležom* (Zagreb, 1969).
3 His essay 'Are We Still Dreaming about Central Europe?' appeared in translation in Zagreb and Ljubljana.
4 In the above-mentioned gathering in Ljubljana, Marijan Rožanc, recalled in his essay the following names: Hajek, Kakfa, Musil, Broch, Joseph Roth, Czesław Miłosz; in the plastic arts Gustav Klimt and Oskar Kokoschka (I would add Schiele), in music Mahler and Bartók, in architecture Otto Wagner and Adolf Loos, in Prague the Linguistic Circle (Jan Mukarovský), the social democrats and Kautsky, Freud and psychoanalysis. Several Slovene and Croat names were added. Ivan Čankar, Henrik Tuma, Janez Evangelist Krek, Josip Plečnik, Milan Vidmar, Rihard Jakopič, Stanko Bloudek, Miroslav Krleža, A. G. Matoš, Ivan Meštrovič, Josip Broz Tito, and so on. Some of these personalities would not necessarily approve of this classification; others would definitely reject it.

17
Does Central Europe Exist?
Timothy Garton Ash

I

Central Europe is back. For three decades after 1945 nobody spoke of Central Europe in the present tense: the thing was one with Nineveh and Tyre. In German-speaking lands, the very word *Mitteleuropa* seemed to have died with Adolf Hitler, surviving only as a ghostly *Mitropa* on the dining cars of the Deutsche Reichsbahn. Even in Austria, as ex-Chancellor Fred Sinowatz has remarked, 'until ten years ago one was not permitted so much as to mention the word *Mitteleuropa*.' In Prague and Budapest the idea of Central Europe continued to be cherished between consenting adults in private, but from the public sphere it vanished as completely as it had in 'the West'. The post-Yalta order dictated a strict and single dichotomy. Western Europe implicitly accepted this dichotomy by subsuming under the label 'Eastern Europe' all those parts of historic Central, East Central and Southeastern Europe which after 1945 came under Soviet domination. The EEC completed the semantic trick by arrogating to itself the unqualified title, 'Europe'.

In the last few years we have begun to talk again about Central Europe, and in the present tense. This new discussion originated not in Berlin or Vienna but in Prague and Budapest. The man who more than anyone else has given it currency in the West is a Czech, Milan Kundera. (See his now famous essay 'The Tragedy of Central Europe' in *The New York Review of Books*, 26 April 1984.) Subsequently, the Germans and the Austrians have gingerly begun to rehabilitate, in their different ways, a concept that was once so much their own. The East German leader, Erich Honecker, talks of the danger of nuclear war in *Mitteleuropa*. The West German Social Democrat, Peter Glotz, says the Federal Republic is 'a guarantee-power of the culture of *Mitteleuropa*', whatever that means. And Kurt Waldheim's Vienna recently hosted a symposium with the electrifying title *Heimat Mitteleuropa*. A backhanded tribute to the new actuality of the Central European idea comes even from the central organ of the Polish United Workers' Party, *Trybuna Ludu*, which earlier this year published a splenetic attack on what it called 'The Myth of "Central Europe"'.

There is a basic sense in which the term 'Central Europe' (or 'East Central Europe') is obviously useful. If it merely reminds an American or British newspaper reader that East Berlin, Prague and Budapest are not quite in the same position as Kiev or Vladivostock – that Siberia does not begin at Checkpoint Charlie – then it serves a good purpose. So also, if it suggests to American or British students that the academic study of this region could be more than footnotes to Sovietology. But of course the voices from Prague and Budapest that initiated this discussion mean something far larger and deeper when they talk of 'Central Europe'.

The publication in English of the most important political essays of three outstanding writers, Václav Havel, George Konrád, and Adam Michnik, a Czech, a Hungarian, and a Pole, gives us a chance to examine the myth – and the reality. Of course it would be absurd to claim that any one writer is 'representative' of his nation, and anyway, Havel, Michnik, and Konrád are different kinds of writer working in quite dissimilar conditions.

Havel comes closest to general recognition as something like an intellectual spokesman for independent Czech intellectuals, although there is a great diversity of views even within Charter 77 (as we can see from the other Chartist essays collected under Havel's title *The Power of the Powerless*)[1]. His 'political' essays are rich, poetic, philosophical meditations, searching for the deeper meaning of experience, 'digging out words with their roots' as Karl Kraus once put it, but rarely deigning to examine the political surface of things. (He nowhere so much as mentions the name of any of the present communist rulers of Czechoslovakia, magnificent contempt!). He shows a great consistency, from his seminal essay 'The Power of the Powerless', written in the autumn of 1978, through his 1984 address on being awarded an honorary doctorate by the University of Toulouse, to his open letter to Western peace movements, published in 1985 as *The Anatomy of a Reticence*[2]. You hear in his writing the silence of a country cottage or a prison cell – for his part in the Committee for the Defense of the Unjustly Prosecuted (VONS), he was himself unjustly prosecuted and imprisoned from 1979 to 1983 – the quiet voice of a man who has had a long time for solitary reflection, a playwright catapulted by circumstances and the dictates of conscience into the role of 'dissident', but not at all by temperament a political activist. Yet his contempt for politics is also more generally characteristic of Czechoslovakia, where most people find it hard to believe that anything of importance will ever again change on the immobile, frozen surface of Husák's geriatric 'normalized' regime.

Michnik, by contrast, has seen the earth shake in Poland. Though a historian by training, he has spent most of his adult life actively engaged in political opposition. A central figure in the Social Self-Defence Committee – 'KOR' – and then an adviser to Solidarity, he, unlike Havel or Konrád, writes with the knowledge that he will be read for immediate political advice[3]. Activists of underground Solidarity, students involved in *samizdat* publishing, look to him (among others) for practical answers to the question, 'What is to be done?'. This gives a sharper political focus to his work, but also makes it more controversial.

Like Havel, he is a hero to many of his compatriots. Unlike Havel, his views are fiercely contested. The KOR tradition, of which he is perhaps the most articulate spokesman (and certainly the most lucid essayist), now vies for popularity in Poland with views that may be characterized, with varying degrees of inaccuracy, as Catholic positivist (in the very special Polish usage of that term), Catholic nationalist, liberal, libertarian, or even neoconservative. Astonishingly, the greatest part of his work has been written in prison and smuggled out under the noses of General Jaruzelski's jailers. (Besides almost three hundred pages of political essays, including *Rzecz o kompromisie* ['These times ... On Compromise'][4], he has also produced a 285-page book of literary essays.) His style is often polemical, full of rasping irony – the rasp of an iron file cutting at prison bars – but modulated by a fine sense of moral responsibility and a keen political intelligence. Like Havel, he also displays a great consistency in his political thought, from his seminal 1976 essay 'The New Evolutionism' to his 1985 'Letter from the Gdansk Prison' (first published in English in the *New York Review of Books*[5]) and his most recent long essay ' ... On Compromise' which has so far appeared only in Polish.

Konrád is different again. He is writing not in and out of prison but in and out of Vienna or West Berlin. We hear in the background of his long excursive disquisitions not the slamming of prison doors but the clink of coffee cups in the Café Landtmann, or the comradely hum of a peace movement seminar. In his book *Antipolitics*[6] (German subtitle: *Mitteleuropäische Meditationen*) and subsequent articles, Konrád, a distinguished novelist and sociologist, has developed what I might call a late *Jugendstil* literary style: colourful, profuse, expansive, and ornate. *Antipolitics* is a *Sammelsurium*, an omnium gatherum of ideas that are picked up one after the other, briefly toyed with, reformulated, then abandoned in favour of prettier, younger (but alas, contradictory) ideas, only to be taken up again, petted, and restated once more a few pages later. This makes Konrád's essayistic work both stimulating and infuriating. Contrary to a widespread impression in the West, one finds few people in Budapest who consider that Konrád is a 'representative' figure even in the limited way that Havel and Michnik are. On the other hand, they find it difficult to point to anyone else who has covered half as much intellectual ground, in a more 'representative' fashion.

So Havel, Michnik, and Konrád are very different writers, differently placed even in their own countries, neither fully 'representative' nor exact counterparts. Yet all three are particularly well attuned to the questions a Western reader is likely to raise, and concerned to answer them. And all three are equally committed to the dialogue between their countries. Havel's *The Power of the Powerless* was written specifically as the start of a projected dialogue between Charter 77 and KOR. In discussing the richness of Polish *samizdat* Michnik singles out the work of 'the extremely popular Václav Havel' and both Havel and the Hungarian Miklós Haraszti have appeared alongside Michnik on the masthead of the Polish independent quarterly *Krytyka*. Konrád refers constantly to Czech and Polish experience, and in one striking passage he apostrophizes a Pole identified only as 'Adam' – but the 'Adam' is clearly Michnik. So if there really is some common 'Central European' ground, we can reasonably expect to discover it in the political essays of these three authors. If we do not find it here, it probably does not exist.

In the work of Havel and Konrád there is an interesting semantic division of labour. Both authors use the terms 'Eastern Europe' or 'East European' when the context is neutral or negative; when they write 'Central' or 'East Central', the statement is invariably positive, affirmative, or downright sentimental. In his *Antipolitics*, Konrád writes of 'a new Central European identity', 'the consciousness of Central Europe' a 'Central European strategy'. 'The demand for self government,' he suggests, 'is the organizing focus of the new Central European ideology'. 'A certain distinctive Central European scepticism' Havel comments in *The Anatomy of a Reticence*,

> is inescapably a part of the spiritual, cultural, and intellectual phenomenon that is Central Europe.... That scepticism has little in common with, say, English scepticism. It is generally rather strange, a bit mysterious, a bit nostalgic, often tragic and even at times heroic.

Later in the same essay he talks of 'a Central European mind, sceptical, sober, anti-utopian, understated' – in short, everything we think of as quintessentially English. Or Konrád again:

> It was East Central Europe's historical misfortune that it was unable to become independent after the collapse of the Eastern, Tartar-Turkish hegemony and later the German-Austrian hegemony of the West, and that it once again came under Eastern hegemony, this time of the Soviet-Russian type. *This is what prevents our area from exercising the Western option taken out a thousand years ago, even though that represents our profoundest historical inclinations.*
> (my italics)

In this last passage, history has indeed been recast as myth. And the mythopoeic tendency – the inclination to attribute to the Central European past what you hope will characterize the Central European future, the confusion of what should be with what was – is rather typical of the new

Central Europeanism. We are to understand that what was *truly* 'Central European' was always Western, rational, humanistic, democratic, sceptical and tolerant. The rest was 'East European', Russian, or possibly German. Central Europe takes all the '*Dichter und Denker*', Eastern Europe is left with the '*Richter und Henker*'.

The clearest and most extreme articulation of this tendency comes from Milan Kundera. Kundera's Central Europe is a mirror image of Solzhenitsyn's Russia. Solzhenitsyn says that communism is to Russia as a disease is to the man afflicted by it. Kundera says that communism is to Central Europe as a disease is to the man afflicted by it – *and the disease is Russia!* Kundera's Central European myth is in frontal collision with Solzhenitsyn's Russian myth. Kundera's absurd exclusion of Russia from Europe (not endorsed by Havel or Konrád) has been most effectively criticized by Joseph Brodsky. As Brodsky observes, 'The political system that put Mr Kundera out of commission is as much a product of Western rationalism as it is of Eastern emotional radicalism.' But can't we go one step further? Aren't there specifically *Central* European traditions which at least facilitated the establishment of communist regimes in Hungary and Czechoslovakia, and traditions which those regimes signally carry forward to this day?

A superbureaucratic statism and formalistic legalism taken to absurd (and sometimes already inhuman) extremes were, after all, also particularly characteristic of Central Europe before 1914. That is one reason why we find the most exact, profound, and chilling anticipation of the totalitarian nightmare precisely in the words of the most distinctively *Central* European authors of the early twentieth century, in Kafka and Musil, Broch and Roth. And then, what was really more characteristic of historic Central Europe: cosmopolitan tolerance, or nationalism and racism? As François Bondy has tellingly observed (in a riposte to Kundera), if Kafka was a child of Central Europe, so too was Adolf Hitler. And then again, I find myself asking, *Since when* has the 'Central European mind' been 'sceptical, sober, anti-utopian, understated?' For a thousand years as Konrád seems to suggest? In 1948, when, as Kundera vividly recalls in *The Book of Laughter and Forgetting*, the most Central European of intellectuals joined hands and danced in the streets to welcome the arrival of heaven on earth? Or is it only since 1968?

The myth of the pure Central European past is perhaps a good myth. Like Solzhenitsyn's Russian myth it is an understandable exaggeration to challenge a prevailing orthodoxy. Like the contemporary West German myth of the 20th July 1944 bomb plot against Hitler (the myth being that the conspirators were true liberal democrats, proleptic model citizens of the Federal Republic), its effects on a younger generation may be inspiring. So shouldn't we *let good myths lie?* I think not. And in other moments, or when challenged directly, Havel and Konrád, among others, also think not.

In the late 1970s, the Czechoslovak historian J. Mlynářik (writing under the pseudonym 'Danubius') started a fascinating and highly fruitful discussion in Prague when he argued that the expulsion of the Sudeten Germans by the non-communist Czechoslovak government in the immediate aftermath of the Second World War was itself an inhuman and 'totalitarian' act – a precedent and path-breaker for the Communist totalitarianism to come. 'Let us not forget,' the Czech writer Jiří Gruša movingly reminded us at the unofficial cultural symposium in Budapest last year, 'that it was us [the writers] who glorified the modern state' and that 'our nationalist odes may be found in all the school books of Europe.' Havel goes out of his way to underline the lesson of his fellow intellectuals' 'postwar lapse into utopianism'. And Konrád declares bluntly: 'After all, we Central Europeans began the first two world wars.' So if at times they indulge the mythopoeic tendency, there is also, in this new discussion of Central Europe from Prague and Budapest, a developed sense of historical responsibility, an awareness of the deeper ambiguities of the historical reality; in short, an understanding that Central Europe is very, very far from being simply 'the part of the West now in the East'.

Besides these historical ambiguities there are, of course, the geographical ones. Like Europe itself, no one can quite agree where Central Europe begins and ends. Germans naturally locate the centre of Central Europe in Berlin; Austrians, in Vienna. Thomas Masaryk defined it as 'a peculiar zone of small nations extending from the North Cape to Cape Matapan' and therefore including 'Laplanders, Swedes, Norwegians and Danes, Finns, Estonians, Letts, Lithuanians, Poles, Lusatians, Czechs and Slovaks, Magyars, Serbo-Croats and Slovenes, Rumanians, Bulgars, Albanians, Turks and Greeks – but no Germans or Austrians! As with the whole of Europe the most difficult frontier to locate is the Eastern one. The reader may wonder why I have thus far talked so much about Prague and Budapest, but not of Warsaw; of Havel and Konrád but not of Michnik. The reason is simple. Michnik himself never talks of Central Europe. His essays are full of illuminating references to European history, and to the current affairs of other 'East European' countries, but in the whole corpus I have found not a single reference to 'Central Europe'. And in this he is quite typical: the concept hardly surfaces in all the acres of *samizdat* produced in Poland over the last few years.

In the Polish part of old Galicia there is still more than a touch of nostalgia for the elegantly chaotic laxities of Habsburg rule – what Musil called the '*kakanische Zustlände*'. (At the offices of the Catholic weekly *Tygodnik Powszechny* in Kraków a portrait of the emperor Franz Josef hangs next to a row of popes.) For Michnik, as for most of the democratic opposition, it is self-evident that the small states between Russia and Germany contributed to their own destruction by the nationalist rivalries of the interwar years, and therefore that, were they ever to become independent again, they should co-operate as closely as possible – if not actually confederate. (The London-based Polish government in exile and the New York-based Council of Liberation of Czechoslovakia recently reaffirmed the 1942 Sikorski-Beneš declaration of intent to form a confederation of the Polish and Czechoslovakian states.) But emotionally, culturally, and even geo-politically the view eastward is still at least equally important to most Poles: the view across those vast eastern territories which for centuries were part of historic Poland. It is a lost half-mythical Lithuania that Czesław Miłosz celebrates in his poems and prose. And when Pope John Paul II talks of 'Europe' he looks, with the eyes of a visionary and an exile, not just beyond the artificial, synthetic, truncated 'Europe' of the EEC to Prague, Budapest, and his beloved Cracow, but far, far beyond historical Central Europe, way across the Pripet marshes to the historic heartlands of Eastern Europe, to the Ukraine, to White Russia, even to the onion domes of Zagorsk; and when he preaches his European vision in Polish, he rolls an almost Lithuanian 'Ł'.

To say that Poland is to Central Europe as Russia is to Europe would be, no doubt, somewhat facile. But perhaps I have already said enough to indicate, however sketchily, just a few of the awesome historical, geographical and cultural complexities, the rival memories and resentments that surround you, like a crowd of squabbling ghosts, the moment you revive the term 'Central Europe' – let alone *Mitteleuropa*. If we treat the new Central European idea as an assertion about a common Central European past in the centuries down to 1945, as Konrád and Kundera seem to suggest we should, then we shall at once be lost in a forest of historical complexity – an endless intriguing forest to be sure, a territory where peoples, cultures, languages are fantastically intertwined, where every place has several names and men change their citizenship as often as their shoes, an enchanted wood full of wizards and witches, but one which bears over its entrance the words: 'Abandon all hope ye who enter here, of ever again seeing the wood for the trees.' Every attempt to distil some common 'essence' of Central European history is either absurdly reductionist or invincibly vague. In this forest we find, with Stendhal, that 'all the truth, and all the pleasure, lies in the details.'

Fortunately, the new Central European idea is not only an assertion about the past. It is also, and perhaps mainly, an assertion about the present. Put very baldly, the suggestion is that independent intellectuals from this part of the world *today* find themselves sharing a distinctive set of attitudes, ideas, and values, a set of attitudes which they have in common, but which is also, to a large degree, peculiar to them: just how common and how peculiar they realize when they encounter Western intellectuals in Paris, New York, or California. This distinctive set of attitudes has, it is suggested, a good deal to do with their specifically Central European history – for example, the experience of small nations subjected to large empires, the associated tradition of civic commitment from the 'intelligentsia', the habit of irony which comes from living in defeat – but above all it has to do with their own direct, common and unique experience of living under Soviet-type communist systems, since Yalta. They are the Europeans who, so to speak, know what it is all about; and we can learn from them, if only we are prepared to listen. Central Europe is not a region whose boundaries you can trace on the map – like say, Central America. It is a kingdom of the spirit.

'Compared to the geopolitical reality of Eastern Europe and Western Europe', Konrád writes, 'Central Europe exists today only as a cultural-political anti-hypothesis (*eine kulturpolitische Antihypothese*). . . . To be a Central European is a *Weltanschauung* not a *Staatsangehörigkeit*.' It is 'a challenge to the ruling system of cliches.'[7] (It is in this sense that Czesław Miłosz, too, has declared himself to be a Central European.) The Central European idea not only jolts us out of our post-Yalta mind-set, dynamiting what Germans call the *Mauer im Kopf* – the Berlin Wall in our heads. It also challenges other notions, priorities, and values widely accepted in the West. What is more, it has something to offer in their place.

II

Such are the large claims for the *new* Central Europe. How far are they borne out by the essays of Havel, Michnik, and Konrád? How much do these major independent voices from Prague, Budapest and Warsaw really have in common? And where are their most important differences? How might they change the way we look at 'Eastern Europe'? And at ourselves?

On a closer comparative reading, I believe we can find important common ground – although we have to dig for it. The main elements of the shared intellectual subsoil are, it seems to me, as follows. First, there are the 'antipolitics' of Konrád's title. Havel also says, 'I favour "antipolitical politics"' (in his 1984 Toulouse lecture),[8] and although Michnik does not use this term any more than he does the term 'Central Europe', the thing certainly pervades his writing.

The antipolitician rejects what Konrád calls the Jacobin-Leninist tradition and what Havel (following the Czech philosopher Václav Bělohradský) calls 'politics as a rational technology of power'. In *The Power of the Powerless* Havel delicately criticizes those in Charter 77 who overestimate the importance of direct political work in the traditional sense. This I take to be a reference particularly to those former senior Communists in Charter 77 who still conceive their activity primarily as a matter of seeking *power in the state* – and if not power in the state then at least a little influence on it. Konrád declares grandly, 'No thinking person should want to drive others from positions of power in order to occupy them for himself. I would not want to be a minister in any government whatever.' Since he is unlikely ever to be asked to be a minister in Budapest, this hypothetical sacrifice may not seem too difficult.

But in the case of Poland the statement, 'we do not seek power in the state', has very recently had a real, immediate significance. There were some people in Poland in 1981 who thought that Solidarity *should* go for power in the state. This Solidarity's national leaders consistently refused to do. Of course their main reason, was a pragmatic calculation about what Moscow would tolerate. But there was also a theoretical and ethical underpinning from the dictionary of 'antipolitics'. 'Taught by history', Michnik writes in his 1985 'Letter from the Gdansk Prison', 'we suspect that by using force to storm the existing Bastilles we shall unwittingly build new ones.' And in his latest essay he repeats, 'Solidarity does not aspire to take power in the state.' In the Poland of 1986 this is once again a purely hypothetical statment. But the antipolitical hypothesis – characteristic of KOR – still has to compete with other, now widely articulated views, which urge the pursuit of politics (albeit only on paper) in the traditional categories of left and right.

Michnik and Havel regard the categories of left and right as supremely irrelevant. Talking in his Toulouse lecture about the well-intended but incomprehending questions of Western intellectuals Havel exclaims,

> Or the question about socialism and capitalism! I admit that it gives me a sense of emerging from the depth of the last century. It seems to me that these thoroughly ideological and many times mystified categories have long since been beside the point.

'The very division "Left-Right" emerged in another epoch,' Michnik echoes Havel in his latest essay, 'and it is impossible to make a meaningful reconstruction of it in present-day Poland (and probably also in other countries ruled by communists).' Is the Jaruzelski regime left or right? 'To the vast majority of Poles, "Right" and "Left" are abstract divisions from another epoch.'

In place of the old division between left and right, they offer us the even older division between right and wrong. This, they insist, is the truly operative distinction for those living under such a regime. Moral categories figure largely in the writing of all three authors (though less in Konrád than in Havel and Michnik). All three reassert the fundamental premises of Judaeo-Christian individualism. Reversing the traditional priorities of socialism, they begin not with the state or society, but with the individual human being: his conscience, his 'subjectivity', his duty to live in truth and his right to live in dignity. 'First change thyself' might stand as the common motto of their work. But, they all insist, the attempt to live in truth and dignity does not merely have profound implications for the individual; it can also make a substantial impact on the communist state. For, as Havel puts it, 'the main pillar of the system is living a lie.'

Havel illustrates this with the now celebrated example of the greengrocer who puts in his shop window, among the onions and carrots, the slogan,

'Workers of the World, Unite!' 'Why does he do it?' Havel asks.

> What is he trying to communicate to the world? Is he genuinely enthusiastic about the idea of unity among the workers of the world? Is his enthusiasm so great that he feels an irresistible impulse to acquaint the public with his ideals?

Of course not. He is signalling to the authorities his willingness to conform and obey. That is the meaning of his sign. He is indifferent to its semantic content. But 'if the greengrocer had been instructed to display the slogan, "I am afraid and therefore unquestioningly obedient", he would not be nearly as indifferent to its semantics, even though the statement would reflect the truth.'

The mendacious tissue of ideology partly conceals the true nature of the power in question: more importantly, it enables the individual citizen to conceal from himself the true nature of his submission to that power. It is this canvas of ideologically determined lies which, Havel argues, really holds the system together – and keeps society in thrall to the state. Each of these tiny acts of outward semantic conformity – each in itself so trivial as to seem nugatory – is like one of the miniscule threads with which the Lilliputians bound down Gulliver; except that here men and women are binding themselves. By rendering this seemingly meaningless tribute, or even by not protesting against it, people

> *live within a lie.* They need not accept the lie. It is enough for them to have accepted their life with it and in it. For by this very fact, individuals confirm the system, fulfil the system, make the system, *are* the system.

The 'line of conflict' does not run simply between victim-people and oppressor-state, as in the conventional image, nor just between different social groups, as in a more traditional dictatorship. 'In the post-totalitarian system, this line runs *de facto* through each person, for every one in his or her own way is both a victim and a supporter of the system.' Except, that is, for the few who have decided to 'live in truth' – and in the West are so misleadingly known as dissidents.

Even these few voices have had an impact out of all proportion to their numbers. And if more people try to live in truth, to live in dignity.... Well, look at Poland in 1980, at what George Konrád calls, in discussing Solidarity, 'the peaceful power of the plain-spoken truth.' Certainly that is Michnik's interpretation – 'the politics of truth' – he writes, was one of the two principal traits of the democratic opposition to be taken over by Solidarity. (The other was non-violence.) So all three authors express the conviction that moral changes can have a seemingly disproportionate political effect, that consciousness ultimately determines being, and that the key to the future lies not in the external, objective condition of states – political, military, economic, technological – but in the internal subjective condition of individuals. This is where Central Europe confronts Eastern Europe: in the autonomous sphere of culture, in the kingdom of the spirit.

If not in state or party power structures then where, if at all, are these individual men and women 'living in truth' to combine? In 'civil society'. Both Michnik and Konrád use the term; Havel certainly has the idea. 'In Poland', Michnik writes in his 1985 letter from the Gdańsk prison, 'the structures of independent civil society have been functioning for several years – a veritable miracle on the Vistula', and he entitled his account of Solidarity's first year 'The Promise of a Civil Society'. 'The antipolitician', says Konrád, 'wants to keep the scope of government policy (especially that of its military apparatus) under the control of civil society'. To a historian of ideas, these usages of a term with such a long and chequered history might seem unforgivably vague. Yet the reader in Prague, Budapest or Warsaw will understand exactly what is meant. 'You know, for us the struggle for civil society is a great daily drama', a Hungarian sociologist recently remarked to me. A sentence which might equally well have been spoken in Prague or Warsaw, but hardly in Paris or Moscow. Indeed one could write the history of East Central Europe over the last decade as the story of the struggles for civil society.

As the Hungarian philosopher and social critic János Kis has observed, from the mid-1950s until the late 1960s (the key dates being, of course, 1956 and 1968) the 'general idea of evolution in Eastern Europe was that of reforms generated from above and supported from below.' Meaningful change would be initiated from within a ruling Communist Party which had been enlightened by its own so-called revisionists. Socialism would acquire a human face. This idea was crushed in 1968, under the Soviet tanks in Prague and the police batons in Warsaw, but another has since emerged, gaining wide currency in the late 1970s. Broadly speaking, this second 'general idea of evolution' is that meaningful change will only come through people organizing themselves *outside* the structures of the party-state, in multifarious independent social groupings. The operative goal is not the reform of the party-state but the *reconstitution of civil society*, although of course, if the strategy is at all successful the party-state will be compelled to adapt to the new circumstances (if only grudgingly accepting an incremental de facto reduction in the areas of its total control).

This strategy of 'social self-organization' or 'social self-defence' was outlined by, among others, Adam Michnik in his seminal essay 'The New Evolutionism' and it is, of course, in Poland that it has been most extensively pursued. In 1977, a year after its foundation, the Workers' Defence Committee (Komitet Obrony Robotników = KOR) formally renamed itself the Social Self-Defence Committee – KOR – as a signal of this broader goal. In his history of KOR, Jan Józef Lipski gives a comprehensively detailed and scrupulous account of the very diverse kinds of 'social work' in which this involved KOR members – from *samizdat* publishing and journalism to support for the private farmers and the first Free Trade Union committees[9]. How much the birth of Solidarity owed to KOR, and how much to other causes, is a matter for historical debate, but there is no doubt at all that Solidarity was the child of this 'general idea of evolution'.

The biggest child, but not the only one. Strikingly similar ideas were advanced in Prague, for example by Václav Benda in his 1978 essay, 'The Parallel Polis' and the family likeness of Charter 77 to KOR is unmistakable. The 'general idea' is the same. In Hungary the distinction between reforms initiated 'from above' by the party-state and changes coming from below, from a society aspiring to be 'civil', is much less clear. But here too, the idea of the 'struggle for civil society' is one widely endorsed by independent intellectuals. It is therefore no accident (as Soviet commentators always remark) that we find the leitmotif of 'civil society' in the essays of Konrád and Havel as well as Michnik.

Another common leitmotif is non-violence. The reasons given for the renunciation of violence are both pragmatic and ethical. Practically, because it has been clear since 1956 that violent revolt has no chance of success in the present geo-political order. Ethically, because violence – and particularly revolutionary violence – corrupts those who use it. So also does the mental violence of hatred. Violence and hatred, lies, slanders, beatings, and murders – these are the methods of the Jacobin-Leninist power holders. 'Let these methods remain theirs alone,' Michnick told me when we talked in his Warsaw flat in the autumn of 1984 – a few days after the murder of Father Jerzy Popiełuszko by state-sponsored terrorists from the Polish security service. 'We are not fighting for power,' he went on, 'but for the democratic form of our country; any kind of terrorism necessarily leads to moral debasement, to spiritual deformation.' And in his latest essay he repeats the formula so often used by Popiełuszko and by the Pope: 'vanquish evil through good.' (*zło dobrem zwyciężaj*').

This is not merely preaching. As Lipski records, Michnik personally helped to save several policemen from being lynched by an angry mob in the small town of Otwock in May 1981. (He won the crowd's confidence by declaring, 'my name is Adam Michnik. I am an antisocialist force.') Altogether Solidarity's record of non-violence will more than stand comparison with that of any peace movement in Western Europe – and under incomparably greater provocation. Neither the Czechs nor the Hungarians have recently had the opportunity (or necessity) of putting the preaching into practice on anything like the same scale. But the commitment in principle is as emphatic with Havel and Konrád as it is with Michnik.

As Lipski points out, this is an area where 'the influence of Christian ethics' is most apparent. But, looking sideways at the Western peace movements, Havel and Michnik simultaneously bring forward another ancient and fundamental principle of Christian ethics: the conviction of the *value of sacrifice* ('Greater love hath no man than this ...'). Refering to what he calls 'pacifist movements', Michnik says, 'the ethics of Solidarity are based on an opposite premise: that there are causes worth suffering and dying for.' And Havel repeats the almost identical formula of Jan Patočka: 'there are things worth suffering for.'

Indeed, it is in their response to the Western peace movements that we find the most developed common position: in his 'Anatomy of a Reticence' Havel calls it the 'common minimum' of 'independent East Central European thinking about peace.' They begin by expressing an instinctive, 'prerational' (Havel) sympathy with people who appear to put the common good before their selfish interests. But they also begin with a healthy suspicion – nourished by Central European experience – of the peace movement's tendency to utopianism and 'the various much too earnest overstatements (which, at the same time and not accidentally, are not bought at a high cost) with which some Western peace-fighters come to us.' (Havel's rather contorted sentence repays a careful second reading.) They insist, against much of the Western peace movement, that the danger of war arises not from the existence of weapons but from the political realities behind them.

> The cause of the danger of war is not weapons as such but political realities. ... No lasting, genuine peace can be achieved simply by opposing this or that weapons system because such opposition deals only with consequences, not with reasons.

Thus Havel. And from his prison cell Michnik sent an almost identical message: 'Western public opinion has allowed itself to have imposed on it the Soviet pattern of thinking – arms are more important than people. But this is not true. No weapon kills by itself.'

The main 'political realities' in question are the division of Europe and the continued Soviet domination over half of it. 'It is an unobservant European' declares Konrád, 'who fails to notice that the Iron Curtain is made of explosive material. Western Europe rests its back against a wall of dynamite, while blithely gazing out over the Atlantic.' 'What threatens peace in Europe,' Havel agrees, 'is not the prospect of change but the existing situation.' The key to a lasting peace lies not in disarmament or arms control as such, but in changing these political realities. In the long term this must mean overcoming the division of Europe (which we describe in shorthand as Yalta) and moving toward what Havel calls, 'the ideal of a democratic Europe as a friendly community of free and independent nations.' Hard to dissent from that; still harder to imagine its achievement. In the short to medium term, however, this means above all understanding the symbiotic connection between 'external peace' (between states) and 'internal peace' (within states) – for a state that ignores the will and rights of its citizens can offer no guarantee that it will respect the will and the rights of other peoples, nations and states. A state that refuses its citizens the right of public supervision of the exercise of power cannot be susceptible to international supervision. A state that denies its citizens their basic rights becomes dangerous for its neighbours as well: internal arbitrary rule will be reflected in arbitrary external relations.

Such are the states of Eastern Europe, whose citizens, unlike those of West European states, do *not* enjoy 'internal peace'. Therefore – and this is a message both to the peace movements and to the governments of the West – the key to a lasting, genuine peace between East and West Europe (as opposed to the present state of 'non-war') must lie in working toward greater respect for human rights and civil liberties in Eastern Europe. The struggles for disarmament and human rights do not merely go hand in hand (as a minority – and still only a minority – in most Western peace movements maintain). The struggle for human rights has an absolute, logical priority. Michnik: 'the condition for reducing the danger of war is full respect for human rights.' Havel: 'respect for human rights is the fundamental condition and the sole genuine guarantee of true peace.'

So on the one hand the 'Central European mind' ('sceptical, sober, anti-utopian, understated') comes up with a warning about the true nature of Soviet bloc states that could warm the cockles of President Reagan's heart. Indeed, in his latest essay, Michnik quotes with approval some of Reagan's remarks about the difficulty of reaching arms control agreements with the Soviet Union. On the other hand they talk about respect for human rights as the *fundamental* condition and the sole *genuine* guarantee of *true* peace – to which a Western peace activist might well reply, 'and who is being utopian now?' The message that combines these two aspects might be rudely summarized thus: the best thing that West European peace activists can do for peace is to support the democratic opposition in Eastern Europe.

This concludes my rudimentary short list of what seem to be important *common* positions, approaches, or leitmotifs in the political essays of Konrád, Havel and Michnik. Beyond this however, as we move back up toward the surface from the common Central European subsoil, we find differences and inconsistencies which are quite as striking as the underlying similarities and consistencies. The three authors differ greatly in their analysis of the prospects of change, in their own countries, in the lessons they draw from the history of Solidarity, and in their prescriptions for immediate political (or antipolitical) action in East Central Europe.

III

How might change come about in Czechoslovakia? In his writings, Havel does not give a clear answer to this question. He suggests that very gradually, indirectly, in convoluted and largely unpredictable ways, the pressure of individuals living in truth and dignity, and associating in loose structures of 'social self-organization,' the 'fifth column of social consciousness,' *must* eventually change the way the country is governed: but how and when, he cannot foresee. When we talked recently at his country house in northern Bohemia he gave a slightly more concrete illustration of what he means. After Chernobyl, he said, people in Czechoslovakia were complaining openly and loudly on the streets. True, they did not organize protest demonstrations or sign petitions (that was left to some Austrian students who came to Prague specially for the purpose). But ten years ago most people would not have dared even to complain so openly in public, though of course they would have done so in private. And so perhaps, in another ten years, they *will* be signing petitions. The evolution is so gradual as to be invisible to a casual visitor, or to an angry young man engaged in the opposition. But coming back into society after four years in prison he could measure the difference, as between two still photos, and he was favourably surprised.

To be sure, no one can predict how the regime will respond to this pressure from below. In the book which he has just completed, a volume of intellectual memoirs taking stock of his first half-century (he will be 50 this autumn), Havel describes how, in his view, pressure from below was decisive in the prehistory of the Prague Spring. But is there anyone inside the Party now who will respond to this pressure as Party intellectuals and reformers did then? Then there were still genuine, convinced Communists and socialists inside the Party. Now there seem to be only cynics and careerists – and the younger the worse. The 'fifth column of social consciousness' is at work, slowly, oh so slowly, like tree roots gradually undermining a house (my metaphor, not Havel's). But no one can be confident of their impact. They can be cut. The house can be shored up. Fortunately the roots main purpose is not to undermine the house. 'Dissident' man is, so to speak, a thinking root. His attempt to live in truth and dignity has a value in itself, irrespective of any long-term social or political effects it may or may not have.

As a political analysis and prescription this is, indeed, 'sceptical, sober, anti-utopian, understated' – and present conditions in Czechoslovakia would lead us to distrust any analysis that was not. There are, however, also moments when Havel lifts off into a visionary, almost apocalyptic, mode. 'It is ... becoming evident' he writes in his Toulouse lecture,

> that a single seemingly powerless person who dares to cry out the word of truth and to stand behind it with all his person and all his life, has, surprisingly, greater power, though formally disfranchised, than do thousands of anonymous voters.

Here he is closely following Solzhenitsyn, whose example he cites in the next sentence. Between the lie and violence, Solzhenitsyn wrote in his 1970 Nobel speech ('One Word of Truth ...'), 'there is the most intimate, most natural, fundamental link: violence can only be concealed by the lie, and the lie can only be maintained by violence.' And he goes on to prophesy; 'Once the lie has been dispersed, the nakedness of violence will be revealed in all its repulsiveness, and then violence, become decrepit, will come crashing down.' The first part of the prophesy was realized in Poland in 1981. But, alas, even in Poland, the second part has yet to be confirmed.

In his *Antipolitics* Konrád draws a simple lesson from the apparent defeat of Solidarity by lie-clad violence. The Hungarians tried it in 1956, the Czechs and Slovaks in 1968, and the Poles in 1980–1; 'three tries, three mistakes,' says Konrád. Lesson: 'the national road to Eastern European liberation has not carried us very far.'

> 'Be careful,' I said to Adam [i.e. Michnik], 'the third time around it has to work.' It didn't. Adam is awaiting trial perhaps. 'It's incredible,' he said: incredible that he was able to give a lecture at the Warsaw Polytechnic University on 1956 in Poland and Hungary. The lecture was first-rate: he didn't stammer at all; he was sharp, dialectical, and got to the heart of the matter. Then they said he fell madly in love with a great actress. Then they said he was arrested and beaten half to death. They they said he was all right. What does it all tell us, Adam? You are thirty-five million, but you couldn't pull it off; now what?
> What would you say if I told you: 'now let the Russians do it'?

Well, I think I can make a pretty good guess what Adam Michnik would say to that: (expletive deleted). But perhaps he will now give us his own answer, since he was unexpectedly released from prison in August. The 'it' the Russians should 'do', incidentally, is to go home. This certainly seems a good idea, though not perhaps an entirely original one. To reduce Konrád's *Antipolitics* to a coherent argument would be to do some violence to the text. The peculiar (and peculiarly Central European?) quality of this book is, as I have suggested, the coexistence in a relatively small space of a remarkable diversity of formulations and arguments, as rich and multifarious as the nations of the Dual Monarchy – and as difficult to reconcile. For example, 'the Russians must be afforded tranquility so they can reform their economy and administrative system' but, on the other hand, 'it would be fitting if creditworthiness were reduced in proportion to the number of political arrests.' Yet three main pillars of argument may perhaps be discerned behind the ornamental profusion of the late *Jugendstil* façade.

First, there is the proposition already indicated above: national routes to liberation have failed, let us therefore try the international, all-European one: let us propose that American troops should withdraw from Western Europe and Soviet troops should withdraw from Eastern Europe: let us dissolve the blocs! 'To me, personally, that seems just lovely,' Václav Havel nicely comments on this not entirely new proposal, 'although it is not quite clear to me who or what could induce the Soviet Union to dissolve the entire phalanx of its European satellites – especially since it is clear that, with its armies gone from their territory, it would sooner or later have to give up its political domination over them as well.' *Basta!*

For Konrád the 'who or what' that could induce the Soviet Union is the 'international intellectual aristocracy'. This is his second leitmotif. 'It appears,' he writes, 'that the intelligentsia – not the working class – is the special bearer of internationalism.' 'Dissidents – autonomous intellectuals – are the same the world over, irrespective of their political philosophies.' Therefore we should get together and produce the intellectual framework for going beyond the 'intellectually sterile operations of ideological war.' Incidentally, 'anyone who believes that two systems and two ideologies are pitted against each other today has fallen victim to the secularized metaphysics of our civilization, which looks for a duel between God and Satan in what is, after all, only a game.' (What would Adam say to *that?*). Hence his own 'plan to take down the Iron Curtain,' which the Intellectuals' International should now place on the agenda of world politics. For it was 'our intellectual failings' which ultimately 'brought about the baleful situation in which our continent is cut in two.' Think right, and we'll walk happily ever after.

However, just in case the dolts in the Kremlin and the Pentagon can't see the light which the 'international intellectual aristocracy' is holding under their noses, Konrád has an interim fallback position. This is the Hungarian way. While he has moments of stern fundamentalism ('the Hungarian nation ... will not rest until it has won self-determination here in the Carpathian basin'), for the most part he writes in almost glowing terms about the present condition of Hungary, and in particular about János Kádár, whom he compares to the Emperor Franz Josef. 'The best we can hope to achieve,' he writes,

> is an enlightened, paternalistic authoritarianism, accompanied by a measured willingness to undertake gradual liberal reforms. For us, the least of all evils is the liberal-conservative version of Communism, of the sort we see around us in Hungary.

In these circumstances, the task of the 'creative' or 'scholarly' intelligentsia is to engage in dialogue with the 'executive' intelligentsia, to help make the enlightened dictatorship still more enlightened. 'The intellectual aristocracy,' he declares, 'is content to push the state administration in the direction of more intelligent, more responsible strategies.' And he muses: 'is a moderate, authoritarian reform possible on an empire-wide scale – an enlightened Party monarchy, a "Hungarian" style of exercising power?'

Now these may indeed be realistic assessments and propositions for an independent intellectual wishing to act effectively in the peculiar circumstances of contemporary Hungary. But they find no echo at all in the work of Havel and Michnik. For Havel in Czechoslovakia, such a role for independent intellectuals is inconceivable. Where he lives, the intellectual aristocracy are working as window-cleaners, stokers, and labourers. And even if it was conceivable, his conception of antipolitics hardly makes it desirable. For Michnik in Poland, such a role for intellectuals is entirely conceivable – and entirely unacceptable. A Polish Kádárism is his jailer's dream, not his. General Jaruzelski would sing hallelujahs to the Black Madonna if Poland's creative and scholarly intelligentsia were to accept the role sketched by Konrád. But they won't.

And for Michnik, the fact that Poland does not enjoy a Kádárite dispensation is a measure of success – not failure. Certainly he would never endorse Konrád's formula of 'three tries, three mistakes.' Solidarity, for him, was hardly a 'mistake'. The fact that Solidarity was defeated by force does not demonstrate that Solidarity's fundamental strategy was wrong: it demonstrates that people without guns (and with a conscious commitment to non-violence) can be driven off the streets by people with guns (and the will to use them). And anyway, this was not simply a defeat. The imposition of martial law on 13 December, 1981, was 'a setback for the independent society' but 'a disaster for the totalitarian state.'

The point now is to sustain a genuinely autonomous, strong, well-organized 'civil society.' For Michnik, as for Havel, the key ingredient, as it were the basic molecule, of this 'civil society' is the individual living in truth. Moral absolution is the only certain guide in such times – such is the lesson he draws in his book of literary essays from the example of those like Zbigniew Herbert who were never ever morally 'compromised,' even in the darkest times. On the other hand, just because individuals – and particularly intellectuals – do not accept the roles assigned to them in a would-be Kádárite dispensation, just because there is a strong and wholly independent 'civil society', there is a chance of positive political compromise with the authorities.

Most of Michnik's latest essay is then devoted to exploring, through a vigorous and detailed analysis of the history of KOR and Solidarity, the question of the possible nature of such a compromise. His answers, too, are not always convincing. For example, he says at one point that 'no one among the activists of Solidarity today believes in dialogue and compromise with the authors of the December coup. Nor do I.' But if not with them, then with whom? He cautions that, ' Solidarity should reject the philosophy of "all or nothing"' but a few pages later he suggests that the precondition for any agreement with the authorities must be recognition of the existence of an 'independent self-governing Solidarity' and that such an agreement must avoid even the last vestiges of newspeak which were present (and controversial) in the agreements negotiated by the Solidarity leadership in 1980 and 1981.

If that is not 'all', it is pretty close to it. Throughout Michnik's book, there is a palpable tension between the moral and the political argument. To discuss these problems in detail would require another essay. All I wish to emphasize here is that Michnik is wrestling with questions that do not even arise for Havel or Konrád, and consequently that his answers are not for them. But if George Konrád is occasionally inclined to suggest, as a true internationalist, that the 'Hungarian way' might after all be the best way forward for neighbouring nations, Adam Michnik is not entirely disinclined to suggest the reverse. Poles should feel national pride, he writes, for

> it's the Poles who have showed the world that *something like this* is possible. Sooner or later these deeds will be seen to have set an example. When other nations begin to follow this example, the Soviet order will be faced with its most serious threat.

In short, as soon as we move up from the common subsoil to ask the political question, 'what is to be done?' we find that even these three writers, most keenly interested in the Central European trilogue, most open to other traditions and ideas, offer answers that are widely disparate, and in part contradictory – and their differences largely mirror those of their national circumstances. To say, as Konrád is inclined to do, that these are merely different national 'strategies' or paths towards the same goal is to put an attractive icing over the cracks, but hardly to bridge them.

IV

Beside these deep differences, moreover, there are some major limitations and omissions which are common to all three authors. In their domestic analysis perhaps the most striking gap is their neglect of the entire material side of life – their contempt of economics. One may well insist – against Marx – that consciousness ultimately determines being, that ideas are ultimately more important than material forces; this hardly justifies completely ignoring the latter. Without the refinement of KOR's ideas there would have been no Solidarity (or, at least, a very different one), but the midwife at Solidarity's birth was a vulgar increase in the price of meat. Much the most widespread, indeed the one almost universal form of independent social activity in Eastern Europe today is work – or 'operating' – in the 'second economy'. Black-marketeering is the antipolitics of the common man.

Konrád makes a gesture in this direction when he advocates 'an amalgam of the second economy and the second culture.' But how? Thomas Masaryk pointed the way forward to Czech independence (from the Habsburg 'Central Europe') with a twin commandment: 'Don't lie, don't steal.' But the qualities required for any kind of success in the second economy under a state socialist system are the precise opposite of those prescribed for the intellectual antipolitician. Don't lie, don't steal? Anyone who engages in any kind of independent economic activity anywhere in Eastern Europe will not survive five minutes unless he – well, shall we say – tolerates some terminological inexactitudes and unless he – well – countenances unorthodox methods of procurement.[10] (A priest in Poland once told me that when people confess to him – in the secrecy of the confessional – that they have had to, well, use unorthodox methods of procurement, he instructs them that they should not regard this as a sin. In this godless system, it is a necessity. And how else would new churches get built to the greater glory of God?)

Neither Konrád nor Havel address this issue at all. Theirs is a programme for intellectuals. Michnik seems to assume that the economic demands of Solidarity-as-trade-union will naturally go hand in hand with the moral and antipolitical demands which mainly concern him. This assumption requires a little closer examination.

In their international analysis perhaps the most important common weakness is their approach to what is still the most important regional power in Central Europe: Germany. True, they all recognize in a very general way that overcoming (or reducing) the division of Europe requires overcoming (or reducing) the division of Germany. So they're all for it. True, Konrád avers that the intellectual aristocracy should concentrate its mind on the issue of a peace treaty with Germany. But this really is not the significant level of German thought or action today. None of them begins seriously to engage with the real West German policies – the *Deutschlandpolitik* and the *Ostpolitik* – which are such a pivotal factor in contemporary European politics. The architects and executors of these policies, for their part, largely ignore the voices from below in Eastern Europe, and see their real partners among the apparently all-powerful, in the ruling Communist parties and in Moscow, not among the apparently powerless, in opposition and in prison.

It is perhaps worth recalling that the original East Central European usage of the term 'Central Europe' was developed and articulated by Thomas Masaryk during the First World War in programmatic opposition to the German usage of the term *Mitteleuropa* by Friedrich Naumann, and others, as a justification for imperial Germany's expansionist plans. To compare present Germany's policies and visions to those of 1915 would obviously be quite wrong, and invidious. But it would be neither invidious nor unrevealing to explore the differences between the concept of *Mitteleuropa* as used by West German Social Democrats like Peter Glotz (particularly in the context of their 'second *Ostpolitik*') and the concept of 'Central Europe' as it emerges in the work of independent East Central European intellectuals.

Another line of general criticism would be this (and I exaggerate deliberately): Konrád, Havel and Michnik are merely the latest scions of a tradition that has been present in Central and Eastern Europe since the Enlightenment: the

Westward-looking, cosmopolitan, secular-humanist and rationalist element, what Thomas Mann contemptuously called the *Zivilisationsliteraten* (before becoming one himself). True, the *Zivilisationsliteraten* are now saying different things from what they were saying half a century ago: indeed, in crucial respects they are saying the opposite. But one thing has not changed: they have always been a tiny minority. They were a tiny minority before the First World War, impotent against the nationalism that tore that Central Europe apart. They were a tiny minority before the Second World War, impotent against the imperialisms that tore *that* Central Europe apart.

And today? Why even today, in a region largely and terribly purged of its two greatest minorities – the Jews, of course, and, yes, the Germans – nationalism still has a stronger appeal than Konrád's internationalism, even to many independent intellectuals, let alone to the general public. What is the greatest single issue (apart from declining standards of living and growing inequalities) for public and intellectual opinion in Hungary today? Is it human and civil rights? Is it democracy or 'the struggle for civil society'? No. It is the plight of the Hungarian minorities in Transylvania and Slovakia. I raised the idea of Central Europe with a highly intelligent and sophisticated Hungarian friend. 'Ah yes,' he sighed, ' there could once perhaps have been something like Central Europe. And you know, we rather blame *you* for the fact that it does not exist.' He referred to the Treaty of Trianon.[11]

And then the deepest doubts of all. Isn't all the common ground that I have attempted to describe ultimately no more than a side product of shared powerlessness? Isn't the existence of an imagined Central Europe finally dependent on the existence of a real Eastern Europe? Aren't 'antipolitics' in the end merely a result of the impossibility of politics: since you cannot practice the art of the impossible, you invent the art of the impossible. Western Europe's moralistic criticism of American foreign policy has been characterized as 'the arrogance of impotence': doesn't that description apply *a fortiori* to the moralism of antipolitics? Antipolitics is a product of living in defeat. How much would survive victory?

If I raise all these doubts and questions, dwell on the differences between the three authors, their inconsistencies and common limitations, I do so not because I regard what they say as marginal 'pie in the sky' – a view very widely held among those who shape Western policies towards Eastern Europe – but, on the contrary, because I regard it as relevant and important. Though still vague and half-articulated, the notions of 'antipolitics' and 'Central Europe' are, it seems to me, central both to understanding what *could* happen in Eastern Europe over the next decade and, potentially, to shaping that development.

Of course we cannot entirely ignore the possibility of some large-scale geo-politcal rearrangement with Moscow's agreement: a 'new Yalta', say, a negotiated Finlandization of Eastern Europe. But that is, to say the least, highly improbable. Nor can we wholly exclude the possibility of far-reaching reforms being encouraged by the Gorbachev leadership, and carried forward by a new generation of Communist leaders in Eastern Europe – economic reforms, initially, but with political implications recognized and deliberately accepted by those leaders.

What is definitely possible, however, and even probable, is the continuation of a slow, messy, piecemeal process of differentiation, in which the peoples of Eastern Europe will gradually, in quite diverse and convoluted ways, come in practice to enjoy more and larger areas of *de facto* pluralism and independence – cultural, social, economic – areas partly conceded in a planned and deliberate way by their rulers, but mainly wrested from them by *pressure from below*: not the progress of a 'reformed' and thus revitalized communism, but the regress of a decaying would-be totalitarianism. The Ottomanization rather than the Finlandization of the Soviet empire.

If there is any truth in this prognosis, then it is obviously important to determine what shape the pressure from below will take. Will it be violent or non-violent, individual or collective, organized or disorganized? Now in practice, of course, there is a different and continually changing mix of ingredients in each country: here it is largely the pressure of individual expectations, there it is channelled through the Church, there again, the primitive threat of violent revolt. The formulation of 'antipolitics' in the broadest sense, is an attempt both to characterize and to shape this pressure from below. It is half description, half prescription. Its territory is the space between the state and the individual, between the power and the powerless. Its focus is the middle distance – beyond the immediate selfish concerns of the family nest maker, but well short of the horizon of full national independence. To an imperial system whose main instruments of domination are lies, violence, the atomization of society and 'divide and rule', the antipolitician responds with the imperatives of living in truth, non-violence, the struggle for civil society – and the idea of Central Europe.

But this new Central Europe is just that: an idea. It does not yet exist. Eastern Europe exists – the part of Europe militarily controlled by the Soviet Union. The new Central Europe has yet to be created. But it will not be created by mere repetition of the words 'Central Europe' as the fashionable slogan from California to Budapest; nor by the cultivation of a new myth. If the term 'Central Europe' is to acquire some positive substance, then the discussion will have to move forward from the declamatory, the sentimental, and the incantational to a dispassionate and rigorous examination both of the real legacy of historic Central Europe – which is as much one of divisions as of unities – and of the true conditions of present-day East Central Europe – as much one of differences as of similarities. Happily this process has already begun, in Prague, where the founding of an underground journal called *Střední Evropa* ('Central Europe') has catalysed a sharp debate between

Catholic and Protestant intellectuals about the legacy of the Habsburg Empire and the First Republic. But it still has a very long way to go.

If we look to the future, one crucial Central European issue, beside the articulation and enrichment of the domestic strategies of 'antipolitics' is surely that of minority rights. Can Central Europe be put together again, albeit only on paper, at the very point where it has most often, most horribly, and (from the point of view of the neighbouring empires) most successfully been divided – at the point where different nations, races, cultures, religions try (or fail) to coexist? Even today, the most open, tolerant, and democratic intellectuals in Czechoslovakia and Hungary cannot agree on a common statement on the position and treatment of the Hungarian minority in Slovakia. An interesting discussion has begun in the Polish underground press about attitudes to Germany and the German minority in Poland. At the moment the main focus of discussion is the question, does the German minority exist? (Cardinal Glemp agrees with General Jarulzelski that it does not.) But perhaps the more important question is, would it be a good thing if a German minority did exist? And what about a Jewish minority? And a Ukrainian minority? And *why not* a Hungarian minority in Slovakia? Provided, always provided, that each minority would enjoy those rights which we regard it as our Central European task to define.

Many of the obstacles to such a Central European dialogue are historical, emotional, and intellectual. But others are simply practical. For this is a debate that the Communist authorities have done everything in their power to discourage – or to channel in a chauvinistic direction. And a great deal is in their power. When we talk about the 'division of Europe' or the 'Iron Curtain', we automatically think of the East-West divide, and usually of the Berlin Wall. But perhaps the most impenetrable frontiers in Europe are not those between East and West, and not even (thanks to a decade and a half of *Deutschlandpolitik*) the German – German frontier. For freedom of movement, and hence for genuine cultural exchange, perhaps the most impenetrable frontier in Europe today is that between Poland and Czechoslovakia. That really is an iron curtain. Leading Polish, Czech, and Hungarian intellectuals meet more often in Paris or New York than they do in Warsaw or Prague. They read one another, if at all, in English, French or German: with a very few exceptions their work is not translated into one another's languages. It is easier for the author of this essay to meet with them than it is for them to meet with one another. If they do have a common ground, then by and large this has been arrived at independently. In the circumstances, we may be favourably surprised how much of it there is.

This common ground has a great potential importance for the part of Europe in which they live: Eastern Europe *in acta*, Central Europe *in potentia*. But does it have any broader relevance for intellectuals in the West? This, too, is part of the larger claim for the new Central Europe. In a negative sense, as a guide to the nature of totalitarian power and a source of ideological inoculation, it undoubtedly does. For example, no one who has honestly read and digested what Michnik and Havel have to say can continue to believe that there is any real structural symmetry or moral equivalence between American domination over Western Europe and Soviet domination over Eastern Europe. (I fear that danger remains for the casual reader of Konrád) In this respect they have undoubtedly had a beneficial impact on parts of the West European peace movement. But most of the *positive* ideas they advance are not strikingly new (though none the worse for being old) and where they are new, they are not obviously relevant to our Western circumstances. Attempts to interpret the activity of Western peace movements as part of the struggle for civil society, for example, are not very convincing; and most of us still think we know what we mean – in Britain and America – by the categories of left and right.

And yet I do believe they have a treasure to offer us all. At their best, they give a personal example such as you will rarely find in London, Washington, or Paris: an example, not of brilliance or wit or originality, but of intellectual responsibility, integrity, and courage. They know, and they remind us – vividly, urgently – that ideas matter, words matter, have consequences, are not to be used lightly – Michnik quotes Lampedusa: 'You cannot *shout* the most important words.' Under the black light of totalitarian power, most ideas – and words – become deformed, appear grotesque, or simply crumble. Only a very few stand the test, remain rocklike under any pressure; and most of these are not new. There are things worth suffering for. There are moral absolutes. Not everything is open to discussion.

'A life with defeat is destructive,' writes Michnik, 'but it also produces great cultural values that heal. ... To know how to live with defeat is to know how to stand up to fate, how to express a vote of no confidence in those powers that pretend to be fate.'[12] These qualities and values have emerged from their specific Central European experience – which is the central European experience of our time. But since we can read what they write, perhaps it may even be possible to learn a little from that experience, without having to go through it.

The Russian poet Natalya Gorbanyevskaya once said to me, 'You know George Orwell was an East European.' Perhaps we would now say that Orwell was a Central European. If this is what we mean by 'Central Europe', I would apply for citizenship.

NOTES

1 Václav Havel et al., *The Power of the Powerless: Citizens against the state in central-eastern Europe*, introduction by Steven Lukes, edited by John Keane (London, Hutchinson, 1985).
2 Václav Havel, *Anatomy of a Reticence* (Charta 77 Foundation, Stockholm, 1985).
3 Cf Adam Michnik, *Letters from Prison and Other Essays*, translated by Maya Latynski, foreword by Czesław Miłosz, introduction by Jonathan Schell (University of California Press, 1986).
4 Adam Michnik, *Takie czasy ... Rzecz o kompromisie*, (London, Aneks, 1985).
5 18 July 1985, pp. 42-8.
6 George Konrád, *Antipolitics: An Essay*, translated by Richard E. Allen, (New York; Harbourt Brace Jovanovich, 1984).
7 Quotes in this paragraph are from his essay 'Mein Traum von Europa' in *Kursbuch* 81 (September 1985).
8 Quotations in this essay are from the translation first published in the *Salisbury Review* (January 1985). This has recently been reissued by the Charta 77 Foundation as No. 2 in their Voices from Czechoslovakia series, obtainable from the Charta 77 Foundation, Box 50041, S-10405 Stockholm, Sweden.
9 Jan Józef Lipski, *KOR: A History of the Workers' Defense Committee in Poland, 1976-81*, translated by Olga Amsterdamska and Gene M. Moore (University of California Press, 1985).
10 This applies even to the legal private sector as Anders Aslund shows in his invaluable book *Private Enterprise in Eastern Europe* (London, Macmillan/St. Antony's, 1985).
11 It will be recalled that the 1920 Treaty of Trianon, part of the post-war settlement whose main architects were Woodrow Wilson, Clemenceau, and Lloyd George, stripped Hungary of more than two-thirds of its pre-1914 territory, including the Slovakia, in what then became Czechoslovakia; Transylvania, which went to Rumania; and Croatia, to what then became Yugoslavia.
12 This quotation is from his introduction to a German edition of his essays, reprinted in the Winter 1986 issue of the *East European Reporter*, (London).

Index

absolutism, 66-7, 68, 73, 75
Acheson, Dean, 37
Adenauer, Konrad, 37
Ady, Endre, 126, 129
Africa, 43
alienation, 119, 165
Andrić, Ivo, 134-5
antipolitics, 198, 201, 210, 211, 212
anti-Semitism, 150
aristocracy, 50, 51, 63, 74, 165
Auschwitz, 151
Austria, 99, 101, 102, 127, 191
Austria-Hungary, 109
Austro-Hungarian Monarchy *see* Habsburg Monarchy
Austro-Hungarian Settlement 1867, 100

Balkans, 31, 33
barbarians, 32
Bělohradský, Václav, 198
Benda, Václav, 202
Beneš, Edvard, 102, 105, 108, 109
Berlin, 186-7, 193, 196
Bessarabia, 103
Bevin, Ernest, 37
Bibó, István, 131
Bohemia, 99, 101, 172
Bolsheviks, 35-6
Bondy, François, 127, 195
bourgeoisie, 51, 52, 53, 76
Bratislava, 134
Britain, 37, 42, 43, 46; *see also* England

Broch, Hermann, *The Sleepwalkers*, 151, 189
Brodsky, Joseph, 116, 190, 195
Budapest, 63-4
Bulgaria, 16
Byzantium, 13, 122

Caesaropapism, 13, 20
Canossa, 10, 13
Čapek, Karel, 121; *A Place for Jonathan*, 133
capitalism, 51, 57, 59-61, 64-6, 119, 165
Catherine the Great, 58, 64, 67, 165
Catholic church, 48, 186
Catholicism, 123, 129, 189, 193
Central Europe; compared with Eastern Europe, 58, 194; compared with *Mitteleuropa*, 210; cultural identity, 18-19, 98, 123, 125, 127, 134-6, 140, 153, 157-9, 174, 183, 189, 198; as frontier, 19-20, 98, 128, 129, 186; geographical identity, 116, 145, 186, 187, 196-7; meteorological identity, 185; non-existence, 212; as utopia, 153-5, 185
Charlemagne, 32, 39
Charter 77, 192, 194, 198, 202
Chernobyl, 205
Chernyshevsky, Nikolay, 164
Christendom, 31-4
Christian ethics, 202-3

Christianity, 10, 13, 20, 26, 44-5, 50, 53, 56, 98, 186
Ciacchi, Aurelio, 149
cities, and towns, 8, 11-12, 63-4, 134
civil liberties, 53, 55, 204
Comecon, 93, 94
Committee for the Defense of the Unjustly Prosecuted, 192
Common Market see European Economic Community
Commonwealth, 42
Communism, 98, 186; in Czechoslovakia, 195; in Hungary, 195; intelligentsia and, 71, 72, 82-9; in Poland, 87-8; in Russia, 140-1, 160, 164, 167, 174, 190, 195; see also Marxism; socialism
Communists, in Czechoslovakia, 180, 200, 205; in Hungary, 180
Congress of Vienna, 122
Constantine I, 31
Constantinople, 32, 33
consumerism, 44
Copernicus, Nicolaus, 11
Corvinus, Matthias, 101
Croatia, 103, 129
Crusades, 33
Czechoslovakia; Communism in, 195; Communists in, 180, 200, 205; creation of, 101; economic integration with Russia, 95; intelligentsia in, 192; nationalities policies, 101-2, 103-10, 150, 179, 196, 213; reform in, 204-5; Russian occupation, 105, 111, 159, 173, 201
Czechoslovak-Polish Federation, 179, 197
Czechs, in Germany, 105-6

Danube, 187
Danube barrage, 95
democracy, 55, 108-9, 112, 113, 166, 203
detente, 163-4
disarmament, 203, 204
Dobruja, 103

Dostoevsky, Fyodor, 158, 189; *The Possessed*, 121
Droz, Jacques, 146, 151

East-Central Europe, see Central Europe
Eastern Europe, compared with Central or East-Central Europe, 58, 194; economic integration, 94-5; as political entity, 93, 96; Russianization of, 93-4, 213
EEC see European Economic Community
Engels, Friedrich, 57
England, 50, 58
Enlightenment, Age of, 10, 44, 72, 122, 125, 135
Europe, cultural unity, 9-14, 21-2, 31, 34-40, 46, 91-2, 98, 142; division of, 97, 122, 191, 198, 203; influence of United States, 38-9, 43-4; see also Central Europe; Eastern Europe
European Economic Community, 10, 39, 40, 46, 92, 94, 191, 198
European Parliament 92, 94

Fábry, Zoltańn 104, 111-12, 113
Fascism, 37, 51, 102-3, 111-12, 151, 186 see also Nazism
federalism, 187
feudalism, 11, 50, 58-63
Foucault, Michel, 73, 74, 80
France, 37, 38, 45, 58, 100, 140
Frank, K. H., 105
freedom, 168-9, 170, 177-8
French Revolution, 48, 49-50, 51, 52, 53, 73-4, 75, 82
Furet, François, 73

Gellner, Ernest, 74
gentry, 77, 79
Germans; in Bohemia, 99; in Central Europe, 211; in Czechoslovakia, 101, 102, 104, 105, 179, 196; in Poland, 213
Germany, 74, 145-6, 147, 172, 191; division of, 212, 215; expansionism,

145, 148–9, 153, 210; integration into Europe, 37, 180; pact with Russia, 103, 151
Gerschenkron, Alexander, 64
Glotz, Peter, 191, 210
Goebbels, Joseph, 37
Goethe, Johann Wolfgang von, 149
Gombrowicz, Witold, 130, 131, 135–6
Gomułka, Władysław, 70
Gorbachev, M. S., 212
Gorbanyevskaya, Natalya, 214
Gorizia, conferences at, 148, 149
Gramsci, Antonio, 81
Greeks, 32, 33, 65, 66
Gregory VII, 10
Gruša, Jiří, 196

Habermas, Jürgen, 78, 187
Habsburg Empire, 57, 63–4, 68, 78, 99, 100, 102, 114, 128, 144, 153, 196
Handke, Peter, 185
Hašek, Jaroslav, *The Good Soldier Švejk*, 23, 118, 127, 151, 152, 186, 189
Hauner, Milan, 179
Haushofer, Albrecht, 146
Haushofer, Karl, 145
Havel, Václav, 196, 199–200, 203–5, 206–7, 209; *Anatomy of a Reticence*, 192, 194; *The Power of the Powerless*, 192, 194, 198
Hellenes *see* Greeks
Helsinki Conference 1975, 110
Henry IV, 10
Herbert, Zbigniew, 131, 133, 208
Hilferding, Rudolf, 147
Himly, A., 145
history, 23, 117, 130
Hitler, Adolf, 10, 37, 68, 91, 103, 119, 151, 159, 191, 195
Holy Roman Empire, 31, 32, 39, 100, 144, 153
Honecker, Erich, 191
Hrabal, Bohumil, 127
Hungarian Revolution 1848, 52, 59, 62

Hungarian Revolution 1956, 53, 86, 105, 111, 173–4
Hungarians; in Czechoslovakia, 101, 102, 104, 105–6, 108–10, 114, 179; in Slovakia, 211, 213; in Transylvania, 114, 212
Hungary, 95, 100–1, 103, 129, 140, 150, 160, 172–3, 180, 207, 212; capitalism in, 59–61, 64–6; Communism in, 195; Communists in, 180; immigrant traders in, 65–6; nationalities policies, 100, 112–13; reform in, 202; Russian occupation, 111, 173, 179; Turkish occupation, 100
Husák, Gustáv, 93, 106, 108

identity, 18
individualism, 76, 127–9, 169, 199
intelligentsia, 11, 71–5, 80, 85, 122, 197, 207; attitude towards Russia, 160, 169, 174; and Communism, 71–5, 82–9, 119; in Czechoslovakia, 192, 208; in Poland, 70, 86–7, 88, 89, 208; and politics, 76–8, 80–2, 122, 197, 210; in Russia, 71, 74, 77, 81, 164–6, 167; in Yugoslavia, 187
Iron Curtain, 146, 203, 207, 213
irony, 23, 118, 197
Islam, 13, 20, 31
Italy, 37
Ivan IV (Ivan the Terrible), 12, 58, 63

Jagiellonian Shield, 186
Jaruzelski, Wojciech, 199, 208, 213
Jews, 32, 98, 148, 150–1, 159, 184, 188, 189, 211; in Hungary, 65, 66; in Poland, 173
John Paul II, Pope, 197

Kádár, János, 110, 207
Kafka, Franz, 119, 126, 130–1, 152, 196
Kakania, 27, 187, 188
Kautsky, Karl, 147
Khruschev, N., 87

Kijowski, Andrzej, 88
Kiš, Danilo, 184–5
Kis, János, 201
Kiss, Csaba G., 21
Kocbek, Edvard, *Paris Notebooks*, 133–4
Kołakowski, Leszek, 70, 119
Konrád, György, 196, 198, 203, 207, 209–11; *Antipolitics*, 193, 194, 201, 206; *My Dreams of Europe*, 185
Kopelev, Lev, 157, 169, 170
KOR, 193, 194, 199, 201–2, 208, 209
Kraus, Karl, 187, 189, 192
Krleža, Miroslav, 126, 127, 132, 183–4
Kundera, Milan, 19, 105, 123, 127, 168–75, 178–9, 180, 183, 185–6, 190, 195; *The Book of Laughter and Forgetting*, 195; *Life is Elsewhere*, 152; *The Tragedy of Central Europe*, 22, 139–41, 143 150–2, 157–9, 159, 160, 162, 191

Lampedusa *see* Tomasi de Lampedusa, Giuseppe
language, foreign, 26, 46; national, 78, 99; official, 25, 78; varieties of, 126, 134
Latin, 34
law, 11, 76
Lenin, V. I., 8, 15, 57, 160, 164, 167, 187
Liberals, 166
Lipski, Jan Józef, 201–2
literacy, 11
literature, 117, 123, 125–7, 149, 151–3; Austrian, 127; Jewish, 119; national traditions in, 129–31; Polish, 135; Russian, 125, 128, 177; of small nations, 133–4
Little Entente 1918–20, 102

Magris, Claudio, 187
Malczewski, Jacek, 123
Mann, Thomas, 211
Mannheim, Karl, 72
Marx, Karl, 57, 74, 76, 80, 164, 188

Marxism, 17, 24–5, 64, 118–20, 190; *see also* Communism; socialism
Masaryk, Thomas, 108, 109, 187, 196, 209, 211
Medvedev, Zhores A., 71
Meyer, Henry Cord, *Mitteleuropa in German Thought and Action*, 144, 149
Michnik, Adam, 192–3, 196, 198–204, 206, 208–9, 214
Mickiewicz, Adam, 128
Mills, C. Wright, 70, 82
Miłosz, Czesław, 19, 21, 22–3, 126, 128, 129–30, 130, 189, 197, 198
Mináč, Vladimír, 133
minorities *see under* specific nationalities, e.g. Germans
Mitteleuropa, 117, 126, 143, 144, 145, 146, 184, 185, 191, 210
Mlynářik, J., 195–6
Modrzewski, Andrzej Frycz, *On the Improvement of the Republic*, 122
Molotov-Ribbentrop Pact, 117
Mongols, 33
Muscovy, 13, 33, 34, 36
Musil, Robert, 126, 131, 195, 196; *The Man Without Qualities*, 151, 177, 189
Muslims, 33, 45; *see also* Islam
Mussolini, Benito, 43
Mutton, Alice, 145

Napoleon I, 35, 81
nationalism, 10, 26–7, 35, 98–9, 102–3, 112–13, 118, 151, 179, 211; and Communism, 106–8; in Czechoslovakia, 105, 197; in Eastern Europe, 92; and Fascism, 37, 38; and language, 134; in literature, 131, 132, 149, 196; in Serbia, 185
nationalities policies *see* Czechoslovakia; Hungary
NATO, 40, 92, 94, 148
Naumann, Friedrich, *Mitteleuropa*, 145, 146–8, 184, 210
Nazism, 121, 158–9, 172–3, 178

Németh, László, 129
Nietzsche, Friedrich, 121
nihilism, 121
Novgorod, 12
Nyirség, 60

Orthodox church, 33, 123
Orwell, George, 214; *1984*, 121
Ottoman Turks *see* Turks

Palacký, František, 68, 141
Paris, 21
Partsch, Josef, *Mitteleuropa*, 145–6
Patočka, Jan, 203
patronage, 79–80
Pavlović, Miodrag, 185
peace movememt, 203, 214
peasantry, 51, 74, 79
Peguy, Charles, 30, 39
Peter the Great, 34, 58, 64
pluralism, 112–13
Poland, 57, 63, 103, 105, 122, 130, 140, 150, 160, 206, 213;
Communism in, 87–8; Germans in, 213; intelligentsia in, 70, 86–7, 88, 89, 208; Jews in, 173; literature, 135; nationalism, 209; reform in, 201–2; religion in, 26; Russian occupation, 103, 141
Polish-Czech Confederation, 179, 197
Polish Revolution, 70
Polish United Workers Party, 192
Popiełuszko, Jerzy, 202
Potsdam, conference at, 104
Prague, 134, 190
proletariat, 76
Protestantism, 98, 189
Proudhon, P.-J., *L'Organisation du travail*, 164
Prussia, 57, 144
Pushkin, A. S., 128, 158; *The Great Horseman*, 34

Radl, Emanuel, 102
Reason, 72, 82
Reformation, the, 10, 13, 34

religion *see* Christianity; Islam
Renner, Karl, 147
revolution, 49–50, 51, 74; and intelligentsia, 80; and violence, 48, 52, 54, 202
robot, 121
romanticism, 10, 125, 135
Rome, 32, 122, 129
Rožanc, Marjan, 184
Rumania, 23, 27, 103
Russia, climate, 9; Communism in, 140, 160, 164, 167, 174, 190, 195; compared with Soviet Union, 158, 172; culture, 17, 118, 128, 140–1, 158, 168, 170, 171, 172; Czech attitudes towards, 16; economic integration with Czechoslovakia, 95; European attitudes towards, 16–17, 169, 194; Europeanness of, 7, 161–2, 163–4, 168, 170–1, 175, 195; Europeanization of, 34–5; geography of, 8; influence in Central Europe, 37, 93–4, 97, 101, 114, 117–18, 141, 150, 159–60, 161, 170, 179, 180, 194, 195, 214; intelligentsia in, 8, 71, 74, 77, 80, 86, 164–6, 167; Liberals in, 166; literature, 123, 128, 177; Mongol conquest of, 33; occupation of Czechoslovakia, 105, 111, 159, 173, 201; occupation of Hungary, 179; pact with Germany, 103, 151; Polish attitudes towards, 33; religion and morality, 13–14; towns, development of, 63, 64
Russian language, 26
Russian Revolution, 15, 52, 53, 81, 82, 84, 123, 178

Sakharov, Andrei D., 181
samizdat, 25, 194, 202
Sarajevo, 134–5
Schnitzler, Arthur, *Reigen*, 143
science, 121
seigneurial economy, 57, 58, 61
Serbia, 35, 185
serfs, 58, 60, 62–3, 77

Sikorski-Beneš Declaration, 197
Šimečka, Milan, 163, 168, 169, 172-5
Sinowatz, Fred, 191
Slavs, 186, 187
Slovakia, 211, 213
Slovaks, 103
Slovenes, 184, 189
small nations, 133-4, 151, 197
socage, 57, 58, 59, 61
socialism, 36, 51, 52, 54-5, 123, 199; see also Communism, Marxism
Solidarity, 25, 87-9, 119, 193, 199, 200, 202-4, 206, 208-10
Solzhenitsyn, Alexander, 12, 160, 195, 205-6
Sonnenfels, Josef, 67
Soviet Union see Russia
Spain, 31, 45
St Petersburg, 34
Stalin, I., 103, 151, 179
Stalinism, 24, 52, 187, 189
state; absolute, 66-7, 68, 73, 75; in Austria, 67, 68; in Central Europe, 73, 75, 121, 195; Christian, 122; and Church, 20; in Europe, 14-15, 111; in Habsburg Empire, 66, 67, 68; in Marxist societies, 120; reform, 76; in Russia, 12, 14-15, 67, 166
Stendhal, 197
Svevo, Italo, *The Confessions of Zeno*, 189
symbolism, 123
Szabó, Dezső, 129, 153

Takács, Péter, 59
time, 117
Tomasi de Lampedusa, Giuseppe, 214
totalitarianism, 98, 105, 119, 122, 214
tourism, 95-6
towns, and cities, 8, 11-12, 63-4, 134
Tőzsér, Árpád, 129

Transylvania, 103, 114, 123, 211
Treaty of Saint Germain, 104
Treaty of Trianon, 211
Tumler, Franz, 148-9
Turks, occupation of Balkans, 33, 34; occupation of Europe, 58; occupation of Hungary, 100

Ukrainians, 172
United Nations, 118
United States, 15-16, 38-9, 43-4, 97, 208
universities, 20, 77

Vajda, Mihály, 176-8, 180-2
Vienna, 31, 63, 66, 102, 186, 187, 191, 196
Vienna Exhibition 1985, 126
Vincenz, Stanisław, 129-30
violence, and non-violence, 48, 52, 53-4, 202-3
Vörös, Károly, 61

war, 24, 41, 120
Warsaw Pact, 93
Weber, Max, 64, 76
Western Europe see Europe
Wilno, 19, 116, 134
Witkiewicz, Stanisław, 122-3, 189
World War II, 102
Wyśpiański, Stanisław, 123, 126

Yalta Conference, division of Europe at, 97, 122, 191, 198, 203
Yugoslavia, 183-5, 187, 188, 189

Zagorski, Krzysztof, 87
Zimand, Roman, 87
zsellér, 60, 61
Zweig, Stefan, 152, 153

Index by Chris McKay